THE CAVE DIVERS

THE CAVE DIVERS

ROBERT F. BURGESS

Aqua Quest Publications, Inc. • New York

THE CAVE DIVERS

ROBERT F. BURGESS

AQUA QUEST PUBLICATIONS, INC. ➤ NEW YORK

DEDICATION

To the memory of
Sheck Exley, 1949-1994,
who spent his life pushing back the frontiers
of innerspace so that others might go there in safety.

Library of Congress Cataloging-in-Publication Data

Burgess, Robert Forrest.
      The cave divers / Robert F. Burgess.
      p.   cm.
      Includes bibliographical references (p.   ) and index.
      ISBN 1-881652-11-4 (paper)
   1. Cave diving. 2. Underwater archaeology. 3. Caves—United States.
   4. Caves—Europe. 5. Cave divers—Biography. 6. Scuba divers—Biography.
   I. Title.
GV200.63.B87 1998
796.52'5—dc21

96-39661
CIP
r96

Cover design: Justin Valdes

Printed in Hong Kong
10 9 8 7 6 5 4 3 2 1

Cover: In a halo of light, long experienced
cave diver Lamar Hires investigates a
colorful passage of Sand Bag Spring in
Florida's Suwanee County. Photo by Wes
Skiles.

ACKNOWLEDGEMENTS

I wish to thank my many colleagues who helped make the first and the second edition of this book possible, especially retired Col. William R. Royal, cave diving pioneer and diver extraordinary, along with his always supportive wife, Shirley; underwater archaeologists, Carl J. Clausen, Wilburn A. ("Sonny") Cockrell, and their cooperative staff; oceanographer Garry Salsman, one of the first deep penetration cave diving explorers whose team's work at Florida's Wakulla Springs in 1954 laid the groundwork for all that followed; master diving instructor John C. Crotty, whose basic scuba certification courses taught blacked out cave diving techniques that probably saved our lives during our first tentative cave dives almost three decades ago; NACD instructor and friend, Tex Chalkley, who provided me with invaluable information as to why divers were dying in caves, at a time when everyone else in the National Association of Cave Divers was afraid to talk to writers; and my faithful cave diving photographic assistants, Charles Harnage Jr., J. Michael Wisenbaker, David Perryman, Bob Sofge and Doug Bogert, who braved mud, floods, dirty water, errant eels, alligators, the occasional water snake, and irate caretakers, to get the photographs we needed.

Special appreciation for his help on this new edition is also due such auspicious multi-talented cave diving innovators as William C. Stone, whose writings, photographs and insightful ideas enabled me to recreate some of the more dramatic events involving advanced diving technology; Ned DeLoach for his penetrating look at a most extraordinary underwater cave explorer and record-breaking pioneer; Sheck Exley, that extraordinary cave diving pioneer for his overview of world record cave dives; Woody Jasper whose little niche in the cave diving community proved a heck of a lot more important than boring a hole to China; Lalo Fiorelli who brought back some of the first stunning photographs from the Yucatan; Steve Gerrard who has taught many of today's cave divers; and my gratitude is especially due that 16-year-old would-be cave diver I met at an air fill station near Ginnie Springs decades ago who listened to me talk all night about this sport, then went on to become one of its leading explorers, cartographers, and foremost underwater cave photographers: Wes Skiles. Thanks, Wes, for returning the favor.

Thank you all.

Robert F. Burgess

TABLE OF CONTENTS

Preface

Most people think of a freshwater spring as a tiny fountain of water bubbling up out of the ground. As a youngster in a homemade diving helmet I saw them underwater, puffing clouds of sand like miniature volcanoes on the bottom of Spring Lake, Michigan. Years later, diving down for my first look at an underwater Florida spring, I was amazed to see an opening in the bottom the size of a two-stall garage from which issued such a copious flow of water it created a navigable river. Florida has many such springs scattered through the northern half of the state, with concentrations along the Suwannee River.

Since most of the southeastern United States was once an ancient ocean bottom, this land area now contains vast limestone deposits formed from the skeletons of early marine life. In Florida these limestone deposits lie near the surface and are composed largely of calcium carbonate. In texture it varies from hard stone to lime clay and chalky powder. Over the centuries rain has percolated down through the porous limestone and dissolved the softer, more soluble material, creating ever-changing labyrinths of underground passageways whose walls, floors and ceilings are composed of the less soluble limestone. In some places underground, rivers carve their way to the surface and emerge as a fast-flowing stream or river called the spring run. In other areas, surface waters have so eroded the limestone roof over a cavity that a cave-in results, usually revealing a pool of clear, placid water. These are called sinkholes. They may vary in size from a hole no larger than a washtub to one 300 feet in diameter and over 100 feet deep. Besides hundreds of lesser springs and sinkholes, Florida has 22 springs of major magnitude, meaning that their average discharge is at least 100 cubic feet per second, or 64.6 million gallons daily. Many are popular tourist attractions featuring glass-bottom boat rides, jungle cruises or an underwater theater.

But big or small, on or off the tourist trail, the water in the basins of these springs and sinkholes is usually so free of suspended particles that on a bright sunny day a strange blue luminosity is cast above the surface and can be seen from some distance. In fact it was this telltale blue glow amidst the tangled vines and gray, moss-festooned cypresses of a flooded Florida swamp that always guided me unerringly to a small, half-forgotten sinkhole. This characteristic reflection of sun-kissed water so deep and clear that it appears blue has led to these unique pools being called blue holes or blue sinks.

No matter where this interesting geographical feature occurs it attracts attention. Generations of Maya worshipped gods that supposedly inhabited the depths of similar sinkhole formations dotting the Yucatan Peninsula. In Florida, circa 10,000 B.C., Paleo-man may have performed some rather grisly rites around a major spring. Many centuries later, an armada of tourists in glass-bottom boats plied the popular springs years before the invention of the self-contained underwater breathing apparatus.

But once scuba appeared on the scene in the early 1950's, more venturesome sightseers soon donned the diving gear and plunged into the crystalline depths of these azure pools for a closer look.

Once they exhausted all the peripheral pleasures of the pools, the next logical step was to investigate the springs' enticingly mysterious caves. Thus began the sport of cave diving in the United States.

In the next two decades thousands of scuba divers around the world dived into submarine caves and lived to tell about it. Others, however, were not so fortunate.

As in any hazardous sport, cave diving suffered its fatalities. Divers drowned in caves and no one seemed to know why. Was something bizarre happening in there? If so, what? Some people blamed the caves. KILLER CAVE CLAIMS ANOTHER VICTIM, often read the headlines. Sparse, inaccurate news accounts spread the myth. But only the fact was valid: death by drowning; cause unknown. The public wondered why anyone in his right mind would want to swim into the bowels of the earth anyway.

Certain experienced cave divers knew why. Members of the National Association for Cave Diving had a pretty good idea what was killing the divers. Quietly they shared this information among themselves. But they were unwilling to share this information with the general public on the grounds that it put their sport in a bad light. Their ultimate fear, of course, was that bad publicity would result in legislation closing all spring caves to divers. Consequently, uninformed novice divers continued doing the same fatal mistakes as their dead predecessors. Only later was it realized that the key to this problem was to properly educate all divers to these dangers, and to offer training programs that included introductory courses, such as "Cavern Diving" for divers who might not intend to go into deep penetration cave diver training.

Today's cave diver education and training, plus recent developments in diving technology and equipment such as exotic breathing mixtures and the innovative Cis-Lunar Mk-3R mixed gas rebreather, have put us on the very threshold of mankind's greatest period of exploration beyond the old frontiers. With this new knowledge, we are about to cross over into one of the greatest adventures ever: the exploration of both inner and outer space, where the only boundaries ahead are our own imaginations. This book is about the pioneers who led to this point of departure.

Twenty Thousand Years
in a Cave

In southwestern Europe between France and Spain for a distance of about 240 miles, the earth's crust pushes up to a
height of over 11,000 feet to form the rugged Pyrenees Mountains. Scattered throughout their length like beads on a string
are many caves and caverns in such places as Alquerdi, Labistide,
Gargas, Trois-Freres, LaVache and Niaux. Where prehistoric man
inhabited these caves, he left behind unique evidence of his presence, including some of the earliest art in existence. At the Grotto
of Marsoulas, early spelunkers found frescoes and engravings
made by cavemen. At Gargas the walls are covered with curious
ancient hand-prints, many with missing phalanges resulting
from intentional mutilations. The cavern of Niaux has some of
the most beautiful historic designs known; other remarkable
works of art appear in the caves of Portel, Trois-Freres and
Isturitz. In 1913 a Count Begouen, while exploring the depths
of the dry cave of Tuc d'Audoubert with his three sons, made
the astonishing discovery of the first clay animal statues modeled by cavemen. The figures were still malleable.

Then, in 1932, a dedicated French speleologist, Norbert
Casteret, made one of the most daring plunges into prehistory
ever known, for a find unique in the annals of exploration.
Casteret was more than a dedicated cave explorer; he was obsessed with the sport. One would almost think he had been born
in a cave, but actually he was all of five years old when he entered his first. And then it was only the modest Grotto of Bacuran,
near Toulouse, where his parents showed him its wonders by
flashlight. He was not overly impressed. Nor was he much moved

by his preadolescent visits to various lofty caves at Saint-Martory while on his way to rob hawks' nests. These were nothing compared to what he called his "first cavern." Casteret dated all his future caving experience from his exploration of a cavern he read about in a pamphlet called *The Hyenas' Lair in the Cavern of Montsaunes*. The grotto was only two miles from his home. From the text Casteret learned that about 1890 a scholar named Harle entered the cave to do a little paleological digging. As a result he found a veritable prehistoric animal boneyard made up of the bones of such species as elephant, hippopotamus, wolf, beaver and porcupine and even a monkey's jaw, believed to have been brought into the cavern by a pack of hyenas. The idea of being able to explore such a fantastic subterranean boneyard appealed to the boy's sense of adventure almost as much as did Jules Verne's *Journey to the Center of the Earth*, which he had reread so many times he had worn out the book.

With the enthusiasm of a Tom Sawyer, the boy grabbed a candle and some matches, leaped on his bicycle and pedaled off to the Montsaunes quarry where the cavern was located. Just before twilight, with candle in hand, he crawled into his first real cavern, feeling like "a new Argonaut, on the brink of an unknown world, trying to pierce the darkness of the past." He wriggled through a labyrinth, dropping down into a gallery where he barely skirted a deep pit. Pausing at another pit, he listened to the sounds of an underground stream. There was much more beyond, but he had gone as far as he cared to go with nothing more than a candle.

The next night Casteret returned with his younger brother, and the two went on what certainly must rank as one of the most exciting candlelit journeys in the history of spelunking. "Explorer's fever had hold of us and nothing short of collapse would stop us," he wrote years later. Carrying a Boy Scout knapsack containing a rope, a hammer, matches and a package of candles, they reached and crossed the second pit and wandered ecstatically through a grotto full of strange stalactites. Skirting more pits, they roped down a 40-foot precipice, squeezed through stone loopholes, splashed through a sunken brook, fought their way up steep mud banks the consistency of butter, broke their way through a forest of stalactites to a hidden corridor that they followed to a dead-end where they found a small animal's skeleton. After that fantastic journey they retraced their steps and toured it all again. Finally, at three o'clock in the morning, the two muddy apparitions emerged from the cave none the worse for wear and rode their dew-covered bicycles home.

As the boy grew into a man, the only thing that interrupted his obsession with caves was a three-year tour with the French infantry during World War I. After the war, Casteret began spelunking in earnest with a cave-exploring club from Toulouse. For him and the other enthusiasts, there was more to it than just testing themselves in the unknown reaches of a cave. They sought evidence of man's unwritten past in the hidden grottoes.

During one of his vacations in the Pyrenees where he frequently explored caves by himself, Casteret learned that there was a supposedly impenetrable cavern at the village of Montespan in the foothills of the French Pyrenees. The word "impenetrable" was all the encouragement Casteret needed to hear. Slinging his knapsack over his bicycle, he pedaled to the village of Montespan on the slope of a hill crowned by a feudal castle overlooking the River Garonne.

After visiting the ruins and making discrete inquiries at the village, he learned the whereabouts of the grotto and bicycled to it. Outwardly it was unimpressive, only a small crack at the base of a cliff from which trickled a mountain stream. The villagers had told Casteret that in exceptionally dry summers, one could walk up a natural corridor carved by the stream and easily enter the sizable grotto. But since this was not one of those dry periods, Casteret stripped off his clothes, squeezed through the small opening and waded along the shallow pebble and sand bottom of the stream into a cave about 12 feet wide and 8 feet high. Inside was a fairly uninteresting horizontal gallery 130 feet long. As Casteret waded toward its farthest end, the ceiling sloped down and forced him to walk in a stooped position. The stream deepened until he stood at the edge of a dark pool, where the roof of the cave disappeared into the water. It was a dead-end. Or was it? he wondered. Examining the cave more closely, Casteret saw that it consisted of a type of soft limestone that was easily eroded by water. He wondered if it might be possible that the stream had carved out grottoes elsewhere in the mountain. If it was true that there were long periods without rain toward the end of the glacial epoch, then perhaps the cave would have been dry and possibly inhabited by prehistoric man. The stream had to come from some source within the mountain; perhaps there, too, would be found a hidden cavern. It did not take long for Casteret to decide what had to be done.

Dripping hot wax onto a rock projection, he placed his lighted candle there. Then he slowly waded into the ever-deepening pool, determined to try and follow the stream underground, to swim into its flooded tunnel, its siphon. When the water was up to his neck, he paused to consider all the ramifications of this risky undertaking. The stream could go on endlessly with no air pockets; he might lose his way and never come out; he might get caught in quicksand or hit his head on a rock projection or maybe even fall down some sunken shaft. None of these possibilities frightened him enough, however, to dampen his spirit for learning what, if anything, was beyond the rocky barrier in front of him.

Casteret prided himself on being an excellent swimmer capable of holding his breath for long periods. Now, as he prepared to duck underwater, he filled and refilled his lungs with air. Taking a deep breath he knew he could hold at least two minutes, he dived down and felt his way underwater along the rough contours of the sloping ceiling. Pulling himself along, he used his fingertips like eyes, knowing that he would have to retrace this same route without a mistake.

Suddenly, first his hand, then his head emerged, and he could breathe. It was totally dark. He had swum through an underwater tunnel and surfaced in an air pocket. Knowing it would be even more foolhardy to go further without any light, he turned back, again diving down under the ceiling and surfacing in the glow of his candle sitting by the edge of the pool.

The next day Casteret returned with his simple but effective caving equipment—a handful of candles, matches and a rubber bathing cap to keep them dry. Again hiding his clothes in the bushes outside the cave's entrance, he waded into the grotto and went directly to the pool at the other end. Using the cap as a waterproof container for his candles and matches, Casteret clutched it tightly in his hand and cautiously felt his way down under the sloping ceiling, then swam as near a course as he had before. When he came up, he was again in the air pocket. Shaking the water free of his bathing cap, Casteret lit a candle.

He was in a long, shallow opening with a ceiling just inches above his head; yet there was enough trapped air to breathe as he cautiously moved along the passageway for 100 yards.

Ahead of him, in the flickering candlelight, he was surprised to see the shallow air pocket widen into a large chamber some 35 or 40 feet high. Nearby was a clay bank. He crawled out of the icy waters to recuperate, his heart pounding from the excitement of what he had found.

Awed, he looked around him. In his limited circle of light he saw great frozen waterfalls of white calcite cascading down the walls of the chamber. The creek itself was almost buried in boulders fallen from above. As many caverns as Casteret had explored in the past ten years, he could never remember feeling quite so alone and isolated with such a sense of foreboding and apprehension. Yet, he was drawn on by the gnawing curiosity to find out what lay beyond, knowing full well that some simple little accident like getting his matches wet could be fatal. And no one would even know where to look for him. Here he was creeping through an unknown, unexplored cave on the inside of a mountain with no visible means of entry or exit, where not a soul would hear him if he shouted at the top of his voice for as long as his strength lasted. For obvious reasons, Casteret forced himself not to think about what could happen and concentrated on coping with the unknown dangers that might lay ahead of him.

As he made his way past an enormous pillar rising up from the creek bed, he saw that the corridor again came to an end against the slanting ceiling. The water deepened into another pool. Casteret snuffed out his candle, carefully put it in his bathing cap and, shivering, he waded into the deepening pool and dived.

This time long, pointed stalactites thrust down from the roof of the underwater siphon like sharp teeth, obstructing his way. He pushed and pulled his way through them, scraping his body painfully on their rough edges. There seemed to be no end to this torment. Terror tightened his throat as the black water swirled around him, and he wondered if this time he may have pushed his luck too far. But just at the point where he knew he either had to go back or find the surface somewhere, he again came up in a pocket of trapped air.

This time it was a small, low-ceilinged gallery where water dripped so incessantly from the overhead stalactites that his candle was repeatedly extinguished. By now he was so chilled from the stream's icy waters he had to stop and exercise his arms and legs vigorously to start the circulation again.

He had guessed right about the underground stream carving out the cavern, but now he began to wonder just how extensive it was. It might go on for miles. The stream kept flowing, sometimes slowly in placid pools; other times it babbled noisily over shallow cataracts. Casteret picked his way through the rock-strewn rubble of the gallery, crawling the entire distance. Finding his way blocked by a pile of rocks he thought was the end of the gallery, he crawled over them and found that the tunnel went on. After wriggling through a series of limestone columns, he came out of the low-ceilinged passageway onto a clay bank where he was able to walk upright, leaving behind footprints to follow on his way out. Casteret went on until he realized that for some time he had been traveling along a gradually narrowing tunnel. Finally he reached a bottleneck, a hole too small to get his entire body through. Still, he squeezed in as far as he could, thrusting his head and one arm through the opening. And as he did there was a sudden movement in the water around him. He shouted happily for in the flickering candlelight he saw swarms of black tadpoles. Their presence told him that somewhere nearby was an opening to the outside world because tadpoles seldom travel far into underground water. Indeed, a few days later, Casteret found the spot where the spring entered the cavern by a crevice too small for anything much larger than a tadpole to squeeze through.

Now he had to retrace his steps, a task more difficult than when he came in because now he was almost completely exhausted. The only trouble he had, however, was a few moments of indecision as to which branch of a tunnel to take, and at the most treacherous underwater siphon he had to dive twice to find the linking passageway through the rock.

He had entered the grotto in the bright light of day. When he left, it was nighttime. It had taken him five hours to cover what he later measured to be a mile and seven-eighths inside the cave.

For the rest of the summer Casteret made repeated expeditions into the cavern, wandering through a maze of new halls and low galleries on a second level, ever watchful for some signs of prehistoric habitation.

Finally the seasonal rain set in and the underground stream swelled to such proportions that he was no longer able to enter the cavern. Before it was completely flooded, however, he tried to get beyond the first rock barrier but found he had to swim too great a distance underwater to find any trapped air pockets. So he gave up the venture for that summer. He had recovered one small artifact from the bed of the stream inside the hidden cavern that gave him hope that man had once used it during dry periods. He had found a bison tooth.

The next year Casteret returned to Montespan with a caving friend, Henri Godin. This time the water in the cave was so low that they could carry lighted candles and swim through the first siphon with their heads out of water. They went as far as the huge pillar that rose up out of the stream just before the second siphon and with chattering teeth, climbed out of the icy water into a dry gallery that looked like a fairyland. The walls rippled in cascades of limestone, long, slender stalactites glittered from the ceiling, the floor was fluted and scalloped, each miniature stone terrace containing a small crystalline pool of water. Before them arched a bright yellow granular floor. They crossed it, the slap of their bare feet echoing loudly in the stone vault. Turning a sharp corner they found themselves standing on the threshold of a gallery 650 feet long, 16 feet high and 13 feet wide, paved with wet clay. Eagerly they went on, following each other in single file, slipping and sliding their way along the tunnel with its ever-sloping ceiling. For the last 100 feet, the roof was so close to them that they had to crawl the rest of the way, finally being forced to return to a place where they could again stand upright. While Casteret's companion held the lighted candles, he vigorously attacked the clay floor with a small hand

FIG. 1.

FIG. 2.

(FROM PHOTOGRAPHS BY CASTERET)

These 20,000-year-old clay statues confronted Casteret deep within the sunken cave of Montespan. Fig. 1 is a 16-inch-thick, life-size wall relief of the forelegs and chest of one of three lions, destroyed perhaps by prehistoric man's ritual spear thrusts. Nearby, Fig. 2, crouched the form of a bear, the skull of a real bear's head lying between its outstretched forepaws.

pick. The heavy clay stuck to his pick. Casteret began digging with his hands. Suddenly his fingers closed on a hard object. "Even before I had freed it from the surrounding clay, I knew I held one of those chipped flints that delights any archaeologist," he said. "This simple flint, barely formed but indubitably chipped and used, did in fact prove that primitive man had frequented the cavern."

Casteret held his candle high and immediately scrutinized the walls for the rock engravings he knew must be there. "It was then that I stopped suddenly before the clay statue of a bear." Nearly four feet long and two feet high, the headless effigy was crouching with forepaws extended in the position of the great sphinx of Egypt. Between its paws lay the skull of a real bear that had once been pegged to the sculpture. The clay figure was coated with calcite drippings from the ceiling, proving its great age. Subsequent study revealed it to be about twenty thousand years old.

Casteret excitedly called Godin to see his find but his companion had difficulty recognizing the shape as that of a bear. Casteret moved his candle and, "...one after another, as I discovered them around us, I showed him horses in relief, two big clay lions, many engravings."

Godin was convinced. For over an hour the two reveled in their discoveries. "On all sides we found animals, designs, mysterious symbols, all the awe-inspiring and portentous trappings of ages before the dawn of history," said Casteret.

Not far from the huge pillar, in a kind of antechamber to the main gallery, they found fifty shaped reliefs of animals either long extinct or emigrated from the area. Skillfully carved with flint tools were intaglios of mammoths, horses, wild asses, goats, bisons, stags, chamois and hyenas. In many instances the prehistoric engravings were strikingly original. At other times the primitive artist had added symbols and embellishments that were not clear. One of the horses, for example, bore the deeply engraved picture of a hand on its flank. Was this Magdalenian man saying that he had mastered the wild horse? In another, the horse was fashioned in such a way that a slightly curved ledge was used to designate the profile of its back. In yet another, a chamois head was engraved around a pebble embedded in the wall so that the pebble formed the animal's eye. Several of the engravings showed arrows or wounds on the animals depicted. Among the carefully incised animal pictures Casteret found an engraving that looked like a human caricature with a domed head, large bulbous nose, enormous round lidless eye and a short beard similar to those found in other Pyrenees caves. Archaeologists believe that these depict masks that had strong ritual significance to primitive man. Interestingly, human statues always showed great figure detail, but the faces were always left blank. On the ceiling at the far end of the Montespan gallery, a spot Casteret found only by crawling, he discovered the smallest rock engraving ever found—the picture of a hyena only two inches long.

There were 30 clay statues in what was later to be called the Hall of the Bear. Near one wall were the tumbled remains of three felines that had been sculptured as if they were stalking one behind the other. All were about life-size, 16-inch high reliefs modeled against the wall. The body of the first had been five feet seven inches long and two feet four inches high. Large chunks of clay lying on the ground still showed the chest and forelegs still stood upright. Following the line on the wall opposite the missing head, which lay as a chunk of clay between the animal's forepaws, Casteret found still remaining, contoured on the wall, one rear paw and the end of its tufted tail, identifying the relief as that of a lion. The parts that remained standing were riddled with the angular holes of spear thrusts. The two remaining lion statues were in worse condition than the first, possibly entirely dismembered by spear thrusts.

Within a radius of 30 feet in the inner gallery was a vast array of clay animal figures, the most prominent being the statue of the bear. In its crouching position the hind paws were hidden under its belly, but its right forepaw was outstretched, the claws clearly indicated. Shoulders and haunches were well rounded. Apparently the primitive sculptor had fashioned it purposely without a head because beyond the characteristic hump of the bear's back, where the head belonged, the surface was carefully smoothed. A real bear's head had been attached there with a wood peg, remnants of which were still visible. The skull between the animal's paws was all that remained of that head.

Like those of the lions, the bear's clay torso had been repeatedly mutilated with at least 30 spear thrusts. But instead of leaning against the wall as had the lions, it stood about a yard away on a platform made for that purpose. Nearby, the outline of a horse was deeply dug into the clay floor. It was surrounded by 30 other high reliefs measuring from 1 to 2 feet long and from 4 to 16 inches thick. Most had been disfigured by the passage of water through this area; however, enough remained to indicate that these reliefs all represented horses, many bearing symbolic marks or figures.

In the corners of the gallery were pits still showing the marks of stone tools and finger strokes, where the primitive artists had dug the clay used in the sculptures. In the wall a stone crevice several yards long had been carefully chinked with clay and numerous finger holes punched in it. Jutting out of one of the holes was a large polished bone spatula like that used by sculptors for executing detailed work in clay. Closer investigation also revealed a rock cavity full of chipped flints. Along the wall ledges sat fist-size clay balls shaped by human hands. Sometimes a nest-shaped pocket of clay was purposely molded to the wall. Nearby a flat disk of clay was attached, its center cut out in the shape of a horse's head. Most of these items were encased and further cemented to the wall by calcite drippings.

Many of the figures on the floor had been clawed and obliterated in places by bears. Often, bear and naked human footprints were together. "Sometimes the claw marks are on top on the footprints, sometimes the other way around; man and beast struggled for possession of the cavern," said Casteret. "One can hardly think without shuddering of the fearful combats which must have taken place, nor ever cease to admire the courage of our distant ancestors who ventured into this lair of the wild beasts armed only with javelins and stone axes."

No evidence of cooking or living areas was ever found in the cavern. Casteret suspected that the Hall of the Bear was a sanctuary for sacred rituals in which Magdalenian cavemen, in the flickering light of smoking firebrands, fought mock battles with the clay effigies, repeatedly stabbing and "killing" the figures in some strange ceremony possibly to guarantee their success in the hunt. Whatever the reason, the Grotto of Montespan provided us with the oldest statues in the world, all because a curious Norbert Casteret had the courage to strike out into the unknown and cross a threshold into a wonderland as marvelous to him as Alice's was to her, when she stepped through the looking glass.

In the wake of his discovery came archaeologists, French and foreign scientists, reporters and photographers. And from then on the quiet little village of Montespan was never the same again. To the unassuming Casteret, who once wrote, "Where can one find such excitement, see such strange sights, enjoy such intellectual satisfactions as in exploration below ground?" it was the culmination of a lifelong ambition. After his findings were officially confirmed and the grotto was classified as a historical monument, he received awards and accolades from scholars, professors and learned institutions, including a large gold medal from the Academie des Sports—all of which pleased him enormously. But none of this fanfare seems to have turned Casteret's head, because as quickly as he could he went back to doing the thing he most enjoyed: crawling through unexplored caverns in search of new horizons underground.

2

THE WET SPELEOLOGISTS

Somersetshire in southwestern England is a basin surrounded on three sides by hills and bounded on the fourth by the sea. From the north, the Mendip Hills drop from a 1,000-foot height along a series of gorges and caves to the southern lowlands. Through the years the Mendip and Cheddar caves have yielded valuable evidence of Paleolithic cultures (seven hundred and fifty thousand years to about fifteen thousand years ago) and later, following the Claudian conquest of Somerset in A.D. 43, the much scattered remains of that Roman occupation.

It is not surprising then that, in 1934, Somersetshire experienced an awakening interest in exploring the caves for archaeological treasures, whether prehistoric or Romano-British artifacts. The latter especially appealed to two young Englishmen, Graham Balcombe and J. A. Sheppard. What particularly fired their imaginations was not what might be found in the labyrinthine passageways of the dry limestone caves, but what lay below and beyond the pools of cold green water at the end of some of those passageways. As far as they knew, no one had ever summoned either the courage or know-how to investigate those forbidding depths. What incredible treasures must await the first to do so! Surely every cave inhabitant from prehistoric man to Roman soldier had dropped or thrown something from their period into the pools. And, to these young men's way of thinking, those treasures were still there, somewhere underwater, waiting for the first brave man clever enough to find a way to go down and get them.

So they went to work on the project. On their first attempt

to plumb the mystery of one of the pools they attacked it with no more elaborate equipment than a waterproof flashlight and a pair of homemade diving goggles. This effort quickly provided them with the following information: (1) the pool was deep, dark, cold, and exceedingly scary, and (2) they needed some kind of breathing apparatus that would enable them to explore farther than they could by holding their breaths.

This line of reasoning led to a number of penciled sketches of possible diving rigs, most of which were too expensive to build. Eventually, however, by pooling their resources and scrounging materials, Balcombe built what was later described as "a crazy respirator out of an old bicycle frame and forty feet of garden hose."

Like the intrepid inventors they were, they carefully tested the device both on land and in the shallows of a neighborhood pond. On all occasions it worked flawlessly. So there was nothing for it but to make the historic dive.

Their choice of sites—a scummy, odoriferous pool that punctuated a dead-end limestone passageway 2,000 feet inside Somersetshire's Hole.

On the day of the dive, had any passersby seen them carrying their odd-looking equipment into the cave, they surely would have wondered what was amiss; for it was certainly not often that you saw people carrying bicycle frames and hoses into such as Swildon's Hole. But Balcombe and Sheppard couldn't have cared less. They were too intent on their adventure and what they hoped to find in the drowned treasure room at the end of the limestone passageway.

In the yellow glow of their lights they set up the diving apparatus on the edge of the shadowy black pool. Balcombe would dive first. Sheppard would remain behind to tend the hose and lend any necessary assistance.

Balcombe stripped to his swimming suit, shivering in the chill moist air of the dark cavern. He wore a nose clip, his homemade goggles, and a waterproof flashlight tied to his forehead. With one end of the air hose clenched in his mouth, and the crazy bicycle respirator feeding him air, he gingerly waded into the pool, which deepened rapidly as he walked. When the icy water reached his neck, he sucked hard and fast on the air hose, his heart pounding.

He ducked his head under the surface. His light poked a feeble yellow finger into the all-encompassing green gloom surrounding him. With a last glance and wave to Sheppard, Balcombe summoned his courage, filled his lungs with air and pulled himself down.

Instead of sinking as he intended, he tended to float. Trying again, his hands brushed against jumbled rocks lying below him on the sloping bottom. Grasping a sizable chunk, he found that it provided the weight he needed to sink slowly into the gloomy green depths of the pool.

Despite the shock of the incredibly cold water and the heart-quickening experience of sinking into an unknown black abyss, Balcombe, still eager, strained to see what the feeble rays of his light would reveal of his surroundings. All he saw was a uniform brownish green gloom with bubbles of marsh gas rising around him.

As he continued downward, his ears began aching from the increased water pressure. Not knowing what was wrong or how to stop it, he simply gritted his teeth and hoped it would disappear. And surprisingly it did, accompanied by a high-pitched squeaking in his ears. Momentarily he wondered if he had burst his eardrums and would never hear again.

Then suddenly he was plunged into total night! His light had gone out!

His heart double-timed. He sucked rapidly on the hose, wondering why he was not getting air faster. He immediately dropped the rock and pulled for the surface.

As abruptly as it had gone out, Balcombe's light reappeared. Glancing down, he saw the reason. He had reached bottom and become completely immersed in its velvet-soft mud without realizing it.

He rose rapidly now, and moments later Sheppard helped him stumble ashore; his body was racked with spasms.

"Cold water and my nervy condition quickly reduced me to a state of uncontrollable shivering," he reported later. Dressing hurriedly, he ran from the cave to warm himself in the sunlight outside.

Sheppard reassembled their gear and prepared to make his

maiden voyage into the watery pit. Balcombe's experience had in no way diminished Sheppard's eagerness to try his luck in the uninspiring pool of murk. Enthusiastically he donned the diving gear, waded into the chilly water and sank from sight.

His reactions to the subterranean submersion was much the same as Balcombe's. Knowing the danger of sinking into the soft mud bottom, however, he avoided it, and kept himself out of trouble.

As Sheppard made his way along one wall of the pool, he dimly saw the opening of a narrow passageway leading off to the right. Cautiously he entered and followed it, tugging at the tightness of the air hose he had slipped under his left arm.

Turning his head from side to side he swept the faint yellow beam of his light over the angular walls ahead of him. They stretched on as far as the short limit of his visibility, the bottom thick with the soft, silty mud that boiled up before his goggles like smoke whenever he moved his hand too close to it.

Enticed farther into the tunnel by the tantalizing thought of what might lie just beyond the blurred and gradually constricting passageway he was following, Sheppard was unprepared for his air hose to abruptly stop him.

Thinking it had snagged, he reached back and tugged smartly. Forty feet behind him on the surface his action jerked the hose off the respirator and into the water.

The life-giving stream of air stopped. Sheppard's last surprised gasp got little more than firm resistance from the fast flooding hose. Not waiting around for the mouthful of water that would surely follow, he dropped everything and started back the way he had come, holding his breath.

Everything was different now. He saw only stirred up, muddy water. But he could feel both sides of the narrow tunnel and he pushed on in the only direction left.

When he lost contact with the walls he almost panicked. Then he realized he was in open water again, but so badly in need of air his lungs felt ready to explode. As he frantically pulled for the surface, he could hold back no longer. His last breath burst from his mouth just as he shot through the surface. Gasping and sputtering in relief, Sheppard was thankful to be alive.

An anxious Balcombe helped him ashore. Although not aware

of it at the time, their dive into Swildon's Hole made them Britain's first modern cave divers.

The two adventurers realized that if they were to do any serious exploration of underwater caves they needed safer, more professional equipment. By the following year they obtained a somewhat damaged but repairable helmet diving suit and pump. Once everything was made serviceable again, they rounded up six other similarly minded individuals and made their way to Somersetshire's Wookey Hole Cavern, source of the River Axe.

Again, the sight of six people carrying deep-sea diving gear into a cave must have given the locals pause, but there was no restraining the inquisitive team of Balcombe and Sheppard.

Into the hole they went with helmet, hoses, suit and pump. The group, including pioneer cave diver of her sex, Penelope Powell, made its way through the first two dry chambers of the cavern, where earlier spelunkers had already recovered artifacts dating from the Iron Age to the period of Roman occupation. Five hundred feet from the mouth of the cave they reached the third chamber, which ended at a pool of water.

Here they established base camp and prepared to make their underwater assault on whatever lay beyond the watery barrier. They successfully dived through the "water gate" to the dry shore of chamber four. Then on into a partially dry fifth chamber. From there they negotiated a short 16-foot-long passageway down into the sixth chamber. Each time, they moved their base camp forward until they penetrated chamber seven. The total experience was a unique sensation to Penelope Powell, who vividly described how it felt to slip down from the surface and the dazzling glare of powerful hand lights into a shadowy world of green, crystal clear water. It made her think of green jelly, this place where even the shadows cast by the boulders were green, but of a deeper hue; and, as the divers advanced, green mud swirled up around their knees and settled back into the greenish black void behind them. "So still, so silent, unmarked by the foot of man since the river came into being," noted Powell, who found the experience "awe-inspiring but not terrifying."

Twelve years later, members of the British Cave Diving Group, founded in 1946, continued exploring Wookey Hole Cavern's unique wishbone-shaped subterranean system using

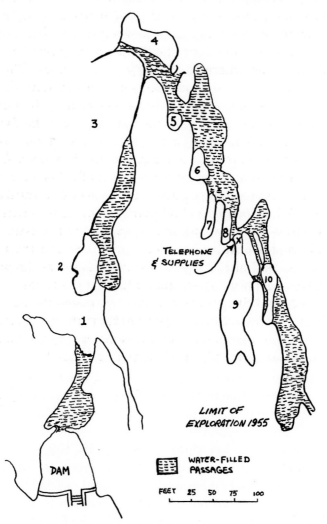

PLAN OF SOMERSETSHIRE'S WOOKEY HOLE CAVE
SHOW THE TEN CHAMBERS REACHED BY 1955
(after Dugan)

TELEPHONE & SUPPLIES

LIMIT OF EXPLORATION 1955

DAM

WATER-FILLED PASSAGES

FEET 25 50 75 100

The extensive Wookey Hole cave system creates an inverted "V" with its flooded eleventh chamber near its entrance. Numbered chambers show the dry areas used as successive "beachheads" for new explorations.

an early type of diving gear called an oxygen lung, or rebreather. Essentially, it was a waterproof canvas pouch connected to a chemical filter and a small cylinder of oxygen. The diver's exhalations were filtered, recharged with oxygen and rebreathed. Although less cumbersome than scuba tanks, rebreathers were inherently dangerous and limited their users to a depth of 30 feet. By staying within this margin and setting up advance camps in the semi-flooded chambers, the British team pushed on to the eleventh chamber, where they reached an impasse. The limestone-walled room was entirely flooded; it provided no shore for an advance camp. Interestingly, the whole cave system had reversed itself, so that the ninth chamber was near the first, yet separated from the mouth by a 1,000 feet of limestone galleries.

And what of the treasures Balcombe and Sheppard sought? Ironically, most were found by the Somerset Section of the Cave Diving Group between the mouth of the cave and its third chamber, where Balcombe's team had started. The more modern-day divers scoured the river bottom and excavated the sand banks with high pressure water jets to uncover ancient Roman pots, wide-spouted lead pitchers, over a dozen human skulls and assorted bones, and several seventeenth century bottles.

Balcombe and Sheppard's team had bypassed the finds even before they began their dives. But then they, like most dedicated treasure hunters, were more profoundly affected by the challenge of the hunt. For them, this was the real treasure.

3

FORTY FATHOMS TO THE GREAT HALL OF NIGHT

Near the French city of Avignon, there is a famous spring called the Fountain of Vaucluse. It lies in a somber crater under a 600-foot limestone cliff beside the River Sorgue. Most of the year it is a crystal-clear placid pool barely trickling spring water into the river. But come March, the entire character of the spring changes. Then the trickle becomes a torrent and the spring a violent fountain of raging waters that boil forth from the mountain for five weeks before subsiding. This strange phenomenon has occurred every year since man has recorded history, as it undoubtedly had for centuries before that. No one knows what causes this strange annual upheaval, but in the past France's poets have had their opinions. One Frederic Mistral (1830-1914), the Provençal poet, wrote that one day a traveling minstrel fell asleep beside the Fountain of Vaucluse. The nymph of the fountain appeared as a beautiful young girl and, taking the minstrel by the hand, led him down between the crystal clear walls of Vaucluse's liquid corridors to a wonderful meadow lushly carpeted with supernatural flowers. And there they stopped, before seven huge diamonds. When the girl lifted one of them, a powerful torrent of water flowed forth. "Here," she said, "is the secret of the spring and I alone keep it. To increase the flow I have but to lift the diamonds. When I lift the seventh and last diamond, the fountain rises to the fig tree whose roots drink but once a year."

While the spring nymph and the diamonds might strain one's credulity, the part about the fig tree was true. The level of the spring varies as much as 75 feet. High up the barren rock wall, far above the normal level of the pool, a lone fig tree clings to the vertical surface. Its roots are indeed watered but once a year, when the fountain rises up in full rampage.

Through the years scientists and speleologists have tried to find an answer to the mysterious workings of the spring. Where did the water come from? What was the source that powered this periodic, violent emission? One theory held that the 600-foot limestone cliff concealed an inner chamber that captured runoff seeping through the porous limestone. When this hidden pool overflowed, the water rushed through a siphon linking it to a lower chamber, and the Fountain of Vaucluse erupted.

In an effort to find some connection between surface waters absorbed from above and those coming out of the fountain below, fluorescein dye was introduced to the area during torrential rains but no one had ever been able to track it to the lower spring. "It was," to quote one speleologist, "the most exasperating enigma of subterranean hydraulics."

In 1878, a helmet-and-hose diver from Marseille named Ottonelli decided that the only way to answer the mystery was to dive down into the throat of the fountain and see what he could find. In his cumbersome gear, his air pumped down through hoses from above, Ottonelli was lowered into the narrow, black opening in the bottom of the spring basin and found himself in a tunnel sloping downward at an angle of about 50 degrees. Thirty feet below the surface he encountered a large, triangular boulder that blocked his way. Squeezing past it he continued downward for another 100 feet. At this point in the inky blackness, cold fear crept over him. The thought of being caught in a landslide in this black, rocky tomb was enough to prevent him from going any farther. But he did lower a weight that went down another 25 feet. Then he returned to the surface with the news that he had reached the bottom of the fountain. Still, this accomplishment provided no answer to the mystery.

In the course of Ottonelli's dive, his zinc boat overturned and sank down the rocky corridor into the depths of the spring. But he never saw it again, apparently passing it in the dark.

In 1938, another Marseille hard-hat diver, one Señor Negri, decided to see what he could find in the fountain. Most of the populace of Vaucluse turned out for the dramatic occasion, seat-ing themselves around the rocky amphitheater and discussing the anticipated spectacle excitedly. In this circus-like atmosphere, Negri descended into the spring. Treating the spectators to a running commentary of the event by broadcasting from a microphone attached to the inside of his helmet, Negri reported the details of his plunge to 120 feet. He said he reached the elbow of the tunnel and a siphon leading uphill, supposedly to the inner chamber. And at that moment the voice from the depths dramatically announced that he had found Ottonelli's zinc boat, completely intact despite the sixty years that it had lain in its watery grave. At this point Negri could go no farther because, he reported, his air hose was dragging alongside a huge pivotal boulder, which he was afraid might dislodge and topple on him.

Once again the whereabouts of the secret room and the workings of the fountain remained unknown. Then, on August 24, 1946, during one of the spring's quieter moments, a small group of French naval officers from Toulon arrived in Vaucluse with an impressive array of unusual diving equipment. The divers were Guy Morandiere, Jean Pinard, Maurice Fargues, Philippe Tailliez, Frederic Dumas and Jacques-Yves Cousteau. With them were Cousteau's wife, Simone, a few friends from Sanary and Marseille, and several interested speleologists. The young divers intended to solve the mystery of the fountain once and for all.

Their preparations for the attempt were based on what they could learn from reports of the two early divers, Negri and Ottonelli. Repeatedly they had tried to contact salvage contractor Negri in Marseille to question him in more detail about the topography of the cave. But for some strange reason Negri purposely avoided them. Therefore the best they could do was to go by the details in the reports.

On the predawn drive that morning to Vaucluse, Tailliez felt that his companions were not as exuberant about making this dive as they usually had been when they dived at sea. Dumas especially seemed full of forebodings. Tailliez himself was apprehensive and had made a list of seven possible dangers that might confront them: fear of the unknown and their instinctual dislike for diving underground; physical exhaustion in the cold 54°F water that would quickly sap their strength; poor visibility in the absolute darkness where flashlights would be of little value if they worked at all; accidents—the rope might break and they would be lost in an uncharted maze; suction or underwater currents could sweep them into the unknown; nitrogen narcosis—the intoxication Cousteau called "rapture of the depths" caused by an excess of nitrogen in the bloodstream at depths from about 100 feet and below—could rob them of reason and prove fatal. While these were possibilities none of the divers cared to dwell on, each man was fully aware of them.

Practically the whole population of Vaucluse, including the mayor, accompanied the divers to the spring and prepared to watch the spectacle. Among the crowd Cousteau noticed a priest who, he figured, was standing by in case his services were needed.

In the same way a group of mountain climbers would plan and launch an assault on a particular mountain, the men planned their attack on the Fountain of Vaucluse. It was to be done in a series of two-man teams. The first would go as far as it could before returning. The next team would use the farthest point of penetration as a springboard for its own effort. Subsequent teams would continue in this leapfrog manner until they reached their ultimate goal—the hidden inner chamber, the source of the fountain.

From a Canadian canoe lent to them by the mayor of Vaucluse, the men lowered a heavy piece of pig iron through the dark doorway of the spring into the shaft beyond, and continued paying out line until the weight stopped at a depth of 55 feet. Jean Pinard, without a protective suit, made a free dive down to the weight and freed it, pushing it on down the rocky slope to a depth of 90 feet before he surfaced, as red as a lobster and thoroughly chilled by the 54°F temperature of the water.

Dumas and Cousteau were to descend first. Both wore rubber diving suits to help insulate them against the cold. Dumas wore an Italian frogman suit, and Cousteau had on an outfit he made himself called a constant-volume diving dress. It not only had a unique hood that trapped enough air for Cousteau to be able to communicate for short distances with another diver underwater, but he could control his buoyancy by inflating it from his own exhalations, the suit adjusting its volume to pressure changes through escape valves at the ankles and wrists. He wore this suit over heavy woolen underwear. Both divers were loaded down with gear. On their backs each wore triple-cylinder Aqua-Lungs, the tanks containing 3,000 psi of air from a recently acquired new air compressor. Dumas also carried two additional air cylinders, one mini Aqua-Lung on his belt for emergencies and another small tank for inflating his frogman suit to control his buoyancy. In addition they had face masks, diving daggers, rubber foot fins and two flashlights apiece, one to carry in the hand, the spare on the belt. And in anticipation that they might have to fight underwater currents, both divers wore extra-heavy weight belts. Each man was encumbered with one further item: Dumas, considering the underwater mountaineering aspect of their dive, carried a mountain climber's ice ax; Cousteau, again relying on Negri's reported distance to the siphon, had coiled 300 feet of line in three pieces around his left arm. Considering what the men must have looked like under all that equipment, it is no wonder that almost everyone in Vaucluse had turned out for the occasion. Not even Negri had showed them a sight like that.

The length of the 400-foot-long guideline that Cousteau and Dumas planned to follow down to the bottom of the cavern had been determined by Negri's measurements to the siphon he said branched off from the main shaft. But what Cousteau and the others did not know at the time was that Negri's description of various features inside the cavern was the result of his overworked imagination. Not only was Ottonelli's zinc boat not there, as Negri reported it was, but Cousteau later came to suspect Negri of descending no farther than 50 feet, where he continued his dramatic broadcast describing things and events that never existed.

Unaware of this, however, the men decided on the following plan: Cousteau and Dumas, with a 30-foot rope tied between them, would follow the guideline down to the pig iron weight. They would then take the pig iron down with them, the guideline serving as the only means of communication between themselves and the surface, where Maurice Fargues would be tending it. They had agreed on a set of signals. One tug meant that Fargues was to tighten the rope to clear it of snags. Three tugs meant that he was to give them more line. Six tugs indicated an emergency, and he was to haul in line as swiftly as possible. Once the divers reached the elbow in the tunnel and the siphon going upward, as Negri had described, they would set down the pig iron, attach the end of one of Cousteau's segments of rope and move up into the branching tunnel, paying out rope behind them; eventually they hoped to reach what they suspected would be a partially air-filled inner cavern from which came the spring's annual raging torrents.

After thoroughly checking their equipment on the surface of the pool, Cousteau and Dumas swam down and entered the narrow, black opening into the shaft. The tunnel beyond angled down sharply, and the men swiftly followed the guideline. Cousteau snapped on his flashlight and was surprised when he could not see its beam. Then he realized the spring water was so clear it lacked the suspended particles that would have reflected the beam. At first the light seemed to be winking on and off until he saw the yellow disk reflecting on rocks he passed.

At one point in their descent Dumas abruptly pulled back on the rope around Cousteau's waist. A shower of rocks swept past Cousteau who, looking back, saw Dumas trying to brake his rapid descent with his feet while, at the same time, fumbling with the cylinder of compressed air that would inflate his now-flooded frogman suit. He had lost his ice ax.

At 90 feet Cousteau collected the pig iron weight and started downward again. He forgot to signal Fargues. All he could think of was that he had to get down through the frightening darkness to the bottom and get the job done. He kept moving his light around in circles, watching the beam when it hit the stone walls and wondering why there was no one else in this subway tunnel.

Abruptly there were no walls to reflect the light. They were passing through a black void and Cousteau's ears were aching. This seemed strange to him because he had been diving all summer and his ears normally adapted easily to the pressure changes. Then his light reflected on a flat, gravel bottom.

There were no walls around them. Cousteau thought this must be the farthest Negri had come. Somewhere overhead was to be found the opening to the siphon. For the first time now he noticed that he no longer had the coil of rope around his left arm. He had somehow lost it on the way down. He turned his flashlight on Dumas who was floating supinely over the bottom. In all his cumbersome gear he looked to Cousteau like some ridiculous glowworm. Dumas was still fumbling with his small air cylinder, trying to inflate his flooded frogman suit. Cousteau shined his light on Dumas' depth gauge. It read 150 feet but there was water in its dial. It had broken. Cousteau suspected that they were at least 200 feet down and some 400 feet along the sloping shaft somewhere in the black void above them.

He knew they were both feeling the effects of narcosis, but Cousteau suspected Dumas was worse off than he. Their safety depended on their staying with the guideline. Cousteau clamped Dumas' hand onto it and shouted for him to stay where he was, that he was going to look for the siphon. Dumas misunderstood him to mean that Cousteau had run out of air. He immediately started fumbling with his emergency Aqua-Lung, trying to get it off his belt. Meanwhile, Cousteau swam upward, looking for the roof of the cavern, swinging his light back and forth in the hope of spotting the opening into the siphon leading to the inner chamber. The rope tightened about his waist and he was dragged backward.

Swimming back down to Dumas, Cousteau found that his companion had let go of their guideline and was scudding backward along the floor of the cave, still trying to get his emergency cylinder off his belt. Cousteau drew closer and realized that Dumas was only semiconscious. When Cousteau touched him, he clamped a hand on his wrist like a drowning man's last grasp. Cousteau wrenched free, turning his light on Dumas' mask where he saw his friend's eyes rolling wildly. Cousteau's own mind was unclear but he remembered that they had to find the guideline. It was their only way back. At least there was no current in the cavern. Had there been, he knew there would be little hope of their recovering the rope.

Cousteau began moving back and forth over the bottom until his flashlight picked out the rusted mass of pig iron, and, above it, the guideline trailing off into the blackness. Tugging on the tether to Dumas, he drew the inert form up beside him. Dumas was in bad shape. In his semiconscious state, he had lost his mouthpiece. He had swallowed water, getting some in his lungs before recovering the mouthpiece, which he forced his jaws to hold once again. After that he was unable to do much more than weakly move his arms and legs. Cousteau too felt something more than the stupefying effect of nitrogen narcosis. He was completely exhausted. And yet it would be up to him to haul Dumas up the rope to the surface, a feat that he felt totally incapable of because in his waterlogged condition, Dumas weighed at least 25 pounds. But Cousteau knew he had to climb the rope and pull his companion along behind him as best he could.

Grasping the guideline, he started to climb. "My first three handholds on the line were interpreted correctly by Fargues as the signal to pay out more rope," said Cousteau. "He did so with a will. I regretted with utter dismay the phenomenon of the rope slackening and made super-human efforts to climb it. Fargues smartly fed me rope when he felt my traction. It took an eternal minute for me to form the tactic that I should continue to haul down rope, until the end of it came into Fargues' hand. He would never let that go. I hauled in rope in dull glee."

Cousteau kept collecting rope and Fargues kept feeding it to him, thinking that the divers were ascending the siphon toward the secret inner chamber. When Fargues came to the end of the 400-foot length of line it did not stop him. He efficiently tied on another length. Meanwhile, over 300 feet of loose rope piled up behind Cousteau who stubbornly kept pulling in slack, certain that the end would have to come sometime. When at last he felt the knot where Fargues had tied on the extension, Cousteau dropped the guideline in disgust. He would have to climb the wall of the cavern, hand over hand, foot by foot, dragging the helpless Dumas behind him.

As he began to climb, his head ached and he panted for air. His hands moved from one slippery outcropping to the next. Slowly he made progress until suddenly his hand slipped and he fell backward with Dumas' dead weight pulling him back down to the cavern floor. Cousteau's head throbbed unbearably now. A wave of nausea swept over him. He could not avoid vomiting. With his jaws locked on the mouthpiece, the contents of his stomach passed through an air vent no larger than a paper clip and through the demand regulator without blocking it.

Again he turned back to the guideline and struggled to remember the signal. Six tugs meant for Fargues to haul in line.

Cousteau tugged hard six times, but in the 400-foot crumbling rock passageway above him the rope was snagged and slack in a dozen places. Dumas clung to him. Cousteau knew this was the end. Dumas was dead, and now his body was preventing Cousteau from saving his own life. He reached for his sheath knife to cut the rope tying him to Dumas. But even in his stupefied, chaotic thinking Cousteau had flashes of reality. Before cutting Dumas free, he would try once more to reach Fargues.

He grasped the line and tugged the distress signal.

Four hundred feet away Fargues was holding the line lightly in his fingertips, trying to sense what was happening below. If he had interpreted them correctly, the earlier signals had called for a lot of slack line. Apparently the men were exploring something really enormous down there for the amount of rope they were using, thought Fargues. But now something, a slight tremor of the line made him wonder. Was it a signal or not? If he was wrong what could he risk but a reprimand? Fargues' hands clamped onto the rope and he began hauling.

Deep in the cavern Cousteau felt the guideline moving upward. He let go of his knife and grasped the line with both hands.

Swiftly the two men were hauled up. In less than a minute Cousteau saw the faint green opening, the narrow door of the tunnel. Then they were through it and were being pulled into the pool. Fargues leaped into the water after the unconscious Dumas, while Tailliez and Pinard waded in after Cousteau.

On the beach Dumas was violently sick to his stomach, but soon revived. Stripping off their wet gear, the men warmed themselves with the help of brandy and a fire.

Once Dumas was back to normal the divers discussed what had happened. Nobody knew. Both men felt as if they had been drugged. But there was no logical explanation for it.

That afternoon the second pair of divers prepared to go down. This time it was Tailliez and Guy Morandiere. They decided to travel lighter than Cousteau and Dumas. Beside their face masks, lead weight belts and swim fins, each carried a knife, a flashlight in his hand and another on his belt. Instead of rubber suits to insulate themselves against the cold, they wore light woolen underwear which provided little protection but gave them more freedom of movement.

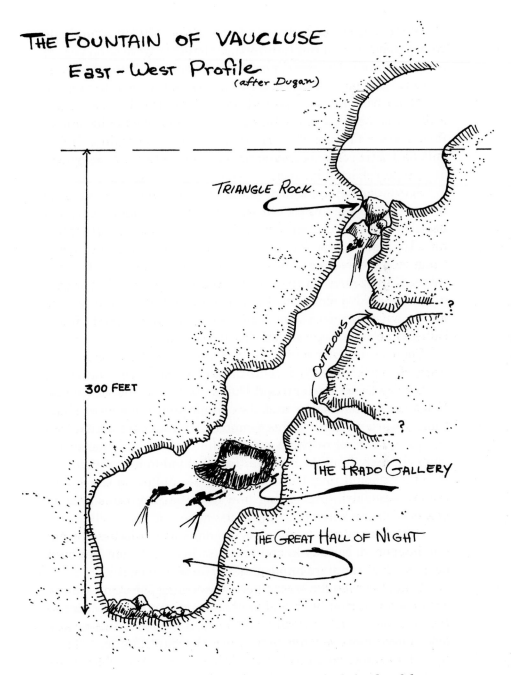

Cousteau and Dumas descended into the cold, dark depths of the mysterious Fountain. Both were in immediate danger of losing their lives by the time they reached the Great Hall of Night.

According to the signals arranged with Fargues, one tug meant they were all right; three tugs that they were to be hauled up immediately. The two divers decided between themselves that if either one shouted they were to return to the surface at once.

At 4:13 P.M. the two swam down through the dark entrance. A guideline was tied to Tailliez's belt. A ten-foot safety rope linked them together. Inside the dark tunnel they turned on their lights and, like their companions, were surprised not to see the beams until they reflected off rocks.

Side by side they swam down the steep incline, following their agreed tactic of staying close to the roof of the passageway. Tailliez kept his flashlight shining on the ceiling. Swimming rhythmically they quickly penetrated the icy depths. Lacking a depth gauge but possessing an uncanny ability to judge depth accurately, Tailliez guessed they were down about 120 feet, when he paused to analyze his sensations. Following the roof of the cave this far gave the men a strange feeling of swimming upside down. But more than that, Tailliez was filled with a nervous apprehension that was not quite fear, but a feeling he could not overcome. He guessed they were at the top of the water mass over the place where Cousteau and Dumas had had trouble. Surely, just a few yards further and they would find the siphon shaft leading upward. Tailliez was tempted to strike out and look for it until he turned his light on Morandiere and saw him trembling violently from the cold. Tailliez shouted to him, indicating that they should turn back and go up. He pulled on the guideline. It was slack, preventing him from sending the signal to Fargues. A strange feeling of exhaustion swept over Tailliez. He started breathing erratically. His mind played tricks on him. He fumbled for the guideline and had it in his hands, but he could not feel it. Morandiere bumped him. His movements were awkward. Tailliez thought Morandiere was feeling the same kind of lethargy as he, that he was groggily pushing Tailliez toward the surface, trying to save him. As if in a dream Tailliez saw Morandiere move around him, grasp the guideline and tug it three times and then fall back.

Far above them Fargues' sensitive fingers felt the signal. He responded by hauling on the rope. Suddenly it tightened; it was snagged!

Tailliez saw the rope move, then stop. He suspected that a loop had caught on a wall projection. Morandiere seemed unaware of it as if he were in a trance. Tailliez knew it was up to him to free the rope.

He caught the line in his hand and wound it several times around his left wrist. Then he took out his knife to cut it. For a moment he tried to think whether he should cut it above or below his wrist. Finally he just cut it somewhere.

"We're going up now," Tailliez later wrote in his diving log. "I gripped the piece of cut rope in my right hand, but I have no hope anymore. The blackness that surrounds us has numbed my brain. I tell myself that when I open my hand it will be two lives that I shall be throwing away with that torn bit of rope.

"Before long I see a faint glimmer of light, and very high above us, very far away, surrounding a solid dark block cut out like the map of an island, three little windows of sky. We rise up and up toward the beauty of God's light. In passing I catch sight of an unusual object, it attracts my attention almost as if it were a human being, and I realize that it is the ax that Dumas dropped this morning."

They scraped through the opening and were hauled into the pool. Tailliez staggered out; behind him Morandiere collapsed. The others rushed to their assistance. Tailliez's left hand gripped his knife blade tightly. Blood flowed freely from the gash in his palm.

Once again the welcome warmth of the fire and brandy rapidly revived the two men. They had been down nine minutes but they had only reached a depth of 130 feet underwater, taking out some 300 feet of the guideline. Why they had not been able to go further and what had happened to give them the same strange sensations experienced by Cousteau and Dumas, was still a mystery. Whatever it was, however, both Tailliez and Morandiere had the feeling that, only minutes before, they were close to death.

After that one more group went down: Pinard, Cousteau and Dumas. But they advanced no further than a triangle rock Ottonelli had described at 50 feet. They mapped the mouth of the fountain and that night left Vaucluse. On the drive back to Toulon they discussed the strange feeling that had come over them in the spring. A comment from Tailliez suddenly made Cousteau wonder if anything was wrong with the air in their tanks. The next morning a laboratory analyzed it. The results showed that their air contained deadly carbon monoxide. At the depth they were diving the effects of carbon monoxide poisoning, which prevents oxygen from being absorbed into the blood stream, would kill a man in 20 minutes. Further checking revealed the culprit to be their new diesel-powered air compressor, which had sucked in its own exhaust fumes and added them to the air in their tanks. It had almost cost the divers their lives.

For many years the Fountain of Vaucluse remained inviolate. Then, in 1955, one of the largest diving expeditions of all time was organized to solve the riddle. Sponsored by the French Office of Underwater Research at Marseille, seventeen divers and a substantial backup force of technicians and scientists with truckloads of special equipment, including recompression chambers, hydroplanes, powerful underwater lights, depth meters, inclinometers, cameras and other gear for measuring, photographing and analyzing the underground passages of the springs, gathered at Vaucluse for a major assault on the fountain.

Day and night, pairs of divers descended, working as teams, leapfrogging each other progressively deeper into the cavern, bringing back measurements and photographs to the scientists waiting beside the fountain along with the townspeople of Vaucluse.

At 165 feet beneath the surface two unknown siphons were discovered. When divers tried to swim up these narrow tunnels, strong outflowing currents forced them back. Other divers, descending down the main shaft, entered a large gallery 170 feet below the surface which they named the Prado. One hundred feet into this chamber put them 200 feet down. Then, at a pressure depth of 230 feet, the shaft simply seemed to end in a black void. This was where Cousteau and Dumas had had their most difficulty, the enormous cavern that appeared to have no walls or ceiling. Appropriately they named it the Great Hall of Night. Directing powerful light beams down through the perfectly clear water far below, the divers saw jumbled boulders lying at an estimated depth of 285 feet, too far down for safe compressed-air diving.

And what of the mysterious workings of the Fountain of Vaucluse, the siphons and the possible hidden chamber?

Considering all the evidence from the dive, the scientists from the French Office of Underwater Research believe this to be the answer: in the upper plateau over the River Sorgue, a series of cave-ins and sinks created a network of subterranean breaks. Periodically these fill with water until the expanded runoff annually surges out through the lower levels, creating the rampaging spring.

This may or may not be true. No one knows for sure. But one thing is certain—the Fountain of Vaucluse guards its secret well.

4

LINDBERGH AND THE
UNDERGROUND LAKE

Every major achievement usually triggers a steady progression of firsts. The first man to jump off a cliff flapping his arms to fly like a bird inspired another to be the first to try it a different way. The Wright brothers' first successful flight at Kitty Hawk in 1903 led to Charles Lindbergh's first successful transatlantic flight in 1927. Similarly Cousteau's invention of the Aqua-Lung that freed man for unrestrained underwater flights, provided the means for that transatlantic aviator's son, Jon Lindbergh, to make the first successful U.S. cave dive.

In March, 1953, the 20-year-old marine biology student from Stanford University volunteered to swim alone into California's Bower Cave. It was no publicity stunt, no act of bravado. It was simply something he wanted to do quietly on his own. Lindbergh's curiosity had been whetted by a theory that the clear, cool popular swimming spa in the gold-bearing hills of northern California was fed from a secret inner chamber. When the man behind the theory, San Francisco speleologist Raymond de Saussure, organized an expedition to learn its whereabouts, Lindbergh offered to make the exploratory dives.

Their first visit was to reconnoiter the pool. Since no one else was a diver, all efforts were directed toward assisting Lindbergh. The water in the pool was cold, clear and deep. Besides a single-tank Aqua-Lung, dive mask and flippers he wore a hooded rubber dry suit to keep himself warm. A six-inch army trench knife was strapped to his leg. He carried a waterproof flashlight, a carbon dioxide-inflatable rubber diver's float to buoy him if necessary, and two small tanks of oxygen in case of an emergency. For safety's sake his companions tied a light nylon line around his waist.

A crowd of curious spectators watched the burdened diver swim out into the pool and sink from sight. Some wondered about the young man's sanity, but then they came by this naturally. Their fathers once wondered the same thing about a young man determined to try and fly single-handed across the Atlantic Ocean.

Less awkward now that he was submerged with all of his gear, Lindbergh cruised along just below the surface examining the basin. As he descended for a closer look, the chill of the water penetrated his thin rubber suit. Increased water pressure molded it tightly to his body in folds and creases that would leave their red welts on his skin long after the dive.

Carefully he scrutinized the fretted niches and fractured limestone walls stretching into the dim green depths below him. The unfamiliar line tugged at his waist. He pulled more slack, then dropped deeper. Pain built in his ears. He worked his jaws, and the pressure equalized with a begrudging squeak that instantly eased the discomfort.

The underwater basin grew larger as the walls receded; cautiously he moved into the shadow of an overhang. Below him he saw what it concealed—the huge black opening of a cave. It was about 30 feet high. Long, jagged, toothlike rocks thrust down into the awesome maw.

Lindbergh paused before it, gathering slack in his safety line and probing the cavern's inner darkness with the thin yellow beam of his flashlight. Despite the general loss of daylight under the limestone overhang, the water visibility was still good. He could see with his flashlight for 25 to 50 feet.

Staying well below the overhead rock snags he moved into the cave, playing the beam of light back and forth in front of him. Slowly he swam about 150 feet along the gradually rising tunnel, his rhythmic exhalations rumbling loud in his ears. Suddenly he saw his air bubbles cease forming the flattened silvery balloons that marked his progress along the roof of the passageway. Instead, they disappeared overhead and were replaced by ripples. The bubbles were breaking on a surface; an air pocket was above him.

Lindbergh rose cautiously, an arm overhead in case it was only a shallow cavity in the ceiling. He did not want to shoot headfirst up into a thin air pocket only inches away from skull-fracturing rock.

His hand went through the invisible barrier first, then the rest of him, his heart pounding as he surfaced with a loud slapping and echoing of waves in a large air pocket. Saussure was right! It was the chamber they were looking for!

Lindbergh pushed up his mask and looked around. It was a large, vaulted room. Long slender stalactites reached down from the ceiling, glittering wetly in the beam of his light. In some places along the undulating limestone walls he saw brilliant white cascades that looked like stiffly starched curtains. He snapped off his flashlight. The room was immediately plunged into darkness. But as his eyes slowly adjusted, he began to see the vague outlines of the walls reflected in a dim light from the underwater entrance.

After a last look at the room, Lindbergh retraced his way down through the siphon, coiling his line as he went. He was anxious to tell the others what he had found.

Lindbergh and his friends returned to the resort the following month. During the intervening weeks he had figured out a way to photograph the inside of the cave and show them what he had seen. Today this might seem like a trivial chore, but in the early 1950s it was a bit more complicated. Waterproof cameras were not readily available then. If a diver was to photograph underwater he usually built his own waterproof wooden box with a glass port, or fashioned something more costly and elaborate of metal. Since no such equipment was available to Lindbergh, he planned to use an ordinary small camera, flashbulbs and reflector that he could wrap in plastic bags until he got them inside the underground room to take his pictures.

This time he would make two journeys into the cave: the first to take in a collapsed rubber raft to inflate and use as a dry, stable platform from which to photograph; and the second trip with his camera.

Getting the one-man raft from the pool to the underground lake was slightly awkward. Despite its small size, the thing was determined to float prematurely. During Lindbergh's long swim through the siphon he kept the ungainly bundle clutched to his chest with all the determination of a quarterback driving for a badly needed first down.

Once again surfacing inside the chamber, he unfolded the raft and ducked underwater to inflate it. As he tried to manipulate the raft, his flashlight and the cylinder of compressed carbon dioxide all at the same time, he wished for at least two more hands. Somehow, however, he got the gas cylinder attached and turned on.

With a whoosh, the raft inflated and popped to the surface. There it continued to balloon into a grotesque rubber bubble while Lindbergh fumbled frantically to shut off the oversized cylinder of gas that he now realized was too big for the job. Seconds before the weirdly swollen craft would have burst its seams, he stemmed the flow.

Bobbing around on the surface, he hastily valved off excess gas until the raft shrank back to normal and floated more supinely. Lindbergh quickly checked its seams for bubbles. It was all right. The stage was set. He clamped his jaws on his mouthpiece and swam back down the siphon to the other pool.

The next morning Lindbergh checked all his gear for the last time. Camera, flash and bulbs seemed waterproof enough in their triple thickness of plastic bags. If anything leaked, the entire two-day dive would be wasted. So he made doubly sure that the package was well sealed and tied to his flashlight before he entered the pool and dived.

Again, Lindbergh made his way into the siphon. As he passed its entrance, his lifeline snagged on the jagged rocks. Caught in mid-stroke, he went back and freed the line without difficulty. How deep was this hidden lake, he wondered? Aiming his light down he began a vertical descent, finning slowly toward an unseen bottom. The yellow beam of his flashlight pierced the green darkness like a slender probing finger, reaching for something it could not touch. It never crossed Lindbergh's mind that if his only light went out he would be left suspended in an inky void blindly trying to find his way back to the surface without crashing into some obstacle.

When nothing solid appeared in his moving beam, he more carefully noted his progress on the slowly moving black hand of his depth gauge. With some surprise that he had not found bottom yet, he continued down...70...90...100 feet. Finally, at 120 feet, he stopped and swept his light below him in wide arcs. Water clarity was perfect, but there was still no bottom. Apparently by then he was beginning to feel the first effects of nitrogen narcosis, because as he later reported: "I found I had difficulty concentrating on more than one thing. I looked at the depth gauge and would forget about the rope. I would remember the rope with something of a shock. As soon as I went to a depth of 60 feet, there was no trouble at all."

Lindbergh returned to the surface of the hidden lake. With a sweep of his light, he picked out the pale oval shape of his raft. He swam to it, dropped his light and camera package inside and prepared to climb in. He got one leg over the side, but in the process he flooded the raft.

He tried scooping out the water but was hindered by his heavy diving gear. Finally, he towed the waterlogged raft over to the side of the chamber, tied it to a stalactite and began shucking his cumbersome equipment. He put his weight belt in the bottom of the raft and tied his Aqua-Lung beside it. Lacking an implement to bail out the raft, he used his face mask. The raft was almost empty when he accidentally hit his air tank and smashed the glass in his mask.

Muttering darkly to himself, Lindbergh climbed into the raft to ponder the situation. The loss of the mask meant that he would be virtually blind trying to find his way out of the cave. But he thought he would at least be able to see well enough to follow the reflected daylight through the siphon back into the pool. About then he realized he had also torn a fist-sized hole in the seat of his rubber suit. It provided him with a chilly reminder that if a piece of his broken face mask glass sliced a similar hole in the raft, his tank, weights, and all could sink from under him. Then there would be no way out of the cave.

Lindbergh cautiously felt around the bottom of the rubber raft, and threw stray pieces of broken glass overboard. Then he placed the camera package in his lap and unwrapped it. He attached the flash, set the shutter speed at 1/25 of a second and methodically shot a roll of pictures of the cave's interior. Then he repacked and sealed the equipment for his return trip through the siphon.

Donning his diving gear again, Lindbergh held his nose and dived down toward the blurred semicircle of light marking the mouth of the siphon. Once he negotiated the sharp rock pendants at the entrance, he had no trouble swimming up into the basin where his waiting friends gave him a hero's welcome.

The incident of the holed suit and smashed mask in no way dampened Lindbergh's desire to explore this new-found system more thoroughly. In fact, he stayed out of water only long enough to get another face mask and stick a tire patch on his seat, and then he dived back through the siphon. This time he swam 300 feet back into the cave, at which point he felt dizzy and returned to the basin. The last he saw of his one-man raft it was still drifting aimlessly around the hidden underground lake, deep within Bower Cave.

5

INTO THE WELL OF DEATH

From the court in front of these theaters runs a wide and handsome roadway as far as the Well, which is about two stone's-throw off.

Into this Well they have had and still have the custom of throwing men alive as a sacrifice to their gods in time of drought, and they believe that would not die, though they never saw them again. They also threw into it many other things they prized, and so if this country had possessed gold it would be this Well that would have the greater part of it, so great is the devotion that the Indians show for it...

Thus wrote Bishop Diego de Landa in his *Relacion de las Cosas de Yucatan*, "An Account of Things of Yucatan," in 1566. De Landa was a Franciscan missionary, who followed in the wake of the Spanish Conquistadores after they conquered Mexico. On his way to becoming the second bishop of Yucatan, he burned all the sacred books of the heathen Maya in an effort to convert them to his own uncompromising creed. Two centuries later De Landa's book was discovered in the Royal Library in Madrid and published. In 1878 the account was read by a budding young Worcester, Massachusetts, archaeologist named Edward Herbert Thompson, who was much impressed with it. Some scholars felt that Diego de Landa's fabled Maya city of Chichen Itza and its sacrificial well were pure fiction; a zealous missionary's way of dramatizing the savagery of a heathen religion. But not Thompson. He was so sure that De Landa spoke the truth that he vowed to go to Yucatan, find Chichen Itza and search the waters of the Sacred Well to produce evidence of the human sacrifices it contained.

While the whole idea sounded like ambitious fantasy, Thompson was dead serious. But, lacking the funds and finding that the various individuals and organizations he approached had no wish to finance such a hair-brained enterprise, he decided the situation was hopeless. Then, miraculously, the matter was settled so efficiently that one wonders if the all-powerful Mayan god Kukulcan could have had anything to do with it. Thompson himself always maintained that he got to Yucatan by way of Atlantis.

In 1879 he wrote an article entitled, "Atlantis Not a Myth," which was published in the *Popular Science Monthly*. It suggested that the Mayan civilization of Yucatan was actually a branch broken off from the civilization that once flourished on the continent of Atlantis before it sank into the Atlantic Ocean. Thompson argued his point well enough to attract the attention of several influential men with archaeological interests. As a result of the article, the vice-president of the American Antiquarian Society checked into his background, and a few years later Thompson was approached by representatives of the society and Harvard's Peabody Museum at Cambridge, who offered him the chance to go to Yucatan and make a study of the Mayan ruins for them. Moreover, he was told that to facilitate matters the President of the United States had agreed to appoint him the American consul to Mexico. And that was the way 25-year-old Edward H. Thompson, our youngest American consul, went to Yucatan by way of Atlantis.

Arriving with his young wife and two-month-old daughter in Merida in 1885, he took on his official duties at the consulate and spent the next 30 years exploring and investigating the Mayan ruins of the Yucatan peninsula. Describing his first visit to the ancient Mayan capital of Chichen Itza, which was to become the focal point of his lifework, Thompson wrote:

"The gradual ascent and winding of the trail between the boulders and the big trees seemed so like familiar forest rambles at home that it came over me almost with a shock to realize that the boulders I passed by so carelessly had cut surfaces and were once carved columns and sculptured pillars. Then, just as I began to understand that the level, forest-covered surface beneath my feet was a terrace made by ancient man, I peered upward to a great stone mass that pierced the sky, and all else was forgotten. A pyramid with terraced sides, paneled walls of cut limestone, and broad stairways leading upward, was crowned by a temple. Other buildings, high mounds, and broken terraces, were buried in the forest and only the dark green knobs on the horizon told me where they stood.

"Pen cannot describe or brush portray the strange feelings produced by the beating of the tropic sun against the ash-colored wall of those venerable structures. Old and cold, furrowed by time, and haggard, imposing, and impassive, they rear their rugged masses above the surrounding level and are beyond description..."

From the summit of the 100-foot-high pyramid before the temple of the plumed serpent god, Kukulcan, Thompson saw the dim outline of an ancient pathway leading to an opening in the distant jungle. There it ended at a large limestone rimmed pool, or cenote. Thompson suddenly realized he was looking at the Sacred Well of Chichen Itza.

As he shaded his eyes and stared toward the spot, he remembered Diego de Landa's words; could almost see the ancient ritual taking place in this once populous Mayan capital of 200,000 to 500,000 people. According to the old legend, around A.D. 1250 in times of drought, pestilence or disaster, solemn processions of elegantly robed and plumed high priests, devotees laden with rich offerings and the young maidens or captive warriors for sacrifice, moved down the steep stairway from the temple of Kukulcan before the massed crowds of chanting Mayan spectators. Slowly, regally, the procession made its way to the brink of the Sacred Well. And there, with the air filled with the fragrance of burning incense and fresh cut flowers, while the drums throbbed, the flutes wailed and the priests muttered incantations, the victims were hurled one by one off the steep precipice into the gloomy waters of the pool to placate the god that lived in its depths. And with each victim the spectators threw in their offerings—garlands of flowers, strings of beads, pieces of carved jade, "and the things they prized," Thompson heard De Landa's words—"and so if this country had possessed gold it would be in this Well...."

What really was in the slimy depths of the overgrown, grim water pit? Thompson wondered.

Several years passed before he had the opportunity to find out. Then, he quit his position at the consulate and purchased a large plantation that included the entire ruined city of Chichen Itza with its Sacred Well. Now he was prepared to devote all his time to the enormous task at hand. But first, like a military strategist, he carefully planned his assault on the imposing well. He decided the best mode of attack would have to be with professional deep-sea diving equipment—a matter about which he knew nothing. So the retired consul-archaeologist turned planter-archaeologist returned to the United States for a scientific convention, and while there he went to Boston and took lessons in deep-sea diving. At the same time he approached his early benefactors at the American Antiquarian Society and the Peabody Museum for moral and financial assistance in the project. When Thompson explained his intentions, they thought he had lost his mind. In the end, however, he persuaded them to his way of thinking. With some misgivings about their judgment, they agreed to lend him their full assistance.

Thompson returned to Chichen Itza and went to work. He measured the well and found it to be an 187-foot-wide oval of limestone whose sheer walls dropped 65 to 85 feet down to the water's surface. He fashioned wooden logs with the general shape and weight of human beings, tied them to ropes and pushed them in. Then he measured the lengths of rope to determine how far out the victims could have been thrown. Once he established the most likely zone where the victims might be found, he installed a stiff-legged derrick and a dredge on a platform close to the edge overlooking the pit. In the following days the steel-jawed Harwood orange-peel bucket brought up nothing but rocks, leaves, branches and unending muck from the depths of the well. Then a week later, amid the usual nondescript debris, Thompson found two small, yellow nodules, which he discovered was sacred resin, copal, an incense that gave off a fragrant smoke when burned. Now, for the first time, he knew he was on the right track.

In the months of dredging that followed, hardly a day passed without the scoop bringing up unusual relics. Before long, Thompson accumulated a large assortment of broken Mayan pottery, spear points, axes, hammers and chisels chipped from flint and calcite; bells and beaten copper disks covered with designs; beads, pendants and small figurines in jade, copper and gold, along with many human bones, mostly those of young women. There was not the slightest doubt in his mind now. De Landa had been accurate in every detail about the sacrifices in the Sacred Well.

To speed up the operation Thompson built a scow, which he lowered down the 70-foot-sheer limestone walls of the cenote, and from then on the dredge spilled its load onto this floating pontoon platform. The contents were then emptied and the tailings examined at a narrow beach on shore. Before long, however, fewer and fewer artifacts appeared, and finally the scoop brought up nothing but thin, soupy mud.

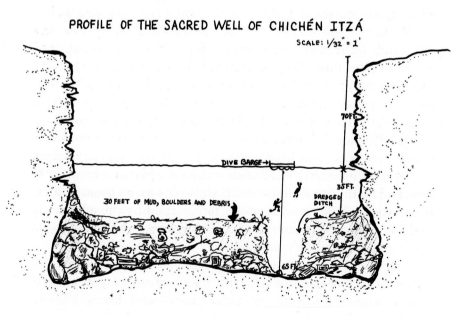

PROFILE OF THE SACRED WELL OF CHICHÉN ITZÁ

SCALE: 1/32" = 1'

Dredging operations in the Sacred Well created the added hazard to divers of being buried beneath walls of mud and debris as they explored the bottom of the cenote.

It was time to cease dredging and begin diving. Thompson had hired two Greek divers from the Bahama Islands to assist him. The pontoon platform now became a diving barge, to which they were lowered each day in the dredge scoop. Thompson and one of the Greeks were helped on with their cumbersome water-proof canvas suits, weighted shoes and 30-pound copper helmets. Then, while the barge crew manned the pumps, the two divers climbed down a short ladder into the water and sank like blocks of lead.

"During the first ten feet of descent, the light rays changed from yellow to green and then to purplish black," wrote Thompson. "After that I was in utter darkness.... The medium in which we had to work was neither water nor mud, but a combination of both, stirred up by the working of the dredge. It was a thick mixture like gruel and no ray...could even penetrate it. So we had to work in utter darkness, yet after a short time, we hardly felt the fact to be a serious inconvenience; for the palpic whorls of our finger-ends seemed not only to distinguish objects by the sense of touch, but actually to aid in distinguishing colors..."

On the bottom, 65 feet down, they could not tell where the water left off and the mud began. But where the dredge had worked, it had dug a 30-foot-deep hole in the sediment. This was Thompson's fertile zone, the area where he felt most of the victims had fallen. While the divers worked blindly at the bottom of it, feeling around in the limestone nooks and crannies for artifacts, 30-foot-high mud walls, punctuated by large boulders, broken columns, stone blocks and massive tree trunks fallen from above, towered over them. Occasionally a boulder or a tree trunk, loosened by the water movement, settled down on them in their super-stygian darkness. Usually, forewarned by the advancing cushion of water just ahead of the object, they were able to dodge the falling debris.

"As for the results of our dredging and diving into the great water pit, the first and most important is that we proved that in all essential details the traditions about the Sacred Well are true," wrote Thompson.

The accumulated evidence was impressive. It included hundreds of masses of copal incense ranging from pieces baseball-size up to those weighing several pounds; wooden implements, usually the notched stick *hul-che*, or dart thrower, of the Maya that, rather than the bow and arrow, was the common battle weapon; flint points; gold-handled flint-bladed sacrificial knives; crude wooden dolls adorned with copal and rubber; thousands of broken potsherds; scores of bones, mostly of young girls between the ages of 14 and 20, along with others of heavy framed powerful men; pieces of gourds; fragments of ancient fabrics; ropes of bark and fiber; copper rings; bells; disks; 42 gold-embossed disks; an openwork gold tiara of entwined feathered serpents; 21 massive gold reptile and animal figurines; 14 small gold candlestick-like objects; 10 gold human or monkey figurines; 20 gold rings; 100 solid gold bells of various sizes; 40 gold washers (probably garment ornaments); a gold *hul-che* of entwined serpents; 15 small jade plaques and tablets; 70 carved ear, nose and lip ornaments; 14 polished jade balls; a small jade figurine; hundreds of carved jade beads and pendants, and many unidentified archaeological items.

Interestingly, most of the finds had been broken intentionally so that their spirits might be free to accompany the deceased on her journey to meet Hunal Ku, the One Supreme God in the Heavens. Even the rattles and clappers had been removed from the tiny bells to "kill" them, make them mute forever. With the exception of the one complete sacrificial knife, two others were found with their flint blades broken off near the hilt, where it appeared they had deliberately been struck with a sharp object for that purpose. While the ritual killing of inanimate objects included many precious items, the breaking was always done in such a way that the head and features of the personage portrayed on the jade plaque or gold disk were left intact.

Thompson found that most of the so-called gold items were of low-grade alloy, with more copper than gold in them. What gave them their chief value were the designs and symbols carved on them. Some experts also feel that gold was not nearly as valuable to the Maya as was jade. Gold was malleable for ornamental use, it was considered of sacred origin (metal of the sun) and it was used for barter. But jade was believed to have been rarer and more valuable. All the items Thompson recovered were genuine jade (jadeite), not nephrite (near jade) or soft serpentine. Yet true jade is not indigenous to America; not a single source has ever been found on the North American continent. Where then did the ancient Maya get their jade? From Atlantis? Or by trade with South American cultures?

Thompson was not a treasure hunter, and his efforts at Chichen Itza were not undertaken with the hope of enriching himself. All he hoped to do was enrich the world with the historical knowledge that could be gleaned from his finds.

"The value in money of the objects recovered from the Sacred Well with so much labor and at such expense is, to be sure, insignificant," he wrote. "But the value of all things is relative. The historian delves into the past as the engineer digs into the ground, and for the same reason, to make the future secure. It is conceivable that some of these objects have graved upon their surfaces, embodied in symbols, ideas and beliefs that reach back through the ages to the primal home of these peoples in that land beyond the seas. To help prove that is well worth the labor of a lifetime."

Thompson planned to spend the rest of his life studying the Mayan culture and working in the ruins of Chichen Itza, but fate in the form of a Mexican revolution intervened. While he was in Merida, revolutionists destroyed his crops, stole his livestock and burned his plantation to the ground. To make matters worse, exorbitant claims from the United States that the golden treasure of the Sacred Well was valued at over five hundred thousand dollars made cash registers ring in the minds of Mexican officials. When Thompson acquired the artifacts and sent them on to Harvard's Peabody Museum, Mexico had no law protecting its antiquities. But since half a million dollars is a lot of pesos, Mexican government officials promptly attached Thompson's plantation for that amount.

It was 40 years later before Mexico's supreme court cleared Thompson of any wrongdoing, but by then it was too late for the venerable archaeologist, who had died in 1935. As a goodwill gesture, Harvard voluntarily returned most of the collection to Mexico. It makes little difference where the bulk of a man's lifetime work lies so long as it accomplishes that individual's original purpose. The archaeological and historical knowledge that Edward H. Thompson gave the world from his work at Chichen Itza and the other ruined cities of Yucatan, speaks for itself.

The next major expedition effort to recover the archaeological treasures of the Sacred Well took place during four months in the fall of 1960. This attempt was made on the part of CEDAM, which translates to mean "Club of Exploration and Watersports of Mexico." The man behind it was businessman Pablo Bush Romero, who first founded the group with a number of distinguished men in 1959 at the University Club in Mexico City. CEDAM was organized for the primary purpose of investigating historical and archaeological underwater sites throughout Mexico and its adjacent waters of the Pacific and Caribbean. Bush and his group hoped to be able to protect these archaeological sites from destruction by treasure hunters.

Several years earlier the Frogmen of Mexico, a diving club founded by Bush, had brought modern scuba diving equipment to the well but found that the waters of the cenote were entirely too murky to accomplish any serious recovery work. Bush figured that there had to be a better way. He remembered that Edwin Link, undersea explorer and inventor of the Link Trainer —aclosed cockpit flight simulator for training pilots during World War II—had explored the sunken city of old Port Royal and had used an air lift, a kind of underwater vacuum cleaner operated by compressed air, to salvage artifacts. George M. Clark, head of the Yucatan Exploring Society that had worked earlier with CEDAM, talked with Link about using the air lift and asked him to join the expedition. Link, however, had other commitments but he referred Clark to Norman Scott, who was using an air lift at Port Royal. Scott enthusiastically agreed to join the expedition and bring his equipment. He was also later instrumental in obtaining the financial and technical assistance of the National Geographic Society, which often supports worthwhile endeavors of this kind.

The various participants and equipment reached Chichen Itza in the fall of 1960. The expedition was led by Ponciano Salazar, head of the southeastern operations for Mexico's National Institute of Anthropology and History. Others included members of CEDAM, working in conjunction with Mexican navy divers; Norman Scott and Raul Echeverria, both expert divers; William Folan, archaeologist; Laverne Pederson, who was to make a motion picture of the event for the American Broadcasting Company television; and well-known diver-photographer Bates Littlehales, from the staff of the National Geographic Society.

Edward Thompson always felt that he had salvaged but a small fraction of the treasure that lay on the bottom of the well. Everyone in the present-day expedition hoped he was right.

The group set up camp around the rim on the well. Thompson would have been pleased to see their sophisticated modern-day equipment which included Aqua-Lungs and air lift, a far cry from his bulky helmet-and-hose diving gear and bucket dredge.

The men hoped to recover enough artifacts for the Mexican government to have its own representative collection from the cenote. The night before the dive individual members of the group were asked which item they would most like to see recovered from the well. Archaeologist Folan said he would like to see them recover some complete Mayan codices. These were the sacred books burned by the *Conquistadores* and Bishop Diego de Landa. Supposedly they contained the lore of the ages and a key to the strange hieroglyphic language of the Maya, which no man has yet been able to read. Only three such codices escaped destruction. So far, however, they have not provided enough clues to answer the mystery. Three of the divers hoped to recover a sacrificial knife, the kind used by the Aztecs and probably passed on to the Maya for carving out the living hearts of victims in some of the more grisly sacrificial ceremonies. Pederson, the ABC television photographer hoped for a complete skeleton wearing jewelry. Littlehales, the National Geographic still-photographer, wanted to photograph a complete set of Spanish armor in the hope that sometime during Cortez's conquest, one of his *Conquistadores* had fallen or was thrown into the cenote. Ponciano Salazar, the group's leader, was more modest. He wanted whatever Thompson had not found.

A derrick was set up on the brink of the well overlooking the pool and used as an elevator for divers and equipment going up or down the vertical limestone escarpment between the lip of the limestone sinkhole and its water surface. An eight-by-twelve-foot divers barge was then lowered down the cliff with block and tackle to give the divers a floating platform from which to work.

On his first orientation dive into the cenote, Littlehales described the experience. "The whole setting was eerie: the water seemed to have turned to ink. With my underwater flashlight I couldn't see beyond my arm. Hearing only my own breathing, I moved hand over hand following the line down forty feet to the rock anchor. By touch I established the shapes of fallen boulders and waterlogged trees. As mud churned up from the bottom my light became useless."

The men spent several days mapping the bottom of the cenote by touch alone, since it was too murky to see. Then, after familiarizing themselves with the underwater topography of the well, they lowered a larger pontoon float above the center of which projected the air lift's outlet pipe. Beneath it a sieve on a conical framework would strain the outflow of any artifacts that would be coming up the pipe.

While divers guided the air lift's maw over the bottom, injected compressed air sucked water, sediment and debris up the wide-mouthed pipe and spewed it high in the air over the sieve on the surface float. The color of this geyser turned from white to muddy yellow. Then suddenly someone grabbed something out of the sieve and shouted that the dredge had sucked up a piece of copal. Moments later more of the resinous incense appeared, then large numbers of pottery fragments. One of the divers surfaced with a perfect ceramic bowl. Another found a crudely made, grotesque rubber doll. He shouted up to the gallery of spectators high above around the rim of the cenote that he had discovered an idol. The onlookers applauded.

As the weeks became months and the air lift ate its way down through layers of silt, dozens of artifacts appeared daily in the catch screen on the surface. With the exception of a noticeable lack of gold items, the artifacts were not unlike those recovered by Thompson. There was a large amount of copal in various sizes, some of it still pressed into small ceramic incense burners; many beads of different sizes and style; and always the seemingly endless amount of broken pottery fragments.

About a month after the search began, the men recovered their first wooden figurine—a crudely carved statue with headdress, ear plugs and downcast eyes, possibly representing the rain god Chac. The wood, still bearing faint traces of blue color-

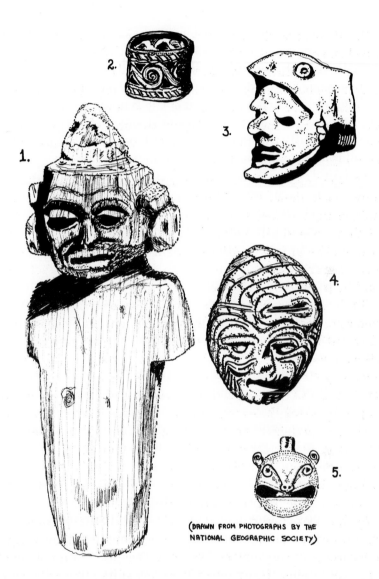

(DRAWN FROM PHOTOGRAPHS BY THE
NATIONAL GEOGRAPHIC SOCIETY)

Artifacts recovered from the Sacred Well by the CEDAM expedition included: 1) Carved wood figurine wearing headdress and ear plugs which may represent the Maya rain god, Chac; 2) Gold-washed copper rings, obviously a set, probably thrown into the Well as a gift of a single donor; 3) Eagle Warrior in fired clay which once adorned a jar, still bore traces of green paint; 4) Small stylized ceramic face which may have represented a deity; 5) Copper and gold bells were frequent finds—many were "killed" by having their clappers or "tongues" removed.

ing on its surface, looked almost as if it had been recently carved; its burial under centuries of muck had preserved it well. Coincidentally enough when the cenote gave up its prize, it also gained one. Professor Fernando Euan, the diver who found the idol, lost his Rolex wristwatch in the mud of the cenote the same day. He proclaimed it as the expedition's first sacrifice to the rain god Chac. Apparently the deity was pleased, because that night they were blessed by an unseasonable rainstorm.

As had Thompson, the divers recovered many metal bells, mostly copper, some washed with gold, and as usual most lacked clappers. Archaeologist Roman Pina Chan called them "death bells," pointing out that they had been "killed" by the Maya, who silenced them by tearing out their tongues before sacrificing them to the Sacred Well.

Not surprisingly, new artifacts kept cropping up in their finds that had not been in Thompson's—contemporary coins thrown into the "wishing well" by generations of visiting tourists. Most of the coins were from Mexico, the United States and Central American countries.

Among the human bones that invariably turned up from the depths of the well was a complete human skull. The expedition's doctor, who examined it, said it was the skull of a young woman probably between the ages of eighteen and nineteen. Typical of the customs of her time she had, as an infant, received the Maya beauty treatment in which boards were strapped to the front and back of her head to flatten these areas. Moreover the doctor noted that where the spine joined the skull, there were indications that the girl may have suffered from arthritis. Again, the impacting cold muck at the bottom of the cenote was thought to be responsible for the fine state of preservation of the skull. Along with the human remains the investigators often found the bones of jaguars, alligators, birds and deer. Some of these animals undoubtedly fell into the well through the years. It was also thought possible that some of them may have been introduced as sacrificial offerings.

Sometimes the work progressed at a snail's pace, the divers in the darkness of the mud-filled world beneath the surface of the cold, unfriendly waters constantly confronted by a seemingly inexhaustible supply of logs, branches, and boulders to interfere with their efforts. Often large rocks sucked up by the airlift got caught somewhere along the way and plugged the whole operation. Sections of pipe collapsed, and everything stopped until repairs were made.

The divers found that one area in particular was extremely rocky on the bottom. When these pieces were brought to the surface they were found to be inscribed blocks and columns, parts of the ruins of a temple that once stood on the brink of the cenote. Some of the pieces were recovered, but most were left on the bottom and their locations noted on a bottom map so that this information could be useful to future investigators wishing to reconstruct the temple.

After four months the work abruptly came to an end when word was received from the National Institute of Anthropology and History in Mexico City that some of the artifacts were being damaged by the air lift. Moreover, this method of recovery was removing the artifacts from their original context, destroying any information archaeologists might gain from knowing exactly where the item was found and in what relationship with its surroundings. During the four months, however, the divers recovered over 4,000 artifacts for the Mexican government, enough material for scholars to study for many years. The outstanding recoveries included a wooden doll wrapped in pieces of fragile ancient fabric; rubber figurines still flexible; wooden spools inlaid with black mosaics and thought to be ear ornaments; a bone blade knife, its handle wrapped with thin gold foil incised with glyphs; and the only solid gold objects found during the entire expedition, two small gold beads. There were also pieces of rare jade; stylized ceramic masks representing some deity; a small clay head believed adorned with an eagle headdress motif; carved jade beads and medallions; gold-washed copper rings; a jade necklace; a copper turtle breastplate from which dangled three bells. Some of the large one-inch-diameter beads were of jade, amber and crystal. Like the gold, these precious items were believed by the archaeologists to have been acquired by the Maya in trade with peoples as far north as the Aztec Empire of Central Mexico and as far south as Honduras and Panama, all areas reached by a network of ancient stone roads and seagoing trade routes.

As the men completed their work at the well, some theorized that perhaps one way to do a complete job of archaeological investigation was to pump the well dry and work it then as one would a land dig.

On the last day the god of the Sacred Well gave back its most recent sacrificial offering. The men had taught one of the local natives how to use scuba gear. On his first dive he surfaced, grinning broadly, with a treasure that fulfilled expedition leader Salazar's wish to find something that Thompson had not found. The native diver was proudly holding aloft the glittering sacrificial "artifact" he had found in the mud on the bottom of the cenote—Professor Euan's lost Rolex wristwatch.

It was another seven years before any serious work was again done at the cenote, and this time the man heading up the group was underwater explorer and treasure hunter, Norman Scott. Not only had he garnered valuable information from the CEDAM effort, but once he thought about the possibility of draining the cenote to facilitate the recovery of artifacts, he spent the interim of those seven years planning and tackling the many problems involved in such a costly undertaking. Setting up an expedition the size of the one Scott thought necessary was a mind-boggling proposition. A multitude of problems had to be worked out. But being a determined man who thrived on adversity, nothing ever stopped him.

Norman Scott grew up around Richmond, Virginia, and graduated from the University of Virginia in 1952 with a major in economics. After discharge from three years in the air force as a fighter pilot, he spent a stint as an assistant director of the National Broadcasting Company television network, then started his own business of building and repairing swimming pools around Washington, D.C. Since he had always been a strong swimmer, his present business got him interested in scuba diving, which in turn brought him to a skin-diving vacation in the Virgin Islands in 1955. Once he saw what the underwater world was like in the islands, it was love at first sight. The following year he found an old nineteenth-century shipwreck and recovered just enough brass ship-fittings to whet his interest in underwater salvage. Before long, he was spending less time with his swimming-pool business and more time getting deeper involved in the highly precarious business of treasure hunting.

He and several friends from Washington, D.C., purchased a cantankerous 36-foot salvage boat, the *Discoverer*, and barely got it down to Florida when major mechanical repairs momentarily put him out of business. Having earlier met Edwin Link, who had been active in the underwater exploration of the sunken city of old Port Royal, Scott had learned from him how to use the injection dredge, or air lift. Since Link felt he had only scratched the surface of the archaeological treasures at Port Royal, Scott headed for Jamaica, and with the permission of the Jamaican government he began salvage activities on the sunken city of old Port Royal. And it was there that Pablo Bush Romero contacted him and persuaded him to join the CEDAM expedition to Chichen Itza.

In the years that followed, Scott became involved in a series of adventurous, but not too remunerative, expeditions seeking treasure from Spanish galleons lost in the Caribbean. In the course of his searches he crossed paths with Texas millionaire, F. Kirk Johnson, who took a liking to Scott. Thinking that he might be able to make a profit from the treasure-hunting business, Johnson lavishly financed all of Scott's subsequent treasure-hunting ventures for many years until his death in 1968.

Ever since Scott had been on the CEDAM expedition to Chichen Itza, he was anxious to return and try out his theories for draining the cenote. Finally he decided he could wait no longer, that the time was right to try to drum up financial assistance from various industries willing to invest in another attempt to wrest the archaeological treasures from the well. For six months he flew around the country, contacting the representatives of various firms. Each time he explained his enterprise and pointed out how the company in question stood to benefit by making their products available and therefore widely promoted in magazine and newspaper articles as well as the film and television publicity Scott hoped would result from his expedition.

The response he received not only indicated the willingness of business firms to associate their products with the endeavor, but it spoke well of Norman Scott's salesmanship.

In Mexico City he outlined his plans to Pablo Bush Romero and Dr. Eusebio Davalos Hurtado, director of the National Institute of Anthropology and History. Scott assured them that he could produce both the financial and technical assistance he needed to accomplish the feat. Bush and Hurtado agreed to assist him in every way possible. CEDAM would make divers and equipment available, and the institute would provide archaeologists and supervisory personnel.

In six months Scott amassed a surprising amount of support, including $177,000 in advances against literary and film rights to the story of the expedition, donations of $20,000 from private industries, the loan of a fleet of twenty-one trucks from Ford Motor Company, a complete filtration system from the Purex Corporation with filtration chemicals furnished by the Johns-Manville Corporation, and a wide range of other contributed equipment and supplies from two dozen other U.S. firms.

Late in September, 1967, the expedition left Florida and the long motor caravan proceeded to Chichen Itza, Yucatan, arriving there 13 days later. The group immediately cleared the area, set up camp beside the cenote and unpacked equipment. A float was constructed and lowered by derrick down the steep limestone sides of the well to the pool where a large water pump with four intake hoses was installed. This system was helped by a booster pump from above with an 800-foot runoff hose leading to a nearby dry cenote.

Scott calculated that the Sacred Well contained 800 million gallons of water, and if there was no influx of water from underground springs or local rains, he could pump it dry in twenty-three days. The water was to be merely shifted from one cenote to another.

Pumping operations got underway on September 23. Periodically during the day the men nervously checked the depth of the well to see what effect the action had. In the first few hours of pumping there seemed to be no difference. Scott felt the bitter pang of doubt; the possibility that he had miscalculated. After all the trouble and expense, the cenote might be getting enough water from some subterranean source to prevent them ever pumping it dry.

Despite their apprehension, the water level slowly began dropping. By the end of the day it had fallen a foot. Six days later with continuous pumping and considerable good luck with

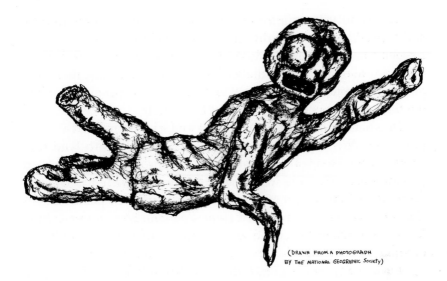

(DRAWN FROM A PHOTOGRAPH
BY THE NATIONAL GEOGRAPHIC Society)

A child's toy or a god's likeness? Whichever it was, this 4-inch gro-
tesque rubber effigy survived 500 years of immersion in the Sacred
Well to become one of the oldest rubber objects ever found.

the weather, the water level in the well had dropped seven feet,
exposing a narrow mud shoreline around its perimeter. The archaeologists immediately began work in this area and were surprised to uncover numerous ceramic shards, jade beads, flint
points and human bones.

The drainage process was slow and tedious. Only a few archaeologists could work the shoreline area at one time. Scott
decided to put the remaining force of divers to work removing
the many stones that had fallen into the well from the small
temple the Maya had built on the lip of the cenote. To make it
safer for the divers, however, he wanted to clarify the water as
much as possible. They decided the quickest way to do this was
by chlorination. But to pump the chlorine gas into the water
meant using the one pump they had for draining the cenote. If
this were done, the well might fill up again during the chlorination project. Rather than risk that, they decided to add the deadly
chlorine gas to the water by hand pump. The two-ton tank of
chlorine was lowered by derrick to the dive raft. Carefully, divers
began pumping the lethal gas into the water. Minutes later they

were in trouble. The chlorine cooled too rapidly as it left the tank and burst the plastic pump hose. Suddenly the poisonous gas was escaping uncontrollably. An open container of ammonia had been placed on the raft to detect any escaping chlorine. Its fumes now mingled with the gas, and within seconds a choking, white fog floated out over the surface of the cenote.

On shore the workmen coughed and gasped in the thickening fumes. What could have become a terrible death trap was narrowly avoided by a quick-thinking crane operator on the lip of the cenote. When he realized what had happened he swiftly brought his crane to their rescue, lifting nineteen people out of the gas-filled cenote in record time. The men were immediately treated for gas inhalation, but fortunately no one was seriously injured.

After the level of the well dropped about twelve feet, its rate of recession slowed to an inch every four or five hours. The men suspected that they had reached the point where the water table was letting water into the well almost as fast as it could be pumped out. It now looked as if the cenote might never be adequately drained even if additional pumps were used.

This new development called for a change in plan. If the water could not be removed entirely or cleared by chlorination, then perhaps it could be filtered to clarity. Not only would this facilitate the recovery of artifacts by enabling the divers to see what they were doing, but more importantly to the archaeologists it would be possible to photograph artifacts in situ underwater on the bottom so that they would have some idea of their original context. Therefore, the remaining water was to be circulated through the sophisticated filtration system, which hopefully would render it crystal clear.

Four days of filtering increased the underwater visibility to eight feet. Considering the conditions they had to work under before, this was almost equivalent to giving sight to a blind man. In the newfound visibility some of the divers eagerly got busy diving for fragments of the fallen temple from the rock pile on the bottom, while others actively used the air lifts in search of more valuable artifacts.

No sooner had these operations begun, when their eight-foot visibility disappeared in a shroud of muddy fallout from the airlift, reducing conditions to about what they were before. Once more everything came to a halt and another decision had to be made.

It was impossible to filter the water clear as long as the divers continued to work and stir up the sediment. Therefore, it was decided to stop the diving operations for a while and let the filtration plant do its job. Six days later the water was so clear that underwater visibility was about forty feet.

It was now possible to see shadowy details of the bottom from the top of the cenote.

This seemed to be about as good as they could get it. Since the men were chafing to get back to work, the air lifts began again. Despite a general clouding of the water from the sediment sifting back into the basin, visibility remained good enough for the divers to be able to see and photograph many of the artifacts on the bottom before they were recovered.

Daily now the finds mounted and proved to be the same kind of items recovered during the Thompson and CEDAM expeditions—many potsherds, jade beads, pendants, copper rings, bells, rubber dolls, fabric fragments and a large assortment of human bones. All went well, with the exception of an accident that could have been fatal for one of the divers.

Norman Scott's nephew, Austin, was on the bottom working with the air lift, when a large boulder toppled off the side of the cenote and pinned him to the bottom so that he was unable to extricate himself. Since he was already just minutes away from exhausting his tank of air, Austin was in a tight spot in more ways than one.

Fortunately, however, a fellow diver, Bill McGehee, saw the accident. Surfacing quickly, he grabbed a fresh tank of air from the dive barge and swam down with it to Austin just in time. Then he lifted the heavy boulder enough for him to wriggle free.

This third and final effort to wrest secrets from the Sacred Well finally came to an end in early April, 1968. The men had recovered some 6,000 artifacts for Mexico's National Institute of Anthropology and History. Included were the first remarkable examples of Mayan furniture ever recovered—two complete ornate wooden stools ornamented with serpent heads bearing the likeness of men's faces.

The Norman Scott expedition was the largest of its kind ever attempted in the Western Hemisphere. Although he was pleased by the large number and caliber of the artifacts recovered, Scott was disappointed that he had been unable to drain the well entirely and learn all of its hidden secrets.

6

THROUGH THE BOTTOM
OF THE OCEAN

The success of the early archaeological efforts at Chichen Itza stimulated renewed interest in excavating other lost Mayan cities. In 1941, Dr. George W. Brainerd of the Carnegie Institution in Washington, D.C., and archaeologist Dr. E. Wyllys Andrews spent several weeks exploring the ruins of Dzibilchaltun (Dzeeb-eel-chal-toon), Mayan for "where there is writing on flat stones." This was believed to be the site of one of the earliest and one of the latest of the cities inhabited by the ancient Maya. Only one temple remained partially standing but Brainerd and Andrews found a large group of hitherto unreported mounds and enough other evidence to indicate that these were the remnants of a most unusual city. World War II interrupted any further investigation, so it was not until 15 years later that Dr. Andrews was able to return to Dzibilchaltun as head of a large, well-equipped expedition sponsored by the National Geographic Society and Tulane University. Gradually the team of archaeologists, surveyors, technicians and artisans uncovered the remains of an enormous Mayan city that sprawled for at least 20 square miles. At its height Dzibilchaltun had a central downtown area crowded with pyramidal temples, a palace and buildings of vaulted stone between which were built thatched-roof houses on stone foundations. "Mainstreet" in this thriving city was a mile-long limestone concourse eight feet high in places, and wide enough to accommodate the equivalent of four lanes of automobile traffic. Quite a promenade for a people who lacked horses and never learned to use the wheel. At one end of this magnificent boulevard stood a great pyramidal temple believed built about A.D. 475. As the archaeologists began excavating its remains they found that the ruins concealed an even older structure buried underneath. Although the uppermost, more "modern" temple had been destroyed, the Indians of a later period had tunneled down through its remains and for some reason excavated the rubble from the older, buried sanctuary. And there, from the bottom of a carefully constructed shaft, the archaeologists recovered seven crudely shaped unpainted clay dolls. Each exhibited some kind of deformity—one was a dwarf, two were hunchbacks, another had a swollen stomach. Whatever the significance, the structure was thereafter called the Temple of the Seven Dolls. Radiocarbon dating in two laboratories showed a sample slice of wood taken from the temple's doorway beam to be 1,450 to 1,500 years old, dating the temple at about A.D 500. At least 50 major Mayan buildings surrounded the temple.

In what would have been the heart of downtown Dzibilchaltun, midway along the concourse and just south of it, was the Cenote Xlacah (pronounced, shla-cah, Mayan for "Old Town,") an oval well believed to have been the city's main water supply. Hundreds of these natural limestone sinkholes pock-mark the Yucatan peninsula. For countless centuries the rainfall had percolated through the porous plateaus to create underground rivers and streams. When the gradually weakened roofs of these subterranean caverns caved in, the results were the water-filled sinkholes the Maya called cenotes. Some were crystal clear, others were green with algae. Most served as a source of water for the Mayan cities. At least one—the Sacred Well of Chichen Itza— was used for human sacrifices during religious ceremonies. And what of Cenote Xlacah? Had it been used for human sacrifices or was it simply a city's drinking well? While Andrews and his group worked Dzibilchaltun's land sites, National Geographic Society's underwater still photographers, Luis Marden and Bates Littlehales, concentrated on exploring the cenote.

When the excavation work began at Dzibilchaltun in 1956, Andrews persuaded two vacationing University of Florida students with Aqua-Lungs to look into the well for him. In a few days of diving, they recovered a surprising amount of artifacts including complete earthenware jars, flint projectile points, carved bone ear plugs and some three thousand potsherds.

Rather than sacrificial offerings, these appeared to be everyday items accidentally dropped into the well over the centuries. In any event, Marden and Littlehales, with their assistant divers Fernando Euan and Earl Becht from Mexico, looked forward to the dive with considerable anticipation, confident that no one had even begun to explore a cenote the size of Xlacah. On the surface the oval-shaped pool was 100 feet across its widest part, smaller than the Sacred Well at Chichen Itza 75 miles away, but it was over 100 feet deeper. Moreover there were no precipitous limestone walls flanking Xlacah; in most places the rim rock was only a couple of feet above water level. Weekend crowds of clamoring children from nearby villages used the pool as a popular swimming hole.

Donning their gear beside the cenote on the morning of their first dive, the men were struck by the beauty of the place. Green trees and shrubs dotted the gently rolling, seemingly white-washed landscape. Limestone walls built for no apparent reason other than to clear the land, rambled aimlessly over the hillsides. At the shallow end of the cenote a thick bed of lily pads carpeted the water, the vivid green swatch dappled with white blossoms. On a rocky beach extending a few yards into the emerald pool several cows waded contentedly, cooling off. It was a typical calendar scene. Xlacah, in all its shimmering green elegance, looked as innocent as a farm pond in the United States.

Wearing a single-tank Aqua-Lung, weight belt, rubber swim fins and face mask, Marden slipped into the water, swam a short way from shore and looked down. The image of sunlit, pristine beauty he had just seen on the surface suddenly became a yawning black bottomless pit beneath him. Gone were any farm pond illusions. The chill he felt came from the fleeting impression that he was staring down into a hole that bored straight through the core of the earth, into the very slag pile of hell itself.

Marden finned back over the sloping shallows and glided downward. Schools of silver-sided minnows swarmed around him like mosquitoes. As the water deepened, a bed of tufted weeds extending downward from the shallows ceased growing for want of sunlight. Twenty feet down, the rock wall behind him faded into the gloom. He paused to clear his ears and snapped on his flashlight. In its yellow glow he saw that the wall curved back under the lip of the cenote to form the roof of a large cavern. Its rubble-strewn floor sloped downward at a 50-degree angle. Looking up toward the pool's mirrored surface, he saw Littlehales' silhouette arcing down toward him, trailing plumes of silver bubbles.

Marden exhaled and continued his descent, gliding in slow motion down through the green water into the darkness below. There was no bottom growth now, only the rock-covered slope. Sweeping his light over the rubble, he noticed a few of the stones were squared and carved, indicating that some of Dzibilchaltun's man-made structures had toppled into the cenote.

At a depth of 80 feet the slope flattened into a velvety mud terrace between two large stone outcroppings. Marden paused and looked back. Littlehales wagged his flashlight at him. Behind him the black walls of the underwater cavern created the peculiar impression of looking through the wrong end of a telescope, the long, black corridor reaching up to the disk of light at the pool's surface far above them.

Beyond the mud terrace the shaft dropped almost vertically. At the edge of the drop-off Marden spotted a large stone lintel balanced on edge between a waterlogged tree trunk and a section of broken column. Equalizing his buoyancy by taking only shallow breaths of air from his Aqua-Lung, Marden stood on his head to avoid disturbing the soft silt with his fins. Carefully he felt along all sides of the lintel, searching for incised hieroglyphics. Finding none, the two men eased over the edge of the terrace and drifted downward, their lights probing beneath the shelf as the rock wall curved back and flattened into another terrace. Following this second terrace came a shallow shelf, then the bottom leveled and continued into the low, black opening of an eight-foot-high tunnel. Checking their depth gauges revealed that they were 120 feet down. Everything was quiet except for the noise of their bubbles. As the bursts moved upward they flattened and separated into myriad silver disks that gurgled, clunked and tinkled all the way to the surface.

Marden started into the tunnel, keeping low to avoid striking his tank on the vaulted roof. Below him lay a bed of silt so fine that his hand could pass into it without feeling it. Suddenly clouds of sediment puffed up around him like smoke. Marden

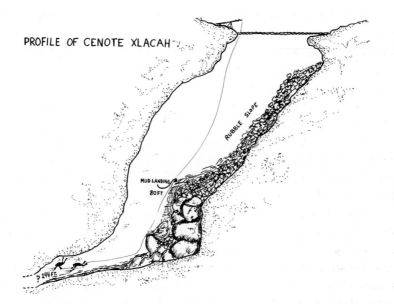

The stocking-shaped cenote Xlacah yielded obsidian implements, potsherds and human bones. Were they evidence of another Maya Sacred Well for human sacrifice?

just glimpsed the green disk of Littlehales' light before it winked out behind a wall of darkness. He turned his own flashlight full in his face and could not see its light. For the next ten seconds Marden teetered on the brink of panic. He fought back the urge to gulp air in sharp, urgent gasps and made a conscious effort to slow his breathing back to normal. Above all, he knew he had to keep his head. With the least disturbance possible, he drifted upward until his tank clanged against the rock roof. There he stayed until the silt slowly began to settle, and he saw a foot of clear water just below the roof of the cave. Slowly he followed it, inching his way back to the mouth of the tunnel. Ahead of him in the roiled water the faint glow of Littlehales' light appeared, and Marden moved toward it.

The two men touched hands reassuringly, then together they followed their bubbles back to the surface of the pool. They had been down 20 minutes.

As they climbed out of the cenote, Marden called over his shoulder to Littlehales. "What stirred up all that mud so quickly?"

"This," said Littlehales, grinning. He held up his arm which was encircled by the broken neck of a large earthenware jar. "I saw it sticking out of the mud and when I tugged it loose the bottom came up in a big cloud that blotted out everything."

After that experience they decided to establish a permanent lifeline down to the bottom of the cenote so that, no matter how bad the visibility got, they could always find their way back. As a support for one end of the line, Euan and Becht, with the help of a couple of Maya, fashioned a kind of four-legged timber derrick that jutted out over the deepest part of the pool. In the next few days they also built a wooden platform just below the surface of the water so that the divers could sit on it to get in and out of their equipment more easily. After tying one end of the lifeline to the derrick boom, Marden and Littlehales each grabbed the side of a 16-pound mushroom anchor and held onto it while it took them to the bottom. Their trip into the black hole this time was somewhat faster than before. The rapid pressure changes during their descent kept them busy clearing their ears. But once they deposited the anchor in the soft silt at the mouth of the tunnel, the long slender white nylon line provided them with a comforting link to the surface.

Swimming back up into shallower water, the men began searching for artifacts. Before long they struck pay dirt at the 60-foot depth. Here, among the two- and three-foot-wide boulders that had fallen from above, the bottom resembled a modern refuse heap. With bits and pieces of earthenware pots scattered everywhere amid the jumbled rocks, they easily filled their wire baskets and sent them up. To conserve air they lay prone, facing up the slope, while picking potsherds from between the boulders. By restricting their movements and at the same time breathing slowly, they could make a single tank of air last up to 50 minutes. But it was like picking away at a large and precariously balanced potential avalanche. Whenever a key stone was moved, something gave. Fortunately, however, the resulting click of one stone hitting another provided an early warning. Inhaling quickly they would float up away from the bottom before the section of boulders loosened and sloughed off down the slope in a great cloud of mud. Then they would move away from the slide area and begin in perfectly clear water.

The pieces of pottery they recovered were crumbly and easily broken from their long immersion. But once they dried in the hot Yucatan sun, they were as hard as the day they were made.

Systematically the four divers worked the slope of rubble, each day taking a new area and exhausting it of artifacts before moving on to another. One day, after a week of finding nothing but potsherds, Littlehales hooted excitedly in his mouthpiece and swam over to show Marden what looked like a long thorn. When Marden examined it more closely, he saw that it was a slender bone awl with hieroglyphics carved on its side. Grinning broadly behind their masks, the two men shook hands and headed for the surface with their unique find.

The awl's ornamentation made them wonder if it had once been used as a woman's hair skewer. Dr. Andrews' theory that the items in the well had been dropped in accidentally, might explain the awl's presence in the cenote. It could have fallen from a Mayan woman's hair while she bent down to get a jar of water.

But after the discovery of the awl or hair skewer, artifacts began turning up that were not particularly the kind of things one might expect to find in a community drinking well. These included a small clay flute that Marden broke trying to extract it from the mud. Underneath one slide area they found a small devilish-looking wooden mask not more than two inches long, a head of a small idol; human bones and skulls, the forehead and back of the craniums flattened by boards in the ancient Mayan beautifying process, scattered in with the usual array of animal bones. Was this evidence of pre-Columbian murder, accidental drownings or human sacrifices? The men could only guess.

Finally, after two weeks of grubbing through the rock pile for broken pottery, the finds became more scarce and the divers decided to move on down to the mud terrace at 80 feet.

Here, an entirely different kind of procedure had to be used. They could no longer lie on the bottom. Now it became a matter of standing on their heads, with their arms up to the elbows in mud particles so fine that they never seemed to settle but only remained in suspension close to the bottom. Any movement in this floating mud aspic immediately stirred up miniature brown tornadoes. Sometimes they puffed up high enough to obliterate the diver's view so that all he had to go on was his sense of touch. Even then it was extremely discouraging to feel a complete pot half buried in the thick ooze of the bottom and despite every effort to dig it free, to find that the upper half of the vessel would often break off in the diver's hand.

It was while working this slope and probing into mud up to their shoulders that the divers found in the muck under a tree-top a dozen buried pots. Despite all the divers' efforts, many broke during their removal, but a few were removed intact. One day Marden slipped his hand into the quaking muck and his fingers closed on what felt like a branching twig. As he slipped it out of the mud and examined it more closely, he was surprised to see a piece of branching gorgonian, a relative of the coral family, with its base attached to a shell. The divers had already noticed fossil evidence in the walls of the well to indicate that they were diving through an ancient ocean bottom. But the gorgonian Marden had found was no fossil. Yet it had originated in salt water seas. What was it doing under the mud 90 feet down in a freshwater sinkhole? Had it been thrown into the cenote as part of some ritual ceremony, possibly one involving a cult worshiping the cenote? Later, when Marden found similar gorgonian fragments, he suspected this might have been the case.

When the men worked in shallower depths, they had no problem with the pressure. They were able to stay well within the safety limits of their air capacity. When they went down to 60 feet, they could, according to the U.S. Navy decompression tables, stay at this depth for 60 minutes after which the accumulated nitrogen in their bodies required them to make a short decompression stop before surfacing. This was still no problem because usually a diver using a single tank of air would exhaust it and surface before it was necessary for him to make a decompression stop. However, now that the men were working at the 80-foot level and beyond, with double and sometimes triple air tanks on their backs, they had to pay particular attention to their time on the bottom. The deeper they dived the less time they could stay down without decompression. Moreover, multiple dives had hidden hazards. When divers make more than one deep dive a day, they accumulate a buildup of residual nitrogen, which not

(AFTER GEORGE E. STUART)

Bone hair skewers recovered by Marden and Littlehales bear Maya hieroglyphs. While cryptanalysts have made progress interpreting numerical and calendric glyphs, the meaning of most Maya inscriptions is still unknown.

only decreases their safe bottom time but requires more decompression than they might anticipate. Failure to take these factors into consideration can result in a case of decompression sickness—the bends—that unpleasant ailment afflicting unwary divers who stay down too long or who rise too fast, causing nitrogen bubbles in the bloodstream which, if not breathed off normally during a decompression stop in shallower depths, can permanently paralyze or even kill them.

After weeks of exhaustive work through the muck and rubble on the flanks of the cenote, the divers wondered what might be found in the sinkhole's deepest and furthermost point, the narrow, black tunnel at the bottom. When they decided to find out, they took more elaborate precautions against the conditions they knew they would encounter. As they followed the lifeline down to the anchor at the mouth of the cave, each man carried a coil of rope attached to the lifeline by a sliding swivel. At the bottom of the pool their swivels clicked against the mushroom anchor. The divers gave each other a sign that they were all right. Uncoiling their lines behind them, they ducked under the rock overhang and swam into the black tunnel, the yellow beams of their flashlights probing the darkness ahead of them. As before, clouds of fine silt swirled up around them. Inside, the curved cave roof rose above them. Cautiously they swam along the level corridor. Ahead of them the eyes of a large black catfish glowed ruby red in the beams of light. They followed the tunnel for 50 feet. That was far enough. The passageway continued, but the divers decided to turn back. Marden shined his light on his depth gauge. It read 140 feet. Since it was calibrated for seawater, they were actually about 144 feet deep.

The men made their way back along the passageway and out of the mouth of the tunnel into the main cavern. Following their lifeline back to the surface, they ascended at the then prescribed rate of 25 feet per minute. This was their third dive of the day. They had been on the bottom for 15 minutes. On both of the earlier dives they had followed the U.S. Navy decompression tables exactly and made the required decompression stops. Five minutes after he climbed out of the water this time, however, Marden felt a surge of pain in his right shoulder. Grabbing a fresh tank of air, he dived down to 60 feet and hung on the lifeline for ten minutes before coming up with decompression stops along the way. The pain was still there.

He dived down to 80 feet where he remained for 20 minutes, hoping that by doing so the accumulated nitrogen in his system would go back into solution in his blood stream and be expelled normally.

After these attempts, Marden surfaced, shivering violently from the cold water. The pain returned. Nitrogen bubbles in his bloodstream had apparently lodged in his shoulder joint. He needed treatment in a recompression chamber, a sort of man-sized pressure cooker where many hours under controlled high pressure air would force the bubbles back into solution so that the nitrogen would be released naturally in his exhalations during his gradual return to atmospheric pressure. While no such elaborate facilities existed in Yucatan, Marden remembered a recent conversation he had with his friend Melvin Art, a construction engineer who was building a new power plant in Merida. Art had mentioned that if he ever needed one, his crew could fabricate a recompression chamber on short notice. The way Marden felt at the moment he knew there was no greater need.

Moments later they were on their way to Merida, driving at top speed over potholed limestone roads better suited for travel on sure-footed burros. During the rough 20-minute trip Marden was in agony. Art was telephoned from Andrews' house, and when they arrived at the plant ten minutes later his crew had already rigged up a large, cubical steel oil storage tank with a pressure gauge, hooked it up to an air compressor and were fitting a linoleum gasket to a circular hatch atop the tank.

Marden explained the procedure to Art and showed him how to use the recompression tables in the U. S. Navy diving manual. Then, Marden and Littlehales climbed a ladder and let themselves down into the tank. Littlehales had experienced no ill effects from the dive, but he decided to take the recompression treatment anyway.

A flashlight and hammer were handed down to them. The workmen attached the hatch, hammering tight its nuts with an earsplitting clangor almost deafening the men inside. The compressor went into action, and air hissed into the cubical. Marden and Littlehales lay on their backs in the darkness. As the pressure increased so did the sound and the temperature. Bathed in sweat they covered their ears against the roar. Suddenly the air compressor stopped.

According to the navy recompression tables they were to be under three atmospheres, a pressure equal to submerging to a depth of 100 feet. But Marden sensed that they had not reached that pressure yet. After a while he hammered three times on the tank calling for more air. The compressor started again but it stopped shortly afterward. The men lay sweating in the darkness for 20 minutes. When it still seemed that the pressure was not high enough, Marden hammered six times on the wall giving the prearranged signal for them to be let out.

The valve was opened and the air shrilled out of the chamber. As it dropped back to atmospheric pressure, the rapid change abruptly chilled the men. When they climbed out, Marden's arm still ached dully.

Art told them he could not give them the three atmospheres of pressure they needed; the tank would not take it. Its walls were bulging and it was in danger of bursting. He suggested that they rig up a cylinder he had that would stand much more pressure. But it would only take one man at a time. Since Littlehales had still not felt any ill effects from the dive, Marden would try the small tank alone.

They planned to raise the pressure to five atmospheres, equal to a depth of 165 feet. According to the navy tables he was to remain at that stage for 10 hours and 48 minutes. In preparation for the ordeal Marden armed himself with a flashlight, spare batteries, his watch and several paperback books for reading material, then he climbed into the cylinder. As the lid was fastened tight, he felt like he was being entombed. The narrow confines were blacker than the inside of a buried coffin. Pressurization came with an almost unbearable roar of air. When the compressor finally shut off Marden knew that he was not only half deaf but half cooked as well. He switched on his flashlight to read. The pages of his books were as limp as lettuce leaves. The next few hours were the most uncomfortable of his life. Periodically he answered the jarring clangor of hammer blows from outside to let them know he had not expired in his own carbon dioxide exhalations. Then finally, six hammer blows on the cylinder told him that they were depressurizing the tank.

When the lid was removed, Marden crawled out feeling about as lively as the pages of his paperbacks. Although he had been in the tank for six hours and twelve minutes, they had only been able to pressurize it to the equivalent of 100 feet. The experience only temporarily eased his pain. That night he had to be heavily sedated to sleep.

The next morning Marden was alarmed when Littlehales awoke complaining of a pain at the base of his spine and was unable to sit up in bed. If this was decompression sickness, Littlehales could end up permanently paralyzed.

There was no time left for experiments. Now it was an emergency. The call for help went out. The U.S. consul telephoned Mexico City where the American ambassador gave permission for the U.S. naval attache to radio for assistance. It came in the form of a four-engine navy airplane that picked up the men at the airport in Merida. They flew across the Gulf of Mexico at 9,000 feet to maintain sea-level pressure in the aircraft's pressurized cabin. A higher altitude in an unpressurized cabin would have further expanded the bubbles in the men's blood streams. The plane landed at Panama City in northwestern Florida, where Marden and Littlehales were taken quickly to the Navy Mine Defense Laboratory and put into a readied recompression chamber for the next 44 hours and 26 minutes. When they finally emerged from the ordeal they were cured.

A few days later Littlehales was called away to another assignment but Marden returned to Yucatan to finish his job at Dzibilchaltun. When he reappeared at the site, some of the Indian workmen were surprised to see him. They firmly believed that the guardian god of the cenote took a dim view of people digging up the household goods and remains of their ancestors and chose this means of punishing him: permanent banishment.

With the help of his other divers Marden continued to photograph and search the deep slopes of the cenote for artifacts. Still suspecting that things dropped into the water from above must have found their way to the bottom of the well, he again went down to the tunnel and reentered it in search of archaeological treasures. But he found none. The bottom seemed devoid of everything but the centuries of accumulated ooze.

Returning to the shallower levels, he and his team hit a fertile area rich in pottery fragments at 60 feet where they worked the vein until it was exhausted. One of the more interesting finds was made by Marden's wife, who turned up the first complete figurine from the cenote—a clay jaguar almost five inches tall.

Their search finally came to an end with the approaching rainy season. The most important items of their find consisted of a half dozen complete or nearly complete earthenware jars, the skeletal remains of several humans, a spatulate bone hair skewer incised with four hieroglyphs, a small cylinder of rock crystal, a single jade bead and a carved bone finger ring with an undecipherable glyph inscribed around it. These artifacts, along with nearly a quarter of a million potsherds, would provide scientists with enough working material for years to come. But as with Thompson and Scott, Luis Marden felt that he had only scratched the surface of the archaeological treasures still hidden in the dark depths of Xlacah. And one day, the guardian god of the cenote willing, he promised himself he would be back to dive again down through that ancient ocean bottom into centuries-old Yucatan to recover more secrets of its past.

7

MASTODON AT
THIRTY-THREE FATHOMS

For years, tourists have gazed in awe into northwestern Florida's mighty Wakulla Spring. Peering down from glass-bottom boats through 100 feet of incredibly clear water, they see a precipitous limestone cliff, schools of catfish and a sloping sand bottom sprinkled liberally with pennies that "turned to dimes" (flashed silver) an instant before they somersaulted into the sand. But what sightseers do not see is hidden in the shadows beyond the overhanging limestone cliff—the mouth of Wakulla cavern, a 100-foot-wide fissure, whose vaulted ceiling may drop to a scant five feet or soar to a height of over 100 feet. From this cavern flows the Wakulla River at the rate of 183 million gallons of water a day. Ranked as one of the deepest and largest first-magnitude springs* in the United States, Wakulla is every cave divers dream of perfection—the ultimate cavern. In actuality, however, for most divers it is a paradise lost, a spring where scuba diving is prohibited. But there was once a time...

"In many ways Wakulla was an obsession with me," diver-oceanographer Garry Salsman told me in 1975 as he reminisced about his feelings toward the once unexplored big hole in the bottom of Wakulla River during his student days at nearby Florida State University in Tallahassee. "I used to spend many hours there, up on the diving tower, just looking at it when I should have been studying, wondering what was in that cave below that big overhang of limestone."

---

* Any spring possessing an average flow of 100 cubic feet per second (64 million gallons per day) or more. Wakulla produces 283 cfs.

In 1954, Salsman, along with his diving buddies, Wally Jenkins, Henry Doll, Andy Harrold, Gordon Whitney and Lamarr Trott, were doing more than just thinking about diving into Wakulla; they were practicing for it.

"We weren't in training just for Wakulla," said Salsman. "We did these things because we were curious about Florida caves and wanted to stay alive. So we embarked on training missions...."

Their practice area was a river that popped up out of nowhere, disappeared underground, then reappeared again. Local divers knew its water-filled maze of interconnecting passageways, siphons, coming-and-going currents as the Natural Bridge Sink.

"We would go back a certain distance laying out a safety line, turn out our lights and make our way back along this line to see the problems we would encounter and work our way out. We learned a lot about how safety lines should be made, how they should be laid, the ways you can get into trouble even if you do take a safety line. We practiced going in with two men, then buddy breathing* back out without lights; with lights; various combinations of these things. We even got proficient enough at 100-foot depths that we could go in with three men and come out buddy breathing on one rig. We got to know each other, got used to each other. We were not doing these things in a daredevil fashion. There was no interest in our minds of going in with a depth gauge to see if we could go deeper than somebody else or farther into a cave to learn things about it; and because of this I don't think there was one man in our group who you'd call a record seeker...."

Despite the training, the off-limits Wakulla Spring remained as elusive as ever. Salsman and his friends spent many days swimming there over the central boil without scuba, holding their breaths to dive down as far as they could, going underneath the overhanging ledge and wondering how much closer they could get to the great maw if they had just one more breath. They tried to talk the manager of the then privately owned spring into letting them dive into the cave with scuba. When this failed they wrote the company that owned the spring, suggesting that

*Two or more divers sharing air from one regulator.

they might make finds that would really enhance the spring for the public. But the company was not interested in what might be in there. In the early days a hard-hat diver had found the bones of a mastodon in the shallow water of the north side of the spring and had recovered it with the help of members of the Florida Geological Survey. Except for the helmet diver, who claimed to have reached the bottom of the spring in 185 feet of water, this was the extent of any underwater exploration. No one had ever penetrated the deep cavern, and it appeared to Salsman and the others that, as far as the spring's owner was concerned, no one ever would.

But then came the movie makers and the break of a lifetime: a short film was to be shot in the spring.

"They weren't interested in the cave or the spring, for that matter," said Salsman. "All they wanted was clear water. If they could have found a washing machine big enough they could have filled it with city water and done what they wanted to do. Sure enough, along in their filming, they were depending on a company in Tallahassee for their air supply, and the company's compressor broke down and they needed air."

Salsman just happened to have an Ingersol-Rand surface compressor coupled to an automobile engine mounted on a two-wheel trailer and capable of filling a 72-cubic-foot tank in about three minutes. And that was about how long it took him to offer the movie makers all the air they wanted from his compressor in exchange for his being allowed to dive in the spring with scuba. The company happily agreed. Moreover, it hired Salsman and two of his friends to help the other divers position camera equipment and set the scenes. When the day 's filming was over in the shallows, Salsman and a companion made their first cautious dive down into the mouth of the huge cavern.

"Wally Jenkins and myself swam slowly down under the ledge to a depth of about 180 feet. The spring was leveling off at this point. We were really equipped, perhaps more so in our minds than anything else. We each had double tanks, and our safety line was on a reel. When we reached a boulder at that depth, Wally gave me a signal that he felt a little narcotic and wanted to stop. We had agreed that the first one that got narcosis, that's when we stopped; we wouldn't go any farther. So we stopped at this boulder. I looked at Wally and he was okay, breathing fine; so I turned and looked a little further on down into the cave, very curious. I saw something down there—a black object—and decided that I had to get to it. I started kicking and no sooner got off that boulder, angling down, than narcosis hit me. But I had a fixation on that object. Somehow or other I had to get to it. I knew it wasn't very far, but it seemed to take me forever to get there. I felt like I was trying to swim through a clear but thick molasses. Every movement was like something in a nightmare where your motions seem to be a lot slower than you'd like them to be.

"I finally reached the object, and it turned out to be nothing but a piece of limestone sitting on a whiter section of the bottom. I looked back up at Wally who was not more than 20 feet away and 10 feet above me. When I recognized that piece of limestone for what it was, I knew I was not operating the way I should. I quickly gave a push off the bottom and was soon up beside Wally where my head cleared. This was a new experience for both of us. We swam up out of the place, and later had many a talk about narcosis and how it had affected us...."

They reread Cousteau's *The Silent World*, closely studying the passages in which the French scuba-diving pioneer described the experience he and his companions had had with narcosis. Salsman and Jenkins had felt nothing like it on their dives in other sinkholes and springs in the area. It was their first experience with narcosis and their first experience with Wakulla. Both impressed them.

"There was no doubt in our minds that we had to go back into that place," continued Salsman. "There was no way that we could have stopped at this place and said that we had seen Wakulla. So we launched another expedition.

"This time, two fellows from the company that had been supplying air until we got the business went with us. Both were good divers. So Wally and myself and these two angled down the slope, reached the boulder where we had our first problems, felt pretty clear-headed at this point, so we eased on down to this black object that I had reached before. Everything was still good. We moved further on in.

"The floor was level at this point, and we were swimming

above it, sweeping our lights back and forth. Suddenly Wally banged his tank twice with his knife, our prearranged signal that he had found something. I turned and swam over to him. He was looking at a mastodon leg bone about four feet long that lay on the bottom. Wally had not touched it. But when he saw it, one of the other divers picked it up. Since it was too heavy for him to swim with he started walking out with it. We helped him get it up to the ledge and that ended the dive."

Wakulla Spring's manager was so excited about the big bone being found 200 feet back in the cave that when the movie company stopped filming, he gave Salsman and his group permission to continue scuba diving there, asking only that they sign insurance releases absolving the company of any responsibilities for their safety.

From then on the real exploration of the cavern began in fine style. Salsman chained his air compressor and trailer to a big tree near the spring, and for the next 18 months it stayed there, refilling their air cylinders as they were needed. The students purposefully scheduled their classes at the university so they would not interfere with their Wakulla dives. The finds that followed were made during many gradual penetrations from 1955 through 1956.

To avoid worry about getting the bends, each dive never lasted longer than 15 minutes, timed from when the divers left the surface until they were back to the point where their safety line began near the entrance of the cave. It was their own self-imposed precaution. Each man observed it just as closely as he did their common agreement that this was no place to play games. If one among them was apprehensive about continuing a penetration, all he had to do was say, "Whoa, that's far enough," and the others respected it. Down there they had nothing to prove to themselves or to anyone else.

The beginning of each dive into the spring was always the same, a kind of long, liquid elevator ride between two worlds. They suited up at the diving tower beside the pool, then finned their way down to the projecting limestone ledge 30 feet below the surface. There they picked up extra heavy weights and stepped off the ledge, descending effortlessly to the sloping sand bottom 100 feet down. Dropping the weights, they continued swimming down the sloping white escarpment into the throat of the gradually darkening cavern.

In the gloom at 180 feet they switched on their lights and tied off one end of their safety line to a limestone boulder. The reel man led the way ; the others followed, sliding their circled thumb and forefinger along the plastic-coated, rayon-cored line.

Six minutes into the cave they approached the area where Jenkins had found the mastodon leg bone. The bottom was clay. Their depth gauges read 200 feet. As they looked closely at the floor in this area, they gradually became aware of more fossil bones. Curved ribs, massive femurs, tooth-studded jawbones and dozens of other bone fragments were embedded in the bottom. It was as if the men had stumbled into the fabulous graveyard of elephants, except that these were the fossil remains of the elephant's early ancestors.

Fixing the safety line permanently to another boulder, the men measured from this baseline to a prominent thigh bone. A diver photographed it in place. A second bulb flashed brilliantly as he recorded the 50-pound femur being rolled free of the clay and readied for removal. Salsman produced a pillowcase lined

PROFILE OF WAKULLA CAVERN

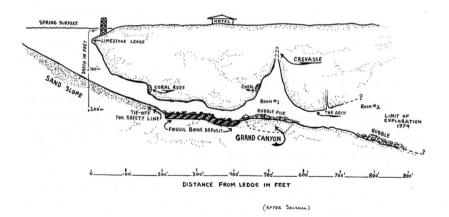

(AFTER SALSMAN)

The exploration of Wakulla Cavern by Salsman and his group took place over a long period of time involving more than 100 dives, each one never lasting longer than 15 minutes for safety reasons.

with a plastic bag. Tying the open end of the sack to the bone he held his mouthpiece beneath it so it would free-flow and inflated the bag with just enough air for the whole thing to have neutral buoyancy. Now the divers had no difficulty pushing the weight-less find ahead of them as they made their way out of the cave.

While ascending with their prize, however, they had to spill air from the bag to prevent it from overexpanding and rocket-ing to the surface prematurely. And, as always, because of the depth and the time spent below, the divers had to make decom-pression stops totaling 46 minutes based on the old U.S. Navy decompression tables at 30, 20 and 10 feet in the spring basin.

Since the students were working closely with the Florida Geo-logical Survey on this project, paleontologist Dr. Stanley J. Olsen was usually waiting on the surface to help identify the mineral and fossil specimens they recovered.

On subsequent exploratory dives, Salsman and his compan-ions found that the area of fossil finds went on for almost 300 feet of the bottom. Scattered across it were the skeletal remains of mastodons, mammoths, giant ground sloths, bears, deer, cam-els, and about 500 feet in from the entrance, the large curved tusks of mastodons. Nearby, the bottom was black with traces of charcoal. Embedded in the same sediments as the fossil bones, the divers recovered 50 or 60 bone-tipped spear points, the same kind that they later found by the dozens in the basin outside the cave.

What was the significance of these finds? Was the cave once dry? Had early man lived there? Was it the diver's imagination or did they detect what appeared to be "sorting?"

"In some areas it looked like all the rib bones," said Salsman. "In another we found three or four tusks and nothing else; in still another place there were only teeth. It looked almost as if they had been sorted that way on purpose. Nature sorts things —gold nuggets settling to the bottom of a stream, for instance. Currents sort sediments, and they are very effective at this. But currents did not seem like a good mechanism for sorting the kinds of things we saw. Maybe it was wishful thinking, but we tried to envision that the sorting agent here was man; that many years ago Wakulla was dry, inhabited by man, and it was a nice cool cave where the animals he killed he butchered here and left their bones. Maybe in the butchering process the ribs got tossed on one part of the cave floor, the tusks in another, and so forth...."

Not far from the boneyard the divers got into one of the few arguments they ever had at 220 feet underwater. Andy Harrold insisted that not only was there charcoal on the floor of the cave at that point and evidence of a camp site, but there were markings on the wall that looked to him as if they had been made by some prehistoric artist. Consequently a silent, pantomimed argument went on down there about what he thought they were, with Jenkins and Salsman shaking their heads that he was wrong. The two small concentric circles that Harrold thought was a man-made petroglyph of the sun, Jenkins recognized for what it was—an impression of the design imprinted on the heels of his full-foot rubber swim fins. Earlier he had placed his foot against the wall to hold his position in the current while taking a photograph. The underwater argument promptly ended when Jenkins flourished the offending foot fin before Harrold's mask, sun sign up.

Just beyond the boneyard at a depth of 225 feet, one wall of the cave made an abrupt right-angle turn while the other fell off into an unusual depression that the divers were to name the "Grand Canyon." When they first saw it they thought they had found a sinkhole in the floor of the cave that might lead down to another level. Shining their lights into it they saw alternating horizontal bands of light and dark layers of clay. It gave them the impression of gazing into the depths of the Grand Canyon with all its geological strata clearly defined.

"From the top it looked fantastically deep," recalled Salsman. "We stopped in amazement and just stared down into it. On our next dive we were all prepared to see just how deep it was. Wally was to stay up on the edge of it, and I was to descend slowly down one of the steep walls with a safety rope tied to me while the others shined their lights on me.

"The lip of the sink was at about 235 feet. So down the wall I went. You can imagine our surprise when we found that the whole thing was an optical illusion. The 'fantastic' depth I descended to was only 20 feet lower than the lip. Those horizontal bands of color, aided, no doubt, by a little narcosis, fooled us. Every time I swim by that depression I smile about it, but we still call it the Grand Canyon. There are a lot of things I smile about in caves now that worried and bothered us in those days. I'm glad they did because it made us cautious. We had to plan how to approach the cave, how to approach narcosis, how to approach the Grand Canyon and the other obstacles that later confronted us...."

Deciding to investigate the roof of the cave near the Grand Canyon, Salsman and his buddies were amazed to find that it soared upward to over a 100 foot-high ceiling. On that trip they carried along a buoyant float, which they tied to a line attached to their permanent safety rope running along between boulders over the floor of the cathedral-sized room. When they released the float, it rose to the ceiling, trailing the safety line behind it until it was strung taut, straight up from the bottom. Then Jenkins and Salsman followed it, giving the others quite a spectacular view as they watched from below and saw the men gradually grow small far above them, their lights illuminating a wide expanse of the domed roof. As they investigated the curved limestone surface, the "flywalkers" passed part of an exposed fossil coral reef similar to a patch they had found on the roof closer to the entrance. When the apex of the dome began forming a peak that became a narrowing crack in the rock ceiling, Salsman and Jenkins continued on into it.

"We came on up to a place where we were just about shoulder to shoulder with vertical white walls on each side," said Salsman. "We went until it got so narrow we could not get any further up into the crevice. I checked my depth gauge. We were 60 feet below the surface. I looked down the way we had come toward the two fellows we had left on the floor of the cave and saw their pinpoints of light down there, 170 feet below us.

"Finally we reached the point in our dive where we had to leave to be out of the cave by the 15th minute. So we came bombing on down and to me that was one of the most fascinating returns, to descend quickly from 60 feet, dropping on down that safety line to 230 feet, and then swimming out of the cave. I don't know why but I felt as if we had literally been back in the bowels of the earth. I've never had that feeling cave diving before...."

Breakdown from the long, narrowing roof crack had left the

bottom strewn with limestone boulders. Moreover, the crevice approached so close to limestone sinkholes located on the surface above it that Salsman felt certain some link must exist between one of the flooded sinks and the spring, even if it was too small for a man to negotiate. In subsequent tests he found that the water level of the sink was the same as that of the spring and he suspected that small fish were able to travel back and forth between the cavern and the flooded sink.

As exploration of the main shaft continued, the team found that just beyond the Grand Canyon the bottom steepened into a brilliant, white sandbar, then sloped back down to the original cave floor. Beyond this it was littered with limestone boulders and scattered fragments of fossil coral, the result, probably, of more roof breakdown. The divers penetrated to a distance of about 950 feet at a depth of 240 feet below the surface. At this point the cavern's passageway continued enlarging and sloping ever downward into deeper, unknown depths.

"Time mostly determined the limit of penetration," said Salsman. "We reached a point where it was just a mad swim in, turn around, and a mad swim out. The idea was against the very thing we wanted to do. We weren't going in there to set a depth or distance record. Sure, we were curious about where Wakulla went, but we were not naive enough to think that we could find it by this method. Some day, with advanced diving systems, manned submersibles small enough to get by some of those places, it might be a fantastic voyage...."

By 1957, Salsman and his associates had made more than 200 accident-free reconnaissance dives into the vast cavern. But that spring marked the high-water point of their early efforts. As heavy seasonal rains turned the spring murky, their cave-diving ended. In June when school was out the group dispersed, many of the team members moving away from the area to pursue their fortunes elsewhere.

Their exploratory dives at Wakulla had opened up a whole new underwater world, but their efforts to dispel some of the mystery of the cavern created more provocative questions than they answered.

Was the cavern ever dry and inhabited? How did the skeletons of prehistoric land animals get 500 feet back in a passageway that was 200 feet underwater? Did early man have anything to do with it? Scientists have long searched for valid evidence of an association between North American man and mastodons, the pachyderms' prehistoric ancestor that became extinct sometime after the last Pleistocene glaciation, possibly as early as 11,000 or 12,000 years ago. After the Wakulla finds of over 600 bone spear points similar to those found with Florida's prehistoric inhabitant, Vero Man, and considering the close proximity of these items to the prehistoric boneyard in the cavern, paleontologist Dr. Stanley Olsen cautiously commented that, "interpreting underwater finds in Florida is no easy occupation and the excitement of this juxtaposition of man and mastodon is quickly dampened by experience. In the Itchtucknee River, one of Florida's most productive fossil localities, for example, it was once possible to find the remains of mastodon and tapir in juxtaposition with pop bottles and beer cans." Today, however, through special efforts the river is again pristine. But until extinct animal bones are found with a spear point actually embedded in the bone—and preferably with the bone growing around the point—positive, contemporary association of the two cannot be claimed in the case of a stream deposit."

As for the presence of the fossil bones in the cave, Olsen speculated that water could carry such objects over a great distance, especially considering the first couple of hundred feet of Wakulla's steep, sloping bottom. "But at Wakulla the flow is in the opposite direction," he said. "Some objects can be easily rolled but not, for example, a crescent-shaped tusk weighing hundreds of pounds. Yet surely," said Olsen, voicing the once popular scientific belief, "Wakulla cavern had never been dry at this depth, and thus had not been visited by these animals at the time when they were alive."

If the remains had not slid down the sloping floor because of the strong outflowing current, and if the cavern was always completely flooded, how then did the bones get there?

Olsen theorized that they had fallen through the roof—a not too farfetched theory when one remembers the crack in the ceiling that Salsman followed up underneath a flooded surface sinkhole. Had these animals fallen into the sink and in time their remains filtered down onto the floor of the deep cavern?

Perhaps. But on a dive into the spring in January, 1969, Salsman, no longer a student but a civilian oceanographer with the U.S. Navy Mine Defense Laboratory at Panama City, and fellow oceanographer, Walt Howard, believe they may have found the mechanism that got the bones into the cavern. Indeed, they had the dubious pleasure of being present when the strange phenomenon occurred: the spring flushed itself!

"In all the years that we had been diving Wakulla," said Salsman, describing the incident, "probably the most forgotten bottom in the whole area was that long steep-sloping stretch of sand angling down under the edge to a depth of about 180 feet. That's about 200 feet horizontally into the cave. This sand floor had a crown in it with occasional blocks of limestone scattered along its east side—all of which we had always swiftly bypassed in our eagerness to get in or out of the cavern in our allotted 15 minutes. Consequently, we had never really looked at this bottom.

"They had heavy rain in Tallahassee the week before our dive and Wakulla was not as clear as usual. So, instead of making a deep penetration into the cavern, we decided to fan around the edges of that sand slope at a depth of about 100 feet to see if we could find any bones. Well, we hadn't been down there five minutes hand-fanning near the base of a couple boulders for artifacts, when Walt came over to me and pointed back toward the cave. I turned and looked down there and saw a lot of white water coming out of the cave toward us. It was really eerie. We hadn't heard anything, but there it was. I swam down to look at it and it was just like a thermocline in a lake, the density layer was so different. It was like a line of demarcation, working its way out. So we swam up to the surface and decided that maybe it was a good thing that we hadn't made the dive. We figured there must have been a breakdown back in the cave system and white water was just getting here.

"We went up to the diving tower and the manager of the spring came down as the basin was turning white. He wanted to know what we had done to his spring. I had visions of our whole diving sequence being terminated at that point. I said there must have been some kind of cave-in back in the system, but I admitted to him that I didn't see how we just happened to be down there when it happened.

"Several days later after it cleared up we went back down to dive, and it was completely obvious then what had happened. In fanning around those boulders we must have loosened a key stone that moved just enough to precipitate an avalanche.

"The domed area on that sloping sand bottom was no longer there. All that sediment had given way, and in its place was a steep sloping V-shaped valley. In some places as much as twenty feet of sediment had moved; in other places along the walls maybe three or four feet were gone. The spring had flushed itself. All this material simply plunged downslope into the system, carrying with it everything that was in those deposits; the turbulence kicking up clouds of sand and limestone that were pushed back out on the outflowing current as white water.

"We found the whole mass several hundred feet back in the cavern, redistributed all the way from the fossil bone area to actually running over into the Grand Canyon. Not only had the action uncovered new fossil bones, but it carpeted the whole fossil area with modern artifacts that had filtered down into the basin outside—coins, keys, Coca-Cola caps, even a plastic boomerang—things swimmers had lost or had thrown into the spring. They were all down there now lying beside the prehistoric artifacts. So, I think that avalanche is the mechanism by which all things get into the deep inner part of the cave. Over the years it probably occurs periodically, each time the slope becomes overburdened with a new mass of fallout. Normally it would trigger itself. But in this case, we apparently triggered it a little sooner than some natural source would have done it. For that reason, we now consider this slope the most dangerous thing in Wakulla. In fact, where we had our safety lines tied off was buried under eight feet of sand. If someone had been in the cave during the avalanche there would have been no way for him to have followed that safety line out. He wouldn't have been killed by the avalanche itself, but the secondary effects would have gotten him."

Once before, something strange had happened in Wakulla Spring. In March, 1964, the night of the great Alaska earthquake, the manager was awakened by the sound of rumbling. Finding nothing wrong he went back to sleep. The next morning white water was coming up out of the spring. The manager and a work-man went out in a glass-bottom boat for a closer look and found a fresh fissure in the limestone on the west side of the spring that had not been there before. Was it coincidence that this fault occurred the same night as the Alaska earthquake on the other side of the continent? Salsman thinks not. He believes that the spring reacted to the earthquake in the same manner as did the large fluctuations of water levels in wells in the southeastern United States; or a premature fluctuation of a tide gauge at Pensacola, twenty-five minutes before the quake; or the one-and-a-half-foot tsunami-type wave that swept across the Gulf of Mexico and caused some problems at one of the ports.

Continuing with the original policy of prohibiting scuba diving in the spring, the management still allowed Salsman and a few close associates to pursue their investigation of the subterranean waterway after their initial discoveries.

"There is so much that could be learned from a place like that," said Salsman. "But we feel that with compressed air, at our age, our dives in this cave are quite limited now. We know that with scuba gear as presently configured we're not going to find the origin of Wakulla Spring, so our explorations have taken a turn in another direction. We're looking for different signals instead of going down with the direct approach and looking with the old Mark One eyeball. We're putting sensors down there...."

Salsman explained how they had wired the spring with sensitive detecting devices—a current meter at its entrance with a surface readout and a tide-gauge water-level indicator by the diving tower on the surface. He told of cave-diving hydrologist Larry Brill's tireless efforts to monitor changes in the spring and to determine the length of time the water had actually been underground, as opposed to in the air or sunlight, through radiocarbon dating of water samples. All of which is revealing more intriguing facts about the spring.

They found, for example, that the water emerging at Wakulla appears to come from a main source no farther away than 60 or 70 miles. The level of the spring not only fluctuates with a delayed sympathetic response to the rise and fall of the ocean tides, and the normal oscillation from local rainfall, but it also responds to atmospheric changes.

"This variation that takes place has nothing to do with tides or rainfall," said Salsman. "This one has to do with atmospheric pressure. The spring acts like an inverted barometer. Whenever the pressure falls, the spring rises. It's a beautiful inverse relationship and quite a large change: water level fluctuations up to 1.4 or 1.5 feet associated with frontal passages. You can actually look at the spring level and tell what has been happening weather-wise when a front passed Tallahassee at such and such a time...."

In 1975, when I interviewed him for the first edition of this book, research oceanographer Garry Salsman did not have as much time as he would like to have to devote to his study of Wakulla Spring, but as far as he was concerned it was by no means a closed project. If it were possible for a man and a spring to have a really close relationship, it existed for this man and that spring. Salsman explained it this way: "Wakulla means many things to me. It's the fantastic voyages of my youth in there. As a kid I always remember reading and enjoying the early sailing expeditions across uncharted waters. Well, there aren't many islands left to be discovered in our oceans any more, but in 1955 Wakulla Spring was that uncharted ocean to us. I think our lives were enriched substantially by our journeys into it." And after a moment's reflection he summed it up:

"I'm not really a religious person," Salsman said quietly, "but Wakulla Spring is sacred to me."

8

DEEP, DARK DESIRES

Interestingly, after Salsman, Jenkins and their team performed the remarkable feat of exploring Wakulla Spring to a then unheard of record depth and penetration, reporting mastodon remains at 33 fathoms, it would be another 33 years before divers put together the technology and know-how to push the exploration of this gigantic system to even more phenomenal record depths and penetration distances.

In those 33 years, however, this mammoth system did not remain entirely virginal. Since the spring was on private property where scuba diving was strictly prohibited, the temptation to see what was really there tempted many a qualified cave diver. Smitten by the explorer instinct to go where no man had gone before, a few figured out ways to sneak into the off limits area. At night, determined divers found they could enter the system through adjoining springs for a forbidden peek at what was down there. Needless to say, on air in Wakulla's depths, few penetrated far. Most were lucky to get out alive. On one occasion, two divers managed to secretly leave air tanks at several underwater sites along the main tunnel to explore in the over 300-foot depths. These experienced cavers had been tested for their tolerances to oxygen poisoning, an insidious and largely unpredictable problem that can occur when a diver breathes compressed air at extreme depths. On this particular trip, when they were over 300 feet down and far back in the system, one individual with an extraordinary high tolerance for the toxicity found his buddy going into convulsions from oxygen poisoning.

Nothing could be done for him. First the convulsions, then

blackout, then death. The first diver tried to tow his buddy's body out, but the effort proved too difficult. He was on the verge of blacking out himself. He finally had to give up, escaping with his life. Later, considering the depth and the distance back in the cave, even an experienced body recovery team had a difficult time recovering the victim.

My first opportunity to view the mouth of Wakulla from the inside out came in 1972 when I was invited to join a local TV crew doing a special on the spring.

Once the shallower water shots were out of the way, a companion and I decided to make a quick bounce dive down to just inside the cav e's entrance. Considering how long we had already spent at depth, even a dive of very short duration would require a lengthy decompression stop afterward. But we figured if we were ever going to see the inside of Wakulla's big open mouth, this was the time to do it.

The sensation of slowly dropping through that cool green void from the surface to the sloping sand floor at a depth of 155 feet, was the most exhilarating thing I had ever experienced in diving up to that time. A TV commercial for a thick green shampoo named Prell was in vogue then. To demonstrate just how richly thick the shampoo was, television viewers watched a pearl drop slowly through that viscous column of green.

"Wow! Like a pearl through Prell!" was my impression of that descent.

As we bottomed out on the slope at 155 feet, our exhaled bubbles rose swiftly like silver chandeliers, each bubble expanding rapidly into a semi-spherical shape as it ballooned musically to the surface. I say musically because divers' exhalations at depths over 100 feet clatter and resonate like glass wind chimes heard in a tunnel as the rapidly expanding bubbles race to the surface. When my depth gauge malfunctioned once while descending a coral wall in the Bahamas, the sound of those chiming bubbles alerted me to the fact that I wasn't really at 70 feet as my depth gauge read, but at 130 feet as my companion's gauge read.

Looking back up from 155 feet of water through the vast opening to Wakulla cavern is like looking through a crack into the world. Indeed, this may be the world's largest stone picture frame.

Everything is black except that giant irregular opening 150 feet wide and 70 feet high, large enough to easily fly a 727 jet through without a problem. In that huge pale green picture you see a slightly wavering blue sky filled with fleecy white clouds, above an encircling cluster of green-boughed cypress trees. Silhouettes of freshwater fish dot the waterscape at different depths. It's a living watercolor you never forget.

In 1981, permission was given professional cave divers Paul DeLoach, Mary Ellen Eckhoff and Dr. John Zumrick to use some of the newer dive technology to explore the system. Employing spaced supply depots of air tanks and speeding up their travel while conserving energy by using electric propulsion units, these divers penetrated Wakulla Cavern to a record 1,106 feet from its entrance while maintaining an average depth of 261 feet. The divers returned with tales of entering chambers so vast their powerful dive lights failed to reach the walls, and of being badly impaired at those depths by nitrogen narcosis.

It appeared that this vast system was being protected from further exploration literally by an air barrier. Simply put, it meant that divers breathing air from a standard scuba system in Wakulla's depths created so many problems that they were extremely limited. One could go only so far for so long and that was it. How odd to think that breathing air in the watery world of Wakulla was the one thing that would keep people out. Was there an alternative?

One man believed there was. At the time Dr. William C. Stone was a brilliant engineer whose early interest in this problem at first had nothing to do with Wakulla Spring. As a dedicated cave diver long ago smitten by the desire to explore the furthest reaches of submarine cave systems, Stone focused his interest on what may well be the world's largest subterranean system, one experts say is the Mt. Everest of caves—the deep, complex tunnels and sumps beneath southern Mexico's Huautla Plateau.

After University of Texas cavers found the system in 1964, subsequent expeditions followed its network of underground passageways to a depth 2,000 feet below the earth's surface. Problems with the area's local Indians delayed further investigations until 1976 when an expedition that included 23-year-old University of Texas engineering student Bill Stone, set another penetration depth record. Stone had grown up in Pennsylvania where he first caught the caving bug. His choice of the university at Austin was based not so much on his academic interests as on the fact that it would put him in contact with world class caving areas, not to mention enthusiasts as keenly obsessed with the sport as himself.

What Stone experienced at Huautla was to change his life forever. For the first time he got a taste of the ultimate challenge, the ultimate adventure. As the cliche phrases of the day go, for the first time he was on the "leading edge" of a thrust to "push the envelope" back on explorations into a totally alien world. Stone's team set a record at Huautla by spending five days underground and penetrating the system to a new depth of 2,624 feet.

Of that experience he said later, "It was exhilarating beyond anything I had imagined. I really felt like I was going into the valley of the shadow of death. I knew I had crossed over the frontier threshold, both physically and psychologically, and I never felt more alive."

What more would you expect from a fellow who when asked recently whom among the great explorers he respected the most quickly responded, "Christopher Columbus."

Months after his first push at Huautla, colleagues added another hard-gained 200 feet until stopped by a water barrier they named San Agustín Sump. Three subsequent expeditions tried to find an air pocket beyond this bottleneck, but failed. In 1981, Stone penetrated 1,000 feet along the sunken passageway, descending another 92 feet, without finding an air passage. Three years later, the obsession had him attempting a link-up through a surface spring where Huautla's underground river emptied into the jungle, seven miles distant as the crow flies over land from the Sump. Entering the system from that direction in 1984, Stone and ten team members spent three grueling months struggling through the labyrinthine passage, a quarter of it underwater.

In the effort, they made 600 dives through six flooded bottlenecks to explore six miles of cave tunnels so serpentine that they only progressed two-and-a-half miles in a straight line. As a seventh water barrier loomed to block their way, the realization that they would now have to haul 72 scuba tanks and thousands of pounds of equipment through miles of that tortuous underground underwater maze just to push a bit further, was too much for them. Stone soon realized that the only hope of continuing would have to await the day someone would invent dive gear that would provide a lot more performance for a lot less effort.

Not being the kind of person to sit back and wait for technology to catch up with him, Stone started his own quest for a solution to his problem. His first thought of course was in the possibility of a closed air system, a rebreather using the basic concept developed for divers during World War II. Essentially, the diver's exhalations were chemically scrubbed of carbon dioxide, oxygen was added, and the diver rebreathed the mixture. There were no exhaled bubbles, and the whole thing required wearing only a couple small canisters and a horse-collar kind of bladder where the exchange took place. But as noted earlier, the only trouble with the early rebreathers was that you couldn't go below 30 feet with them, or fatal things happened to the diver.

Years later, manufacturers tried computerized versions of the idea, but none proved entirely satisfactory. Then along came Bill Stone. He knew little about the new technology of closed circuit rebreathers, but he was eager to learn. Maybe he could learn enough to speed things up a bit, at least enough to let him solve his problem at Huautla.

"In December of 1984—following discussions with Drs. John Zumrick and Noel Sloan after the Huautla Cave expedition—I began design work on a long-range, redundant rebreather for exploration diving," said Stone.

First he founded a Maryland Corporation, Cis-Lunar Development Laboratories, Inc. as his base of operation, forming a research and development team to come up with, then test ideas. His basic concept was to develop a rebreather-type dive unit that would far exceed the current Navy SEAL versions. What Stone was shooting for was a unit that would let a diver breathe underwater for up to 24 hours while operating problem-free at 300-foot depths.

Talk about shooting for the moon! Stone might just as well have said he'd like to explore the inner-workings of volcanoes on that celestial planet. Which incidentally is only the next step down the road in Stone's plans for the future, just in case you were wondering about the word "lunar" in his company logo. All he has to do is figure how to get a slightly modified version of his rebreather into space.

Pipe dreams or reality? For a guy who spins out ideas so fast his friends say he talks without commas, moves in strides or jogs wherever he goes, and said he would do anything to get sponsors to put money into his project, except to smoke, the initial project started with a bang in his basement workshop. For the next eight years, Stone got up at 5 o'clock every morning to put in three or four hours on his pet project in the basement, then hustled off to a full-time job as a structural engineer designing bridges for the National Institute of Standards and Technology in Gaithersburg, Maryland. Hurrying home from work, he ate supper, enjoyed brief prime time with his family, then disappeared into the basement again.

Eight years of this mole-like existence, coupled with the cost of $2 million worth of donated cash and services, added up to what Stone called the Cis-Lunar Mk-1 diving rebreather. Physically, his first model looked about as practical for prolonged underwater diving as the Wright's first contraption at Kittyhawk looked for the future of aviation. Stone's Mark 1 rebreather stacked three gas cylinders horizontally across a back rack with two more larger cylindrical devices mounted atop of them on what resembled the innards of an old vacuum tube radio set, the big robust kind that made it through the depression years. This much a diver was to carry on his back. And that was just the back side. From the front, multiple hoses, redundant backup systems, gauges, electronic monitoring components and a world of other gadgets almost obscured the diver buried inside.

But the kicker was that it worked!

Lest the above description sounds facetious, readers must understand that when a diver plans to penetrate great underwater depths and distances where he will be restricted from surfacing, he must carry a life support system that will function properly for hours at a time.

Should it malfunction, the diver <u>must</u> have, not just another, but multiple backup systems to nullify any chance of recurring failure. Bulky? Sure, but now one can better understand why this first primitive unit resembled the kind of burdens usually reserved for Sherpas back-packing the entire contents of a mountain-climbing expedition into the rarefied region of the high Himalayas.

Stone's job was to figure out how to pack several rebreathers into a space usually reserved for one. And that wasn't all. The whole thing had to have a brain. Someday in the future, this will be looked upon as primitive, but here was the brain behind Stone's first working model as he described it:

"The Cis-Lunar Mk-1 employed a unique onboard computer system, running in excess of 6,000 lines of code, that in addition to automatically controlling the breathing gas mixture, provided instant feedback to the user on the status of all subsystems in the apparatus. Completing this was a manual override console that permitted the user to take control of the system in the event of a complete electronic failure. Unlike all previous rebreathers, the manual override system was combined in a single front-mounted unit within view of the user. This and a head-up display (HUD) were mounted on swing-out arms that gave the diver easy access to both information and control capabilities."

Space Age stuff. But where best to test it? Casting around for a suitable system that would do justice to the device he had created, and after much consultation with the international cave diving community, Stone selected Wakulla Spring. Right from the beginning, this spring seemed the most qualified. After all, it offered deep, unlimited potentials, the kind that had never been reached before. For Stone and the Cis-Lunar Mk-1, it only started out to be a test. But other minds sparked the thought that this might be the first really good opportunity since the Salsman/Jenkins team pushed Wakulla's underwater frontier to its limits 33 years ago, to learn at last what lay beyond that final water barrier.

9

GOING WHERE NONE
HAVE GONE BEFORE

By the late 1980's, Wakulla Spring had become the property of the State of Florida, thereby clearing the way for future scientific exploration of the underground system. In 1986, Dr. Bill Stone applied to the Florida Department of Natural Resources for permission to conduct a research operation there. It would be an opportunity to test his rebreather under extreme conditions, and to explore the deep-water system. The state couldn't care less whether Stone tested his dive unit there. They were interested in having Wakulla explored. So, with Stone as expedition leader, this became the effort's primary goal. The proposal was accepted and in the fall of 1987 the first really hi-tech effort to explore and scientifically document the finding at Wakulla began. This event was the first major effort since the earliest recovery of mastodon remains from those depths in 1850 by helmet and hose diver, George S. King, 137 years before.

It was to be a four-month operation whose team members included more that 20 selected cave divers and scientists. The divers planned to use special gas mixtures, primarily Heliox-14 (86% helium, 14% oxygen) as the bottom breathing mix. By excluding nitrogen, this gas mixture eliminated nitrogen narcosis problems of breathing compressed air at depth. It also controlled potential problems of oxygen toxicity under these extreme conditions.

The logistics of supplying such an effort was considerable. An incredible number of gas cylinders were to be used, including many that were fiber-composite to enable filling to 5,000 pounds psi to provide the volumes needed. Because of the long periods, divers would be at excessively deep depths and decompression times would also be lengthy. Rather than keep the divers in the chilling water during this ordeal, they opted for a dry decompression habitat that could be winched up or down, providing the divers some degree of comfort during these long periods.

Stone designed the habitat. Built of tubular aluminum alloy sheathed in neoprene-coated ballistic nylon, the 10-foot-wide hemispherical dome would be anchored to the bottom with four tons of lead. An additional seven tons of ballast attached to the habitat itself. After snapping off their gear to the outside of the habitat, divers entered through a pie-shaped bottom wedge. Inside, the unit was ten feet in diameter and six feet tall in the center. A food tube provided warm meals. Telephones linked them to the support crew and the outside world. The divers decompressed in the dark. An internal chain hoist allowed those inside to raise or lower the unit from 60-foot depths to the surface, providing warmth, food and comfort during their final decompression stops.

As the team set up at Wakulla, it was plagued by the kind of hardships expected when dealing with new, untested ideas in an alien environment. One major accident occurred when 2 one-ton weights for mooring the habitat slipped off a ledge into over 100 feet of water and buried themselves in bottom sediments. After repeated trials and errors, they were finally recovered five days later and installed where they belonged.

After weeks of set-up, the divers began a series of work-up dives to acclimate themselves to the main thrust ahead. The first dives recreated the efforts of the Salsman/Jenkins team over 30 years earlier. The idea was to discover what it was like to penetrate those depths and distances, seeing it for the first time under the diver's own power, using regular air rather than mixed gas.

Once this experience was behind them, the divers prepared for their major push using the most recent equipment and techniques available, some that originated just for this particular effort. For example, traditionally for deep penetrations, divers spent considerable time and effort setting up spaced air depots, places where air tanks would be cached along the passageways so that reserves were always available. Working from station to station and switching from one set of tanks to another, divers made their maximum progress.

One team member thought perhaps there was a better way. He was Wes Skiles. Wes grew up in Jacksonville, Florida where as a youngster, he and his older brother helped test underwater tow sleds and one-man wet submarines a neighbor was designing in the 1970's. On one of these tests at Ginnie Springs, young Skiles mustered enough courage to enter the narrow opening to that cave and peer into the dark voids within as far as his light would go. From then on his imagination worked overtime as to what might be awaiting him beyond that dark barrier.

In his early teens, Wes began exploring Ginnie and other Florida cave systems, operating with such methodical care that he survived the extremely dangerous endeavors, learning vital techniques and cautions from each unforgettable experience. Rather than sight-seeing, he began surveying and mapping the systems he explored. By 16, he was being called on by local authorities to make cave diving body recoveries, primarily because he kept detailed maps of the different systems. By the time he received his first formal cave diving certification, Skiles had made over 1,000 cave dives and penetrated to a distance of 600 feet in caves. The course he took evolved from much of his own experience and those of other cave diving pioneers of the period such as Sheck Exley, Tex Chalkley, and others who pooled their knowledge so that divers following in their footsteps could live to enjoy the sport. Most of these early enthusiasts went on to become Cave Diving Instructors. Wes began specializing and refining photographic techniques in underwater caves. Exley began setting world records in cave diving.

By the time they were selected to join the Wakulla project, Skiles and the others brought with them a lifetime of cave diving experience, the very least of the requirements for a project of this size. Still, the entire project was a learning experience. One truth everyone realized was the need for innovative breathing mixtures and special decompression tables during the maximum depth and distance penetrations. At the depths they planned to dive, an open circuit standard 80-cubic-foot tank of air was depleted in 30 breaths. Hence the need for multiple tanks and special breathing mixtures. In the course of the project, a total of 36 mixed gas dives were made by various individuals, in addition to 126 dives using air as the primary gas. Decompression schedules were custom designed by gases expert, Dr. William Hamilton. Those pushing the outer limits could expect up to seven hours of in-water decompression, with a final countdown inside the comfortable dry habitat.

As always the divers searched for better ways of doing things. For example, Skiles felt there might be a better way to avoid having to laboriously set up air caches, using the traditional method of switching to reserves.

Believing there might be a way for a diver to carry his air reserves, he designed a tubular aluminum sled that would carry all the spare tanks needed, the whole rig towed behind a diver using a DPV (divers propulsion vehicle). These propeller-driven bomb-shaped battery-operated units enabled a diver to move swiftly through the water without expending much energy. The project's scooter of choice was the German-made Aqua-Zepp, a unit that went further and lasted longer than any other similar device on the market at the time.

Innovative fiber-composite tanks would carry 125 cubic feet of gas in a package no larger than a 50-cubic-foot tank, but it would weigh only 26 pounds. Skiles rigged a manifold system that connected all four tanks to two regulators. In this manner, he could carry 600 cubic feet of gas on a single sled.

While the team of Sheck Exley, Paul DeLoach and Clark Pitcairn chose to use the reserve depots of air tanks, others chose the sleds dubbed *Enterprise I* and *Enterprise II*. When fellow team-member Brad Pecel designed a triple-tank rig of PVC pipe, it became the *Klingon Cruiser*. Since the National Geographic Society was funding part of the project, Skiles was responsible for documenting the underwater sequences on film for this organization.

Initially everyone thought there would be one main tunnel, but as the investigation got underway, they found the system branching into various sub-systems. So the divers divided their efforts into "A" and "B" teams. Exley and his group were the "A" Team, Skiles and his companions were the "B" team. While Exley and his team penetrated "A" tunnel, Skiles and his team Aqua-Zepped down "B" tunnel, both groups laying line and surveying.

The divers penetrated a distance of 800 feet where no one had been before and were seeing it for the first time, perfectly clear-headed, not under the effects of nitrogen narcosis. They now saw four different tunnels which turned out to have three distinctly different water sources. Each tunnel had a different age, origin, and reason for forming. From the surface no one could have scientifically predicted that.

The explorers had no idea where the tunnels were taking them. Every turn was a revelation. Soon they had penetrated over 2,000 feet from the entrance. Though they started out lettering the tunnels "A" and "B," before they finished they were up to "G." At one point the tunnel "B" team reached a depth of 321 feet before the tunnel turned upward. It began ascending a hill, then suddenly the divers found themselves in an enormous chamber.

They were enthralled. Never had they imagined finding something this big. They found it was 320 feet on its floor, and that it was probably 70 feet deep at its ceiling. They were never positive because to check it meant they would risk going into decompression while being 2,600 feet back in an underground underwater system. But from what they could tell, this was a room over 250 feet high. It was 200 feet wide and 300 feet across. In the center of this huge rock chamber was a mound of stones rising up to an apex. Directly on top was a kind of cap stone: a perfectly white rectangular stone standing on edge.

The divers stared at it in awe.

"There it was," said Skiles, "the rock slab similar to the monolith in the movie *2001: A Space Odyssey*. It flashed through my mind that here we were exploring an alien landscape, in one sense, using advanced technology to visit and explore an unknown world, while in another sense, we were the most primitive of beings. The irony of it struck me. There was the monolith sitting right there. It was seven feet tall, three feet wide and pure white. We all felt it. It gave us chills! The only appropriate name for this place was the Monolith Room."

There were many journeys back to the Monolith Room and beyond, but its discovery was one of the high points of the expedition. "A" tunnel, the initial entrance to the system over 100 feet wide, averaging 40 to 50 feet tall, was a huge conduit. "B" tunnel was a narrow, white-walled blue-water tunnel, quite pristine but sinuously winding around. The floor was sand and gravel, sometimes completely free of silt for hundreds of feet at a time.

Skiles had been filming the cave. He had made two 16mm filming dives into the system, using the National Geographic's Arriflex. The only way to carry the Arriflex in a housing into this cave system was by hand. The unit in its housing measured 12 inches by 18 inches. Wes had to hold this camera with one hand, while holding the 400-watt filming light with the other. The other divers had lights on their vehicles. The film crew was a tense team of three. Since he had to hand-carry the camera and light, Skiles was forced to maneuver his propulsion unit by clamping his legs tightly to his vehicle and steering with them.

"That's how I went through the cave filming," he said. "I had done two film dives, but I really wanted to explore and map. The others were getting to lay the line and I filmed it. I would scooter ahead, stop, get off the vehicle in 350 feet of water and film them go by, then get on my vehicle, race ahead, get off and film again. It took incredible concentration."

No wonder. Here were divers already pushing the outer limits of what could be accomplished in this dangerous environment. Each had to ride into the cave while keeping up with as many as eight regulators, four or five pressure gauges of the gas mixtures they were dealing with while keeping track of the guide line and the location of their buddy. When Skiles shot all of his film, he would clip off the camera and survey out.

The things that could go wrong, did. Hoses popped, tanks went down, lights went out. The bombardment of stress just to focus to stay alive was unbelievable. If a problem developed far back in the system, only the coolest of thinking under extreme stress, and the rigid discipline required of this kind of exploration, made the difference between life or death.

The "A" team of Sheck Exley and Paul DeLoach had such an accident far back in "D" tunnel on Thanksgiving Day, November 26, 1987.

The two had explored an offshoot of "A" tunnel, designated "D" tunnel and had penetrated to a point 3,300 feet from the mouth of the cave, when they came to an impasse of fallen rocks. Spotting a balcony near the ceiling of the chamber, Exley thought there might be tunnels leading out in that area. Scootering up to the 50-foot dome to investigate, he discovered there was no exit there. Starting back down, he suddenly heard a loud "thunk" as his vehicl e's batteries broke loose and shifted toward the nose of the scooter.

Instantly, the DPV pitched forward and shut off. Exley got the batteries repositioned but still he had no power. He passed his scooter to DeLoach to take out while he continued survey- ing·the line they had laid coming in on this dive.

Neither was concerned over the event since they knew they had staged reserves of gas awaiting them on their way out.

When Exley finished his survey, DeLoach indicated he would tow Exley and his scooter out. Exley wanted instead to let DeLoach go on while he swam along behind. DeLoach, however, insisted. So, Exley grabbed the T-bar of DeLoach 's scooter and while towing his own inoperable vehicle, they headed back.

They had gone some 600 feet when Exley's compass was ac- cidentally snatched up by DeLoach 's scooter prop. Its bungee cord jammed the propeller and pinned Exley's wrist to the prop.

Exley eventually cut it loose with a forearm knife, dropping both his compass and knife. Now, however, uncertain of how well DeLoach 's scooter would work with a possibly damaged prop, Exley elected to drop his scooter and return for it on a later dive.

They continued on to the next emergency air cache, which was about halfway back to the entrance. Exley felt he had enough gas to be able to swim the rest of the way by himself, letting DeLoach go on with his scooter. Naturally he would have pre- ferred being towed, but by now, additional complications became evident and Exley felt DeLoach should scooter out without him.

The reason was that this new complication was far more se- rious than the initial problem. DeLoach described it later: "Af- ter Sheck cut loose the bungee from my prop, we proceeded for several hundred feet before I began to have irregular breathing patterns. It was like my chest was having palpitations. Hard as I tried, I could not seem to control my breathing and it was ex- tremely difficult to obtain a complete breath. Within 200 feet, I began to get a twitching in my eye and nose. These symptoms continued to build until I began to fade in and out of conscious- ness."

Both divers realized DeLoach was experiencing the onset of oxygen poisoning. Exley recognized the problem when they were at the 1,500-foot air reserve depot and insisted that DeLoach scooter on out of the cave without him.

DeLoach, in no condition to argue, took his advice. As he scootered up the main shaft of "A" tunnel, he switched to his safety tank, hoping to be able to breathe easier, but things only grew worse. Quickly, he switched back to his first tanks. It was not until he reached the 175-foot deep decompression stop that the symptoms finally eased.

Meanwhile, back in the cave, Exley began having problems of his own. The heavy drag of all of his equipment made swimming extremely difficult. His breathing was becoming labored. When he reached their final air reserve depot about 500 feet from the cave entrance, his primary light had gone out and he had switched to his secondary light. He dumped two empty bottles, picked up a reserve 80-cubic-foot tank, and headed out. Near the entrance he encountered DeLoach who, feeling somewhat better, had started back into the system on his scooter to help Exley.

Analyzing the incident later, the divers discovered the cause of the problem. Unlike most of the team, Exley and DeLoach were using Tri-mix, a gas they mixed themselves on the site. On previous dives, this mixture had proven highly successful for them. Since both divers had demonstrated an unusually high tolerance for oxygen toxicity for periods up to 50 minutes in the past, they felt that DeLoach's increased labor in trying to steer the DPV with the added ungainly load of Exley and his scooter caused early symptoms of the malady. After this event, all team members were instructed to use the Heliox-14 mixture for any deep diving at Wakulla.

Then, even that mixture created hidden problems. Without realizing it, divers were losing valuable helium from the microscopic pores in their fiber-composite gas tanks. Helium molecules are so much smaller than the oxygen molecules that they were slowly leaking through the walls of the fiber tanks. As a result, the oxygen partial pressure inside the gas bottles was building up like a time bomb. Being unaware of the problem, the divers kept refilling the same tanks over and over and each time the oxygen level increased.

The realization came almost too late. On one dive into the Monolith Room, two of the divers started feeling numbness coming on in their lips and fingertips. Again, these are the symptoms of early oxygen toxicity.

Though they had no idea what was causing the problem, they knew it was a danger signal. Fortunately, they returned to the surface without further difficulty. Analyzing the situation later, the problem was discovered and corrected.

After all those grueling trips filming the team's progress with the large movie camera, Skiles came up only to be told that the rear lens element of the Arriflex had fallen off. Everything he had filmed for the National Geographic and television, was out of focus!

When he heard the news he was too stunned to believe it. "At first I just sat inside the habitat in shocked disbelief. I had put so much effort into it. You see, I thought the filming was over, I had put it behind me. I was savoring the fact that I was going to get to go exploring the cave after my filming objective. The next time I was going to be the one pushing the unknown with the reel in my hand. There was only a couple days left on the expedition and it set me back right to the beginning again."

Skiles next reaction was to say, "No. Too bad. That's the end of it." But after he slept on it, he realized that the filming was more important to him.

Throughout the dive he had been shooting video as well as film, the small video camera mounted in an unobtrusive way so that it shot everything that occurred. Now, Skiles determined to rig an upright pole behind him so that the movie camera would shoot over his shoulder and get a bird's-eye view of everything they did. At the same time, he would continue shooting video. This was it. He had maybe only three dives left before the whole thing would be over.

As soon as he tried out his idea, he realized the Aqua-Zepp was almost impossible to drive with its unfamiliar load. Skiles had to move the vehicl e 's balancing weights to counter the backward pull of the big camera.

He admits now the idea was impractical, but in his fascination of the moment it seemed the only logical solution.

"It was like attaching a year's harvest of watermelons onto an airplane wing and expecting the airplane to fly," he said. "But I went scootering off into the cave, mad and determined to film and videotape.

"I got down to this critical point where we were diving at a 45-degree angle down into this pit with this tremendous flow, then you have to level back and head up into the Monolith. Suddenly, I misjudged where I was going and the line caught the camera.

"Instantly the vehicle swung up uncontrollably, dropping its 26-pound ballast weight. My vehicle is now close to 30 pounds positive and instead of calling the dive I was just so absolutely determined to ride it out, that I twisted into a line entanglement that I almost didn't come out of.

"I landed on the floor and signaled everybody that I was in trouble. They stopped. The current was ferocious. The coming together of these vehicles was almost suicidal. You can't very well let go of them and you can't get off of them in this kind of difficult place.

"One of the divers, Rob Parker, bailed out and helped extricate me from a very dangerous entanglement at 321 feet. A tank of gas lasts 30 breaths at that depth. Thirty breaths and its gone. We had eight tanks collectively on us. But this was a one-tank solution and we were already three tanks into the dive. So suddenly, I just...this was where I momentarily lost sight of my objectives as far as safety was concerned. The vehicle started getting even more buoyant. Also, my dry suit was now inflating. I had to get the expanding gas out of my dry suit. I started rising faster, being pulled up at a blood-boiling rate of ascent toward the ceiling. If I hit the ceiling, I would be dead. The bends would take me so fast from the fast-forming bubbles in my blood, it would be almost instantaneous....

"So there I was—feet down, head up—holding onto a vehicle that was ballooning me to the ceiling. I thought, let go of the vehicle and all three of us are going to die. Continue on this ascent and I'm going to die.

"I managed to let go of many thousands dollars worth of camera at that point, that being a very low priority. I managed to hook my arm and deflate my dry suit at the same time. Then I made one major effort to get me and the vehicle back down to depth, down to the Monolith.

"I managed to get down and grab hold of rocks and Rob came in and tried to hold me down for a minute. I was at that point... It was like someone saying goodbyes but really not...the whole world was there, all existence being that moment, and saying to yourself...I can't believe I've done this, I can't believe I'm in this situation. I felt awful. It was like a combination of wanting to throw up, and pass out.

"Getting out of the cave was the only choice I had. I got on the vehicle and forced its nose down. It was the only way to make it go. Force it down and push it forward. I had 2,600 feet to go like that with less than half my gas I needed to get out. But we had some safety stations along the way.

"We made it to the safety stations and by then my attitude had vastly improved. Rob carried out the camera and we got to decompression. I cut the vehicle loose, tied a line to it and it went kiting to the surface. There was no way to hold on to it anymore; I was exhausted. The vehicle hit the surface like a jet crash-landing on an air strip."

The topside team knew at once that something had gone wrong down below. The decompression chamber was ready, the people were ready for a bad outcome. But as it turned out everything was all right.

The irony of it all was that Skiles still hadn't filmed. Some footage was shot but it wasn't enough. So, with only two dives left to go in the project, back the camera team went again, with the camera where it belonged and the weights on the vehicle realigned.

This time everything clicked. They shot a stunning 400 feet of film, most of which was used virtually unedited in the National Geographic special on the exploration. It was a total team effort, a collective victory.

For Skiles, this was a major climatic moment. But the biggest was yet to come.

10

PUSH TO THE INNER AND OUTER LIMITS

After the film crew left, Skiles had no experienced team members free to continue with him. Though he had in the past dived solo and actually preferred it, to penetrate such distances as those in the "B" tunnel was another matter. Having a vehicle malfunction that far in would be an automatic death sentence.

Skiles got the National Geographic Benthos camera, the one used to film the *Titanic*. It had already been damaged, but the optics worked and it took still photographs. Tom Morris and Paul Heinerth wanted to accompany him. Neither diver had made repeated deep penetrations in Wakulla, but Skiles was faced with either taking them, or not going. He chose the divers.

Skiles filled three empty line reels with over 1,800 feet of line, more than he felt he could possibly lay at that depth, but he took it anyway.

The divers dived down to 260 feet and penetrated 250 feet where Wes planned to shoot some stills. He fired the camera but nothing happened. Looking at it he saw smoke inside the electrical strobe compartment. That was all he needed. It was his reprieve. With the camera not working, he was suddenly free to do the things he loved most: to push the exploration of "B" tunnel, to lay line as far as he could go. Here's how he described what followed:

"I laid my body as flat as possible, tucking in anything that would create drag. I had my scooter set at the same speed as Paul and Tom, but I flew by them as if they were sitting still."

Morris and Heinerth looked at each other. They realized

Skiles had no camera. It was either catch up with him or be left behind. They sped off in hot pursuit.

"I flew to the back of the cave, tied off the big reel and started laying line," said Skiles. "Before I knew it we had laid the first 800 feet, then tied off. Morris, a biologist, stopped and collected a crayfish that no one had ever seen that far back and at that depth.

"We went through some low spots, then came into a room that had a pit in it. We could see down to about 360 feet and it was either go down that pit or cross this room and go out the other side. We didn't have tables to let us do the pit so we went down this horizontal passageway laying the second reel.

"After that was down, I brought out the last reel, with all three of us still together. Paul looked at me and I signaled to see if he wanted to lay the last reel. He indicated he did, so he grabbed the reel and we ran it to the end. We had laid every inch we had and then some, maybe a short safety reel just to look.

"At this point the cave had taken on a whole new character. There were some catfish and eels in the passageway. There were bones lying on the floor. This was 4,160 feet back inside the cave. We were making progress in solving some of the mysteries of Wakulla. We were getting near some new change, I suspect. Whatever explorations go back to that spot, I think something is happening there. Maybe another entrance out in the woods. Maybe one that has long since been closed off. Maybe an upper cave system that connects down to the Wakulla system, and we know about the upper system but haven't found the doorway between the two."

At this point in the dive, a problem arose. Apparently, Skiles, the more experienced of the three, was the only one who had stayed within the allowable safe air (gas) rule using a third of his total breathing mixture to enter the cave, saving one third for exiting, and one third for emergency. Both Paul and Tom had knowingly gone on to their reserves while following him.

This is one of the dangers of this kind of exploration: getting caught up in it and not wanting to let go.

Morris didn't want to go out on his own. He felt that the only way to make it out was to stay with the others. He didn't want to stop the exploration.

"It's one of the ironies of cave diving," said Skiles. "We have no way to communicate. Here we are on a technological cutting edge of a historical moment in underground exploration and such thoughts as, 'I'm going to die if I leave you, and possibly kill you if I stay with you,' is bouncing around in the heads of people and you're not aware of it. You don't know that that's what the person is thinking. And when we do get ready to turn, to head back, suddenly you're confronted with this near fight or flight syndrome for Tom and Paul who are both getting dangerously low on gas. Actually, I could have gone on if I had had more line. But at this point, I had been doing this passageway in this cave progressively time and time again as I pushed deeper into the system. I had become acclimated to it, they had not. I had been dealing with all of those other problems. Now it was the longest, deepest penetration in the cave and it was the simplest thing I had done. I was in sheer heaven. Nothing could have been better. Mentally I was alert, excited, in ecstasy.

"They looked at me and I looked at them. I pushed my fingers together and signaled them to stay together and go up. Leave. But I wasn't going to leave. The last thing that had to be done was to survey. There would be no proof that we had been there and left unless I surveyed it. My pet peeve for years has been: don't explore unless you survey. Exploration does no one any good unless you bring out the data. I hate being a purist, but it's true. Without a map, the benefits of the entire project would be erased. Who would believe them? I intended to get that data.

As Morris and Heinerth headed back the way they came, Skiles began mapping his way back. It entailed counting the knots on the survey line they had laid coming in, a knot every ten feet. At each knot he put a depth gauge on that station and recorded the depth. Then he shot an azimuth or compass bearing. After that he went on to the next knot and repeated the procedure. As he progressed along the passageway he looked left and right, then at the ceiling and the floor, noting on his slate any side tunnels, type floor sediments, any unusual geological features while also jotting down the dimensions of the passageway. At each new depth, each new azimuth or change in cross-section, he repeated the process, then started counting knots again. The whole thing involves extreme mental discipline.

Skiles mapped his way out of the extreme penetration, highly elated by the experience. As he later described it:

"It was an incredible ending to be passing through all those chambers and tunnels, and rising up into the Monolith and saying goodbye to it in solitude, journeying back down to the deepest point in the cave. And I actually did catch up. At the very end, about 400 feet from our first decompression stop, I caught up with Tom and Paul. They were scrambling for their lives. Tom was flying for one of the gas safety depots. I had finished surveying then. I caught up to watch Tom struggling to get switched over from the gas he was breathing to the safety gas supply. I came down and asked if he was okay.

"He signaled he was okay and Paul was on his way. Five minutes later we three were back together and sitting at 220 feet to began the process of decompressing up."

The epic-making effort at Wakulla Spring resulted in 400 safe dives and a wealth of new scientific data. It was learned, for example, that some of the water in the spring enters the system over 16 miles away. Possibly a new species of blind, cave-dwelling albino crawfish was found living over 3,900 feet from the cave entrance. But equally interesting, crawfish not typically associated with caves, were also found there, along with some eels and catfish. With this final effort, the divers had penetrated the system to a record 4,160 feet back from the cave entrance, reaching a maximum depth of 320 feet. In the process they had found the incredibly large Monolith Room, and proved the efficiency of mixed gas diving coupled with long-term use of a mobile habitat for decompressing divers.

And in the annals of diving, if this undertaking is not epic-making enough, the final results of Bill Stone's initial reason for coming to Wakulla Spring may rival it as the crowning achievement.

During eight test dives of the Cis-Lunar Mk-1 rebreather, the divers spent up to almost six hours underwater, using it to depths of 148 feet, the limiting range of the open-circuit bail-out bottle carried by each test diver.

One thing quickly recognized was the incredible capacity of

the unit to support a diver. The first five dives for more than nine hours underwater under moderate work conditions used only half of the unit's chemical and gas components.

With that data, Stone decided to try for a more prolonged underwater record. On December 3 and 4, 1987, the Mk-1 supported a diver at depth for an incredible 24 hours, again using only half of the system!

In the next few years, Bill Stone modified the unit, improving its performance, creating a more compact version of the rebreather: the Cis-Lunar Mk-2R capable of supporting a diver underwater for up 18 hours. With it he ran test dives to 132 feet in which the diver swam distances in excess of three miles. Such testing usually ended only because of the diver's boredom!

Meanwhile, after the 1987 push into Wakulla by Stone's team, it didn't take long for other highly qualified cave divers to take up that lead and pursue the system to even greater record penetrations. By enhancing techniques used in 1987, the Woodville Karst Plain Project divers continued the exploration to over a mile and a half underwater from any cave entrance.

"What they've done is really a remarkable feat," Stone told me when I phoned him for an update at his Maryland office a little after 8:15 A.M. one fall morning in 1996. He apologized for being out of breath because, "I was on my 65th pushup when you called..." He said the effort made in 1992 by Parker Turner, Bill Gavin, George Irvine and others was essentially an extension of the "A" Tunnel. "They've been 8,300 feet back using dual scooters, basically meditating themselves into low respiration rates because they're still using open circuit scuba," marveled Stone. "Incredible!"

As I might have expected, Stone was preparing for a new push on Wakulla. This time Stone's nonprofit United States Deep Diving Team would use his fifth generation Cis-Lunar rebreather, the Mk-5, throughout the entire effort—the first major underwater exploratory expedition to rely totally on a closed circuit system. In addition, the new Wakulla 2 project proposal sets the same lofty goals and expectations usually associated with Stone's undertakings. Once again this one plans to push cave diving to its outer limits. From the tone of his voice I was happy to hear that this modern day Columbus was still loaded with enthusi-

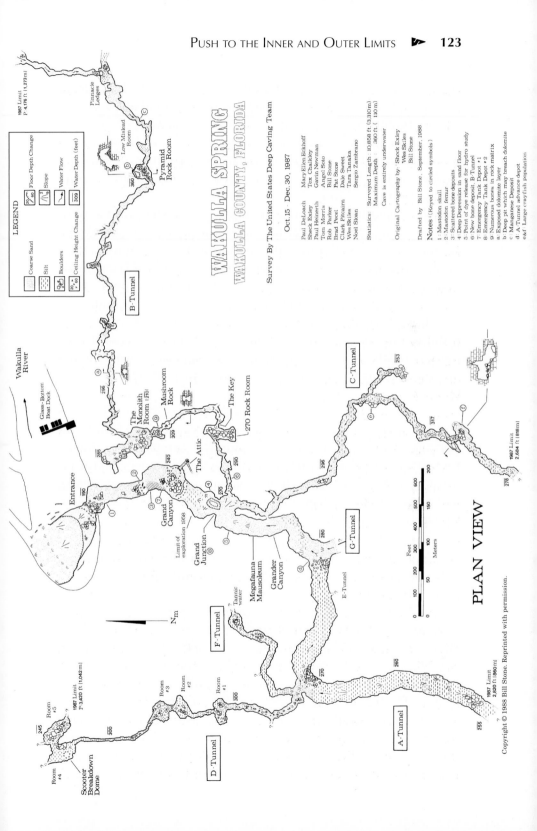

WAKULLA SPRING
WAKULLA COUNTY, FLORIDA

Survey By The United States Deep Caving Team

Oct. 15 - Dec. 30, 1987

Paul DeLoach	Mary Ellen Eckhoff
Sheck Exley	Tex Chalkley
Paul Heinerth	Gavin Newman
Tom Morris	Angel Soto
Rob Parker	Bill Stone
Brad Pecel	Pat Stone
Clark Pitcairn	Dale Sweet
Wes Skiles	Tara Tanaka
Noel Sloan	Sergio Zambrano

Statistics: Surveyed Length: 10,858 ft (3,310 m)
Maximum Depth : 360 ft (110 m)
Cave is entirely underwater

Original Cartography by: Sheck Exley
Wes Skiles
Bill Stone

Drafted by Bill Stone, September, 1988

Notes : (Keyed to circled symbols)

1 Mastodon skull
2 Mastodon femur
3 Scattered bone deposits
4 Deep Depression in sand floor
5 Point of dye release for hydro study
6 New bone deposit, B-Tunnel
7 Emergency Tank Depot #1
8 Emergency Tank Depot #2
9 Numerous bones in rock matrix
a. Exposed dolomite layer
b Deep pit which may breach dolomite
c Manganese Deposit
d A-Tunnel advance depot
e&f Large crayfish population

LEGEND

Coarse Sand
Silt
Boulders
Ceiling Height Change
Floor Depth Change
Slope
Water Flow
Water Depth (feet)

Wakulla River

Glass-Bottom Boat Dock

Entrance

B-Tunnel

C-Tunnel

G-Tunnel

E-Tunnel

F-Tunnel

A-Tunnel

D-Tunnel

PLAN VIEW

N m

The Monolith Room
Mushroom Rock
The Key
270 Rock Room
The Attic
Grand Canyon
Grand Junction
Limit of exploration 1958
Megafauna Mausoleum
Grander Canyon
Tannic water

Pinnacle Ledges
Low Miskoad Room
Pyramid Rock Room

Room #5
Room #3
Room #2
Room #1
Room #4
Scooter Breakdown Dome

1987 Limit
P. 4,176 ft (1,273 m)

1987 Limit
P. 3,420 ft (1,042 m)

1987 Limit
2,820 ft (860 m)

1987 Limit
2,684 ft (818 m)

Feet
Meters

asm and eager to challenge the unknown at full tilt. He told me that each dual Cis-Lunar Mk-5 rebreather unit will allow a diver to stay underwater for up to 12 hours, no matter how deep he dives. Global Marine Industries was providing a chamber that will support all diving operations including saturation diving as deep as 650 fsw. This self-contained system will float on the spring basin enabling six divers to live and work within the chamber, then lock back and forth for their survey and exploratory work. High tech sonar packages mounted atop special propulsion vehicles will automatically make highly detailed sonar readings of the cave system's topography which will later result in a 3D virtual reality program that will provide the public with one of the most sophisticated maps ever seen of this underwater world. Specially designed and super battery powered underwater tandem dive propulsion vehicles currently being built with redundant life support systems will carry divers on penetrations up to 25,000 feet (over 5½ miles) underwater at depths of 300 feet.

Extreme innerspace stuff? You bet! Forty years after Salsman and his pioneers first breached the depth barrier of Wakulla Springs and led us into this unexplored innerspace world with conventional scuba, advanced technology and a new generation of divers imbued with the same pioneering spirit are now ready, willing and able to take us around for a look at the still dark side of this strange new world.

11

DEEPEST QUEST

In 1992 I asked professional underwater photographer Wes Skiles if he intended getting involved in Bill Stone's Huautla Plateau cave project in Mexico. Skiles told me he didn't want to get into anything that meant he had to spend a week climbing through damp caves and living underground like a salamander before he got to dive.

But *National Geographic*'s September 1995 "Huautla Cave Quest" article written by William C. Stone, with spectacular photographs by both the author and Wes Skiles, indicates that Skiles changed his mind.

The Huautla mystery has been baffling cavers ever since the system was discovered in 1966. No one has succeeded in solving it, though not because they haven't tried. In the last 30 years, 18 major expeditions have tried to solve its riddle. Here's the premise: a dye marker poured into a stream atop the Huautla Plateau, emerged from an opening in a canyon 5,492 feet below. There is only one way to verify what the dye suggested, and that is to start at its beginning and go to its end, in person. If the effort is successful, it will prove the Huautla cave system to be the deepest in the world, surpassing that of France's Jean Bernard Cave now holding that distinction at 5,256 feet deep, thus making Huautla perhaps 236 feet deeper.

Wes Skiles may not have wanted to go there, but he accurately summed up why the Huautla Project was such a challenge. First you made your way up the jungle-covered limestone Huautla Plateau towering 7,000 feet over the Gulf coastal plain in southern Mexico's state of Oaxaca. There, you dropped through a hole in the jungle on a thin mountaineer's line into an underground cave where you spent days doing hazardous, uncomfortable, and frustratingly difficult mountaineering-type descents just to get to where you would start your explorations. Once you started any of this there was no coming out of it easily, no swift lift back to the surface where a waiting jungle chopper might whisk you off to some civilized spot for a decent night's meal and rest. Not likely.

Fat chance of that when you spend a week periodically hooked up to ropes that dangle you in black space, then drop you into some drippy rock crypt having all the charm of a long forgotten cistern where you slip and slide your way down perilous rock passageways, taking you deeper and deeper into the unknown bowels of the earth. What you hear are either unearthly echoes of your presence, or the roar of subterranean rivers. No light exists in this world other that what you bring. With you down vertical shafts goes an ungodly amount of heavy gear and compressed grub to sustain you in this prolonged mole-like existence. You sleep on rocks or in slings hanging off them. Everything you see or feel is damp, often slimy. You wear a wet suit or a lightweight jump suit perpetually. You eat liquefied mush, and you carry all your waste with you. Certainly somewhere along the way someone asks the obvious question that must thunder around like bowling balls in everyone's head: "Are we having fun yet?"

Finally, many days later, once you get to wherever you are going, what do you find? Your way blocked by a pool of inky black water known to cavers as a "sump." You must stop here because you are "sumped." There is nowhere else to go except back the way you came. If you are determined to go straight ahead, then at this point you climb into your dive gear which you have sweated bullets to bring along with you, and swim into this sump, dragging along behind you waterproof bags or containers of food and equipment. No one can tell you where or how far the underwater passageway goes, whether it is simply a short water barrier to more unexplored cave passages, or whether it goes on forever, perhaps sucking you along with it into what? Hell maybe. No one knows. Certainly not your fellow teammates. Not even your team leader. That's why you're all there in the first place—

to find out just where in hell it all goes.

The attempt to explore what could prove to be the deepest known cave system in the world has been compared to climbing the highest mountain in the world. It's an unfair comparison. Even before Hillary and Tensing, you could scope out Mt. Everest's hazards and plan your attack accordingly. Not so this explorer's nightmare. You go here knowing nothing. What you find is what you get. If while you are a half mile or more down inside the guts of the earth the narrow shaft you are following suddenly spews you out into oblivion, then it's up to the next team member to avoid that fate. The only similarity between Mt. Everest and what lies underground for explorers on the Huautla Plateau is in the nature of the beasts. One was a visual enigma until it was conquered; the other is a blind one. If it wasn't so impossible to do, people like Bill Stone wouldn't be there trying to do it in the first place.

That March, 1994, the same could be said for expedition diver, Ian Rolland, a Scot who had been one of the ardent 44 team members comprising this expedition for the past two months, pushing hard along with all the others to reach this point almost 4,000 feet below ground—this unknown impasse, the San Agustín Sump—that for 17 years had blocked any further exploration of this cave system. Blocked it as effectively as a solid wall of granite.

Rolland had a wife and three children in Scotland. He was a diabetic. But like Stone and all the others on this expedition, he had to be where he was, doing what they were doing. Ian knew the personal risk he took of a diabetic going deep into one of the remotest holes on the planet. If something went wrong and he needed help, it would be a long time coming. He understood that. He felt that doing it and being there was worth the risk.

His companion, Kenny Broad, had been the first to dive into the watery impasse, trailing a guideline. He finned through the underwater passageway for a quarter mile when suddenly his light reflected off a silver ceiling overhead. Air!

He surfaced, elated. Had he broken through the impasse into a dry passageway? Moving his light around the grotto's walls, he found himself in a large air chamber. He swam back the way he came to report his find to the others.

Broad's dive buddy, Ian Rolland, geared up to go see the chamber for himself. After a period of time, when he failed to return, Broad went looking for him.

After another long time he reappeared in the sump's pool with the startling news that he had found Rolland's body. He had drowned.

When Stone heard it he was stunned. He remembered Ian's diabetes and how determined he had been not to let it keep him from making the cave penetration. Since Ian had already such a strong personal commitment to the effort, Stone, the team leader, had decided not to stand in his way. But now, as he donned his diving gear and swam through the sump to recover the body, he agonized over having made that decision.

He found Ian below the air-filled chamber, lying on his side in nine feet of water. The regulator's mouthpiece had dropped out of his mouth. His dive gear still functioned perfectly. Apparently, Stone learned later, Ian had suffered insulin shock caused by a combination of physical exertion and low blood sugar. He had blacked out and drowned.

The tragedy brought the expedition to an immediate halt. Everything focused now on the sad things one must do in the wake of such events. It took six days for the team to lift Ian's remains back to the surface in a body litter. After a brief memorial service in the local church, the group said goodbye to their friend and one of the team members accompanied the body back to Scotland.

The tragic event brought out the other team members' unspoken frustrations. Stone was criticized for pushing too hard, for being so obsessed with the cave he was taking too many risks. Some team members were ready to call it quits. In the meantime, Wes Skiles flew in to do a documentary for *National Geographic*. After a group meeting everyone decided to stay at least until Wes was able to complete his photographs.

It was already into spring. If the expedition didn't accomplish its goal before the end of May, the rainy season would set in. Runoff waters would flood the caverns where the team was exploring.

A week after the tragedy, hoping to rekindle enthusiasm in the project, Stone returned to the sump. There, with a small

Diver and artifact hunter John Baker stands beside one of two five-and-a-half-foot stone figures he recovered from a cenote in Costa Rica. Photo by Robert Burgess.

Approaching a depth of 160 feet, divers of the 1956 exploration team are framed by the 100-foot-wide mouth of Wakulla Cavern. Photo courtesy of Garry Salsman.

Deep within the Wakulla system, one of Garry Salsman's divers examines part of a mastodon's jaw with two teeth still in place. Notice the redundant dive lights being used, the best "high tech" lights available in 1956. All you had to do was waterproof them! Photo courtesy of Garry Salsman.

Massive mastodon bones were found in a fossil bone deposit extending 500 feet inside Wakulla at a depth of 200 feet. Using a pillow case as their 1956 lift bag, two expedition divers guide a mastodon's massive leg bone out to the cave entrance. Photo courtesy of Garry Salsman.

Sheck Exley during the 1987 Wakulla Springs Project in Florida. Photo by Wes Skiles.

Mary Ellen Eckhoff (right) and Bill Stone inventory cylinders of mixed gas to be used for the open circuit mixed gas dives to 300 feet at Wakulla Springs. Photo by Wes Skiles.

Paul DeLoach checks out a camera mount on his Aqua-Zepp underwater vehicle during the Wakulla Springs Project. Photo by Wes Skiles.

Below: Aboard underwater vehicles, divers Tom Morris and Paul Heinerth wing their way over Wakulla's prehistoric bone bed. Photo by Wes Skiles.

Paul DeLoach and Sheck Exley enjoying the spartan comforts of the underwater decompression habitat the team erected at Wakulla Springs during the 1987 dives. Photo by Wes Skiles.

Opposite: Nancy Morris examines one of the large legbones found among mastodon remains deep within the Wakulla Cavern. Photo by Wes Skiles.

Shown here in 1992, Dr. Bill Stone and his team ran practice dives with his unique rebreather in a Florida spring before taking improved models to Mexico's Huautla cave system for the push on the San Agustín Sump. Photo by Wes Skiles.

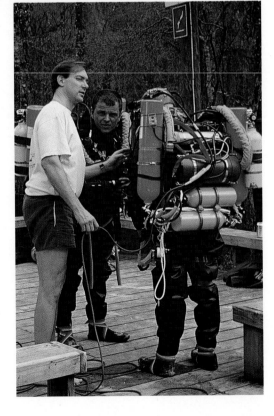

To familiarize themselves with the equipment, team members Jim Brown, Noel Sloan and Bill Stone dive the Cis Lunar rebreathers at Jackson County, Florida's Blue Springs. Photo by Wes Skiles.

Noel Sloan discusses the dive plan with Ian Rolland and Kenny Broad at Devil's Eye Spring, Florida prior to a rehearsal dive for the Huautla expedition in Mexico. Photo by Bill Stone.

On the Huautla Plateau in Mexico, the largest backpacks making the descent into the cave system are readied. The Mk-4s were trimmed to 43 pounds by removing such components as the 15-pound diluent bottles. Photo by Bill Stone.

Opposite: To enter the system, the explorers first had to lower themselves and all their gear down this 300-foot hole in the jungle floor. Here, surrounded by greenery, Noel Sloan dangles like a spider in the mouth of the giant chasm. Photo by Wes Skiles.

Penetrating ever deeper into the dry cave, Barbara am Ende (top) and Bill Stone (below) rappel with their gear bags down the 365-foot shaft leading to their 2,045 foot-deep depot far below. Photo by Wes Skiles.

Team members Steve Porter (left), Noel Sloan and Kenny Broad struggle through the raging torrents of a sudden runoff that fell as rain 2,500 feet above their underground cave camp. Photo by Wes Skiles.

During his 1981 Huautla caving expedition, Bill Stone used an open camera shutter and multiple strobes to paint the walls with light in this series of vast chambers 2,442 feet underground, believed to be a Paleozoic Era lake bed. The room extends 1,419 feet horizontally, is 462 feet wide and 198 feet tall. The photograph shows only a third of its size. Photo by Bill Stone.

Camp 5 was the final outpost before penetrating the San Agustín Sump that begins 10 feet below the camp deck. Fabricated from light aluminum tubing and ballistics nylon, the portable deck was supported by rock bolts and roof slings. Three suspended hammocks provided sleeping areas. Particularly annoying here was the loud low-frequency noise of a nearby waterfall. Photo by Bill Stone.

In this colorful mirror image of her equipment, Barbara am Ende prepares to dive through the San Agustín Sump. Made up of modular parts easily broken down and carried into the depths of the cave, Stone's 97-pound Cis-Lunar Mk-4 diving rebreather that could sustain a diver underwater for 16 hours was the key to the Rio San Agustín. Photo by Bill Stone.

Though spartan, Camp 6 was drier than the suspended Camp 5 over the sump. Sitting on space blankets on the only open patch of gravel they found, am Ende and Stone celebrate breaking through the sump barrier with stroganoff mush. They wear the only clothes they brought—fleece jumpsuits worn for warmth inside their drysuits, the latter used to pad the hard ground under their sleeping bags. Photo by Bill Stone.

After following a side passage's shallow stream, the team discovered the Rio Iglesia waterfall gushing out of the rock walls far above. Its runoff joined the Rio San Agustín. Photo by Bill Stone.

At the bottom of the cave entrance, team members attach gear containers to ropes so they can be hauled back up to the surface. Photo by Bill Stone.

backup crew, he made a solo dive through the water block to the air chamber now named "Rolland Airbell" in honor of their missing comrade.

Once he checked out this air chamber, Stone submerged again and found a major passageway continuing beyond it to the south. After following it for some 600 feet, his light reflected off of a mirrored surface and he came up in an air filled cavern.

This was no small pocket of air. He found a cavern as long as four football fields with a ceiling 40 feet overhead. Then it dawned on him that this at last was a continuation of the passageway beyond the sump. This was what they had been trying to reach for years! As much as he wanted to, he dared not explore any further alone. He had to have a companion who could back him up on the rock climbs and help survey what lay ahead. Stone swam back through the sump to Camp 5 to tell his companions the good news.

From this last established outpost, Stone prepared to make a more determined push beyond the sump with one companion.

Camp 5 was not the kind of rest and recreation site beside a picturesque waterfall that you might imagine. The waterfall was there all right, roaring behind rock walls so loudly your brain rattled. And while the camp had a waterfront view, you might say that view was from the bottomside of the camp. That's because Camp 5 was a 4- by 12-foot aluminum pipe and nylon tarp platform suspended from the rock roof some 12 feet over the water entrance to the San Agustín Sump. Rock fastenings and nylon ropes positioned it over the sump. Other fastenings and a hammock over the deck held bags of food and gear. Communication between camp members at Camp 5 became almost impossible because of the continuous roar of the nearby waterfall. Sleeping there was something you did only because of utter exhaustion. It was a place where you soon learned the real meaning of togetherness.

Stone's choice of a companion on this push was most logically Noel Sloan, the expedition physician. Noel had been with Stone on many similarly difficult expeditions over the last 12 years. Stone knew Noel was a reliable partner, one well versed not only in the specialized diving techniques but also in rock climbing know how. As a youngster Sloan had enjoyed what he called "yo-

yoing" abandoned gold mine shafts in Colorado. That is, gearing up with climbers' ropes and hardware, and rappelling down into long abandoned and often crumbling rock shafts, then climbing back up out of them just for the fun of it.

But now, as Stone prepared to make this push into the unknown, the stresses that had built up among the expedition members to this point had taken their toll. Noel told Stone that he did not feel up to the dive.

His decision literally left Stone between a rock and a hard place.

The rebreathers that they had brought all this way were their only hope for going further. Only nine team members had qualified and been trained in their use. When Rolland drowned, the team began to unravel. Five members decided they wanted no more of it and left. The two that remained felt they had gone far enough. As far as they were concerned, whatever lay beyond that sump was of no more interest to them.

The only remaining rebreather-trained diver was the team's only woman member, Barbara am Ende, a graduate geology student from Chapel Hill's University of North Carolina. Stone knew if Barbara decided not to go, that was the end of the expedition; three and a half months of hard work wasted.

Barbara had 20 years experience climbing in dry caves, but only recently had she become a fully certified cave diver. Though trained on the high tech rebreathers, she was the least experienced of all the expedition's divers.

Whatever Barbara Am Ende may have lacked in cave diving credentials, however, she obviously did not lack in courage. Anyone who has ping-ponged around inside cold, wet, steep-walled caves, often clinging in the dark by their fingertips, or roping off ledges into bottomless abysses, soon finds that courage is about as common as calluses to these enthusiasts, especially hardcore cavers with 20 years of challenges under their belt.

"I've trained for this all my life," she said. "I know I can do it."

Stone believed she could too.

Along with their dive gear, the pair would take food for seven days of exploring. As usual, it was the typical gourmet fare they had been enjoying in their dripping rock caverns for weeks. Such offerings as beef stroganoff and chicken cacciatore, along with more mundane oatmeal and potatoes. Only drawback: everything was freeze dried, ground to powder and compressed into plastic bottles. You mixed it with iodine-treated cave water, then gulped the mush down while trying to recall how the real dishes tasted.

Noel helped the pair get launched into the sump. "Just come back alive," he told them.

Barbara squeezed his hand and submerged. Bill followed, towing their heavy waterproof bag of rations and gear.

Underwater everything looked foggy in the yellow beams of their helmet lamps. As they swam along the passageway, Stone saw Barbara periodically disappear in and out of the haze.

Thirty-five minutes later he followed her up the sand bank at Rolland Airbell. Checking their rebreathing apparatus, they found everything had gone well.

Again they submerged and swam on through the second water barrier, emerging this time on a flat gravel shore, the end of the long dry cavern where Stone had terminated his last exploration. There, they set up Camp 6 where they would leave their gear. They could not afford carrying the dive gear with them because it was their only way back. If something happened and it was damaged, the last hope of their returning would fail with it.

As they took off their equipment, Barbara's helmet lamp fell off and disappeared down a rock crevice. As simple as it might seem, this was critical. With but one light remaining, it would be foolish to try and explore further. If that light was damaged, they would never find their way back to their camp site in the dark.

One thing had to be done: recover the lost light. The two spent an anxious hour while Stone tried to "fish" the lamp out of the deep crevice. Only by sheer luck did he finally manage to get a loop of cord over the reflector and haul it up. With its recovery, relief swept over them.

The next morning they followed the river as it flowed through the dry cavern and shortly came to another pool where it disappeared into the rock. Was this as far as they could go?

They searched the cavern walls. Near the ceiling Stone spotted a shadowy rock alcove. Climbing up the 30-foot wall to investigate it, he found a new tunnel. He had Barbara wait behind while he checked it out.

The passageway rose and fell for about 300 feet, then he glimpsed the gleam of water again. Returning, he dropped a rope to Barbara and pulled her up behind him. He told her the passageway was a way around the sump they had just encountered. At the other end they lowered themselves on their rope only to find another sump. Searching further, they discovered yet another tunnel that led them around this sump. It ended at a large green pool of water with a rock tower in the middle of it.

The river swirled past this obstacle and then they were disappointed to see that it swept away through four separate cavern openings.

"Not so good," said Stone searching the cavern walls to see if there was some way around this last obstacle. When he found none he turned back to Barbara and said, "Looks like this is it. Either we go back, or we swim."

"Through which opening?" asked Barbara.

"I don't know," said Stone.

Stone cautiously waded in in his caving boots and thin jump suit. The chilly water surged up around him. Carefully he moved into the first of the flooded tunnels. To his disappointment, a short distance later it dead-ended. He returned to where he began and checked out the second tunnel. Shortly it too was blocked. The third tunnel looped back to the sump they had just bypassed. That left just one more which looked the largest and the deepest. Stone swam along it for some 30 yards when suddenly he felt his feet hit bottom. This was not really a water barrier, it was a short air and water link leading into a large cavern.

Stone splashed out of the water and joyously ran a hundred yards down a dry gravel bed to a point where his light no longer reached the cavern walls. It simply widened into black oblivion.

How big is this place anyway? Stone wondered. He yelled loudly. The echo rumbled off into the distance. It was like standing in the middle of a blacked out stadium and shouting at the stands, knowing they're there somewhere but you don't know where. Only later did he and Barbara learn just how big a place they had found. At one point the opposite walls were 600 feet apart and the rock stadium's roof simply disappeared into black space above them. Indeed they had found a cavernous stadium that was a mile underground. They named it Perseverance Hall.

The two hurried on, exploring further. The enormous cavern ended in three long lakes. Cautiously they explored each one and decided that the last one had no visible outlet. Had they reached a dead end?

Cold and tired from struggling this far, they decided to halt their exploration for the day. The details of what they had found were carefully entered into their log books. Since they started that morning, they had traveled almost a mile underground through three sumps that had bypasses, reaching a cavernous amphitheater that ended in three narrow bodies of water, all of them oriented to the south in the direction of the Santo Domingo Canyon where Stone knew that all of this would eventually have to end up.

Ten hours later they were back at Camp 6 where they had left their dive gear, celebrating their discoveries with one of their gourmet meals—stroganoff mush.

For the next two days they surveyed the dimensions of Perseverance Hall, finally reaching the three lakes at the end of it. Scrutinizing the last body of water there, Stone saw that where the ceiling met the water there was a small opening. Barbara waded out to investigate. Stone saw her caving helmet disappear beneath the rock roof with just enough room for her head. In a few moments the glow of her light disappeared. Stone stood in the darkness at the edge of the water waiting.

Time passed in leaden minutes. Ten minutes dragged by. The longest ten minutes in his life. Nothing. Nothing but blackness and the gurgling of water from where Barbara had disappeared. Stone refused to let his imagination work on him. He forced his thoughts away from such possibilities as her being swept away. Still, those thoughts kept trying to get at him, trying to push their way into his mind. By the time 20 minutes passed, they had badly frayed his resistance. Stone was about to jump in after Barbara when he suddenly glimpsed the yellow glow of her light coming back through the passageway. Moments later she splashed ashore beside him.

"I've got good news and bad. Which do you want?" she asked.

"Give me the good first," he said.

"Well, the air space goes on for only a few yards, then the roof rises up again. You can follow the water a ways and then abruptly a huge river comes in from the left. It must have four times the flow of this one."

The news excited Stone. He figured this new incoming branch had to be the Rio Iglesia. From past exploration records in this area he knew that back in 1967, a Canadian expedition had followed the Iglesia into a dead-end cavern a half mile from the San Agustín cave entrance. There, the stream went underground over 800 feet below ground level. Geologists figured that it joined up with the Rio San Agustín somewhere underneath the Huautla Plateau forming what they called the Main Drain. Barbara had found the junction of these two rivers.

"Okay," said Bill. "Give me the bad news."

Barbara shook her head. "Just beyond where the Iglesia comes in, there is another sump. And this time there's no way around it."

It looked as if their progress down river was now permanently halted.

Exploring the area Barbara had found, at the juncture of the two rivers, they followed the tunnel beside the Rio Iglesia, knowing from the sounds that were thundering through the caverns that they were soon going to see something unusual in that gallery.

Abruptly they found it. It was one of the most startling sights either of them had seen. Forty feet up the cavern's wall there gushed a huge torrent of water cascading down in a violent white waterfall, the largest Stone had ever seen underground.

Making their way back to the San Agustín tunnel, Stone discovered a crack they had overlooked before. Following the fissure they found that it led them to yet a new passageway. Pursuing it up through a huge breakdown area of boulders, Barbara pushed her way through into a giant cavern. Suddenly their nostrils were assailed by the damp smell of rich earth. Barbara broke into a run down a long slope of soil that they suspected had somehow found its way there from centuries of runoff erosion from the surface.

At the bottom of the slope they searched for an hour, trying to find some continuing passageway beyond this point. In the distance they both thought they heard the faint rush of water.

Following the sound, they came out into an even more gigantic cavern. This one had to have once been a huge underground waterway, for its floor was cobbled from wall to wall with clean, smooth washed stones. Then they found the source of the sound: a river rushing over these rocks. In the distance, in the dim yellow glow of their lamps, they discerned a huge pile of these river rocks rising up into the darkness.

Barbara hurried on, exploring ahead of Bill. In a few moments she returned, breathless.

"It really gets huge over that rise," she said.

"You don't call this huge?" he asked, waving his hands at the vastness around them.

"No, no. You don't understand. I mean HU-MON-GOUS—really BIG!"

When Stone scrambled over the rock rise and moved his light around what he was looking at, he caught his breath. Barb was right. It looked like a gigantic rock funnel angled downward. At its bottom was blackness too deep to be penetrated by their strongest lights.

Cautiously they advanced to investigate. It was a still body of water, a lake they estimated to be at least 150 feet across. As they tentatively felt along its edge they realized that there was no shoreline to this lake; the sides kept funneling straight down below the water.

Where they stood the sand was rippled. The sand ripples were caused by water currents when spring run-off probably filled this entire gallery with water. All of it thundered around in this giant whirlpool and was then sucked down into the apex of this stone funnel. It was a giant drain.

Now, however the giant vortex was still, waiting for the spring floods that would soon come. More than anything, Stone wanted to dive down into this giant sump and find out where it went while it was still benign and they were able to do it. But their diving gear was a long way back behind them where they had left it at Camp 6. To try and bring it this far into the subterranean system, knowing that the spring rains might come any time now, would be madness.

Reluctantly, he and Barbara turned back toward Camp 6.

They had been exploring steadily for 22 hours. In that time they had discovered more than two miles of new passageways containing eight sumps. They had discovered the junction of the Rio Iglesia and its 40-foot-high waterfall, and before that, Perseverance Hall. They had accomplished an incredible amount of progress.

At Camp 6 they rested for a full day, logging new entries in their notebooks. Then they packed up everything the following morning, their sixth beyond the first sump. An hour after they donned their rebreathers and waded into the water, they resurfaced at Camp 5 on the other side of the San Agustín Sump.

Spitting out his mouthpiece, Stone cried, "We made it, Barb!" Somehow he managed to give her a hug, not too easy in their bulky diving gear.

That afternoon they broke down the gear for transport and by the time they climbed back to Camp 3 it was 8:30 in the evening. When Stone saw the distant lights, he shouted. Noel Sloan hurried down to meet them. Extending a helping hand, he hugged Stone. "I can't tell you how relieved I am to see you two," he said. Everyone was laughing and smiling.

After that they made their long tedious way back to the surface. It took them an entire week before they saw sunlight. Each day for ten back-breaking hours, the group consisting of Don Broussard, Jim Brown, Bev Shade, Angel Soto, Sergio Zambrano, Noel Sloan, Barbara am Ende, and Bill Stone hauled their heavy equipment bags up the long seemingly endless shafts by ropes and burdened backs.

Finally, in the end, Stone admitted that trying to follow the Rio San Agustín all the way through the Huautla Plateau to its final destination in the canyon far below had been an unrealistic goal. He had definitely underestimated how hard it would be to haul so much gear through so many obstacles to the bottom. Moreover, the entire effort had been shattered by the loss of one of their teammates.

Months later when they put together all their survey data and calculated how far underground they had been by the time they reached the funnel-shaped cavern and black pool, Stone was amazed to learn that they had reached 4,839 feet below ground level. In doing so, this fact had lifted the Huautla cave system from the 12th to the 5th deepest cave in the world.

When I spoke to Stone in the fall of 1996, I asked him what he planned for the future at Huautla. He told me that he and five others had made a two-month reconnaissance trip back there in April of 1995 and he believed they may have found another way to attack the problem—a passageway that took them 3,200 feet in.

"The tunnel measured 100 feet wide and 40 feet high, and it was still going down...which is either good or bad, whichever way you want to look at it," Stone told me. "The main point is that it's still going and we plan to go back there after Wakulla 2 in 1998."

If Huautla does indeed prove to be the deepest cave system in the world, you can bet that Bill Stone will be there, ready and able to prove it.

12

TO THE CELLARS OF THE SEA

The Great Bahama Bank, a flat-topped mountain of lime-stone over 14,000 feet thick, sprawls in a 750-mile arc across the Atlantic Ocean southeast of Florida. All but its high-est plateaus are underwater. Like white stepping stones, these 690 exposed platforms comprise the Bahama Islands. The larg-est is Andros, an intricately scalloped island 100-mile long and 40 miles wide. Behind it stretch the extensive limestone shoals that once threatened many a northbound Spanish treasure fleet. Before it lies the Tongue of the Ocean, a 6,000-foot abyss. Be-tween the island and the abyss, a relatively narrow, shallow water shelf runs the full length of Andros. This shelf contains holes, some large enough to engulf a three-story building. Seen from afar they resemble brilliant blue gems. Appropriately called ocean holes or blue holes, they are unlike any similar formations in the world. Each hole possesses its own incoming and outgoing currents which may vary widely from the ocean's normal tidal periods. Indeed, their rhythms are more closely linked to those of the deep beyond the wall, the shelf's vertical drop-off.

Geologists tell us that the Great Bahama Bank began form-ing at least 130 million years ago, but the blue holes are thought to be less than a million years old. With the forming of Ice Age glaciers, the sea level dropped some 600 feet. Torrential rains soon etched pockets and crevices in the softer portions of the now-exposed limestone bank. Gradually these fissures enlarged until, after centuries of erosion, they became deep pits and cav-erns, serving as nature's conduits carrying the island's runoff rainfall back to the sea.

As the glaciers melted, the seas gradually rose, covering most of the limestone bank and flooding the now-obsolete drainage system. The blue holes' dark passageways soon became the habitat of strange fish, and the rock-bound corridors pulsed with the violent incoming and outgoing currents.

Native Bahamians have always had a certain awed respect for these sapphire holes in the bottom of the ocean. Especially the natives of Andros Island, home of the Chick Charney—Andros' legendary leprechauns. These large-eyed, birdlike beings that cast no shadow and nest in the tops of pine trees may be small in stature but they stand mighty tall in the hearts and minds of superstitious Bahamians. And so do the blue holes of Andros, for according to some they are the abode of a monster called the lusca, a kind of giant cuttlefish or squid that appears periodically from one of the holes accompanied by a great violent upheaval of water from which the creature's long, slimy arms reach up to engulf anything it finds on the surface.

In February, 1958, Dr. George Benjamin, a middle-aged research chemist and the head of the Benjamin Film Laboratories, Ltd., in Toronto, Canada, decided to dive down and explore some of the mysterious Bahama blue holes. Benjamin, a Latvian, with a Yul Brynner haircut and a striking resemblance to Eric Von Stroheim, was too curious to see what the inside of those labyrinthine blue holes looked like to worry much about the legendary lusca.

At Andros, while Benjamin and his diving buddy, Tom McCollum, waited for the current to slack off at one of the blue holes, their native guide regaled them with stories of the vengeful blue hole monster that inhabited this particular hole. The Bahamian described in no uncertain terms how the lusca had recently stopped a two-masted schooner, reached aboard the vessel with its snakelike tentacles, wrapped them around a seaman, and pulled him screaming over the side and down into the blue hole. Although the Bahamian admitted he himself had not witnessed the tragedy, he swore it was nonetheless true. For the same lusca had attacked his boat only a few weeks later and pulled it down into the blue hole while he swam through the seething waters and was lucky to have escaped with his life. Despite their guide's dire warnings, Benjamin and McCollum were determined to explore the blue hole, monster or no monster.

When the outflowing current slackened, they slipped over the side of the boat in their scuba gear and finned their way toward the sapphire opening. As they approached the mouth of the underwater cave, great silvery schools of pilchards parted briefly to let them pass. Beyond them the smoothly carved limestone walls curved downward into a black pit. Feeding snappers moved fearlessly aside. Looking back up toward the surface, the divers saw that the swarming schools of fish created an undulating, silver curtain over the mouth of the shaft. Gradually the surface light dimmed as they swam deeper, until at 50 feet they switched on their underwater flashlights. Paying out the safety line that they had attached to a rock outcropping at the mouth of the blue hole, they continued downward into the darkness, both men wondering what manner of creatures might be watching their descent from the shadows below.

At 80 feet they reached an underwater amphitheater with a fine, white sand floor. Tunnels radiated out on all sides of them. As they cautiously explored the rock-walled room around them, Benjamin and McCollum were suddenly surprised when their light beams picked up a half-buried boat sticking up out of the sand. Removing the heavy outboard motor from the boat, they secured it to the end of their lifeline, then made their way slowly up the shaft, following their clusters of bubbles back toward the blue circle of light on the surface.

Visibly relieved to see them return safely from their plunge into the lusca's lair, their Bahamian guide was speechless with surprise when he hauled up his motor on the other end of their safety line.

After having made more than a 100 dives in over 50 blue holes, Benjamin has never encountered a lusca, but he has had some rather interesting encounters. On one occasion, he and three other divers, Archy Forfar, Heinz Bolliger and Benjamin's son, George, set out to photograph the interior of a blue hole at Conch Bay at the northern end of Andros. Each of the three divers carried an electronic flash linked by cables to Benjamin's camera. The plan was for the three divers to fan out before Benjamin to the end of their cables and, when he fired his camera,

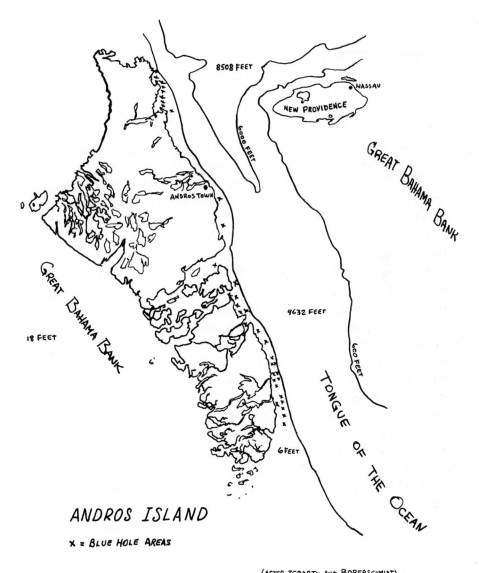

8508 FEET

6000 FEET

NASSAU

NEW PROVIDENCE

GREAT BAHAMA BANK

ANDROS TOWN

GREAT BAHAMA BANK

18 FEET

4632 FEET

6 FEET

600 FEET

TONGUE OF THE OCEAN

ANDROS ISLAND

X = BLUE HOLE AREAS

(AFTER ZEBARTH AND BOBERSCHMIDT)

Fragmented like loose pieces of a jigsaw puzzle, Andros, largest of the Bahama Islands, lies on the edge of the Great Bahama Bank beside the deep Tongue of the Ocean. On the narrow limestone shelf between the two, dotting the shallows like blue gems, are the blue holes.

all three synchronized flashes would simultaneously go off, illuminating the interior of the cavern.

The dive began during the slack period. The men swam down to a depth of 80 feet and entered the big chamber they were to photograph. Moments later they were suddenly confronted by two six-foot-long nurse sharks darting nervously back and forth through their light beams. Everyone knew that nurse sharks were not man-eaters; they were only dangerous if provoked. What nobody knew but everybody wondered at that moment was what constituted a provocation? The divers suspected that if these two were not already pretty provoked, they were certainly putting on a good act.

Swirling the water, the sharks dashed to the opposite end of the chamber. Finding no exit there they charged back toward the entrance through which the divers had just come. One shark swam directly toward Benjamin, veering off at the last instant toward his two companions. Hoping that someone would have his flash pointed at one of the sharks Benjamin triggered his camera, but the cables' contacts were broken and nothing happened. In the next instant his companions dissolved in a melee of arms, legs, cables, sharks and clouds of mud. After that skirmish the sharks disappeared back into the inner chamber. Rather than wait around to see if they would reappear, the divers quickly made their way back to the surface and their boat.

Later, when Benjamin developed his film, he found that although the flashes had malfunctioned, Heinz was so close to the shark that he was actually pushing it away with his floodlight, and when the shutter clicked the shark was illuminated enough for him to get a picture of the panicky nurse shark with a hitchhiking remora on its back.

In all his explorations, nurse sharks are the only species Benjamin has seen in the caves. So far, by sticking strictly to the golden rule, divers and sharks have kept themselves out of trouble.

Where did the tunnels go? Did they have a back door somewhere along the vertical wall in the ocean's depths? It always seemed that a lot of water flowed into and out of the blue holes long after a tidal change. Benjamin wondered why. These were some of the questions he sought to answer. On a falling tide, water would rush out of a blue hole so fast that it was physically impossible for a diver to swim against the current. And on a rising tide, it would surge in with such violence it created whirlpools like water going down a giant drainpipe, sucking everything with it. A diver would never ever consider attempting to enter one of the holes then. At such times they were death traps. But what puzzled Benjamin was that the ebb and flow of these currents continued sometimes long after the tides themselves ceased flowing. After repeatedly observing this phenomenon and mapping the intricate passageways of many of the blue holes, he came up with a logical solution for the delay.

"I think the easiest way to understand this time lag is to think of a blue hole as one end of a tidal river, a saltwater river running underground," he said. "Then make a simple comparison: Atlantic Ocean tides raise and lower the Hudson River all the way from New York City to Troy—the high tide in Troy comes nine and one-half hours later than in New York."

In many cases the currents of the blue holes would continue to flow up to two and three hours after the tidal change.

In an effort to learn whether or not the blue holes had back doors opening along the wall, the sheer drop-off into the Tongue of the Ocean, Benjamin and his team of divers made over 200 descents down to depths of 300 feet along the vertical face of the precipice, scrutinizing it for openings. Although they found numerous cracks and crevices and shallow dead-end caves, they did not find any tunnel connections to the blue holes near the surface.

As Benjamin and his divers perfected their techniques, they were able to penetrate deeper into the side passages of many of the blue holes. Usually they were eventually stopped by rockfalls or walls of sediment. Some of the impasse amounted to a pile of broken rock where the divers released fluorescein dye, and saw its bright clouds of color gently stream toward small fissures in the rock pile indicating that the water was passing through to some point beyond. But at that time, no one had found any major outlet to the caves in the ocean's subterranean basement.

There was no way to know how extensive the passageways were, or how deep they went. One day Benjamin and his companion, Archy Forfar, entered the opening to a blue hole and, looking down the long, gently sloping shaft, they saw a red crab disappear into the floor of the tunnel. When the divers approached the spot they found that the crab had scuttled through a small opening in the floor that they might normally have overlooked. They shined their dive lights down into it but were unable to see bottom. Benjamin attached a small electronic flasher on a line and lowered it through the hole into the darkness. The unit, normally used for safety purposes, kept flashing its brilliant burst of bluish light as it dropped deeper through the black water until Benjamin had lowered it to 200 feet, the limit of his line. The flasher looked like a faint firefly at that depth; still there was no sign of a bottom. Indeed it appeared to be a bottomless pit.

This was too curious a phenomenon to be overlooked. Benjamin and Forfar squeezed through the narrow opening and followed the line down toward the distant winking electronic light.

At 100 feet they stopped, and, pointing his camera downward, Benjamin fired its flash. As the strobe blinked brilliantly at 1/1000 second both divers thought they glimpsed an enormous cavern buttressed by huge columns flanking the massive vault. Had they at that depth actually seen stalactites, formations that could only form in a dry cave?

As Benjamin's photographs later confirmed, they had found one of Andros Island's deepest blue holes. The pit was found to be 230 feet deep. The photos revealed the first stalactites ever found in a saltwater cave.

One day, while searching the wall for outlets, Benjamin discovered the mouth of a large cave at 200 feet deep. It was a photograph of five divers hovering before this vast opening that persuaded Jacques Yves Cousteau, in 1970, to film a documentary of the Bahama blue holes called *Secrets of the Sunken Caves*. And it was Dr. Benjamin's son, Peter, who led Philippe Cousteau 1,200 feet into the largest underwater cavern that they had found up to that time. Benjamin called it "Blue Hole No. 4." Cousteau renamed it "Benjamin's Cave."

The following year this underwater cavern claimed the life of an exceptionally well-trained and skilled cave diver, Frank Martz. In September, 1971, Martz and a companion were making a deep exploratory dive in the cave system. At 280 feet they entered a passageway so narrow and constricting that its shape prevented them from backing out. So they continued on, eventually reaching a large cavern at the excessive depth of 320 feet. Here, they managed to tie off their safety line but stirred up silt and became separated. Martz's companion worked his way out through the narrow tunnel to safety, but Martz did not follow. His body was never recovered.

Benjamin brought a skilled team of divers to photograph the far reaches of the cave. The team included writer-photographer and executive editor of *Skin Diver* magazine, Jack McKenney; diving officer at the University of Miami and president of the National Association of Cave Divers, Tom Mount; and equally skilled cave diver, Ray Hixon. With Benjamin's boat the *Blue Hole* anchored near the cave site, the divers waited until late afternoon for the outflowing currents to slack so that they could enter. They planned to penetrate to 1,200 feet and then come out, with the outflowing currents helping to make their swimming easier. In the inner grotto McKenney would document the dive and hoped to photograph the unusual stalactites and stalagmites, including one formation called the Roman Gate—three stalagmites that rose from the floor of the cavern to support a natural limestone arch across their tops.

In the last rays of the setting sun the men donned their gear. As the current slackened they made their way down to the mouth of the cave. In the clear blue water of the deep basin, hundreds of crevalle jacks swarmed before the opening. At the divers approach, the swirling wall of fish parted and the men entered the grotto, one behind the other, each concerned with the specific job he had to do. Benjamin led the group, followed by Mount carrying a 1,000-watt strobe connected by a 30-foot cable to McKenney's underwater camera. Hixon, bringing up the rear, took up any slack in the trailing light cable.

Each man wore double air tanks with octopus regulators, a system which gives a diver a spare breathing unit in case one fails. All divers carried two lights, a main and an auxiliary, and wore buoyancy compensators, special diving vests that, when partially inflated, enabled them to achieve natural buoyancy, keeping them well off the bottom to prevent stirring up silt. In addition to the regular equipment of knife, compass, and depth gauge, each diver's double tanks were rigged with submersible pressure gauges enabling them to tell how much air they had left at all times.

Benjamin, who always dived with a spare regulator on a rubber strap around his neck, told the others that if anyone needed air, rather than waste time signaling to him to buddy breathe, they were to simply grab the one out of his mouth that he was using and he would then use the spare. If this occurred, they were to immediately abort the dive and return to the boat.

At the mouth of the cave Benjamin and Mount secured one end of their safety line. Paying it out from their reel, they descended into the blue hole to 140 feet where they tied off to a permanent line Benjamin had established during earlier dives into the cavern.

Managing the camera equipment and strobe, McKenney and Hixon followed the line down to join the others waiting below. Then on a signal from Benjamin they moved single file under a ledge and through a ten-foot-wide opening. Thirty feet below them they saw the boulder-strewn floor of a large chamber. They dropped down to it at 170 feet and probed the surrounding darkness with their lights. Unlike the bright colors of coral and sponges usually found on the outer reefs, the drab limestone walls were unattractively festooned with small nodules of colorless sponges. On a sign from Benjamin they rose again like weightless astronauts to the high ceiling and the permanent nylon rope that led them 300 feet farther through a narrow tunnel. Sliding their hands along the rope, they continued into another enormous room where the ceiling soared more than 100 feet above their heads, too far for their most powerful lights to illuminate.

Like a guide leading a midnight tour through a deserted art gallery, momentarily pausing to sweep his flashlight over some remarkable pieces of sculpture, Benjamin led them swiftly along the corridor, briefly pointing out unusual rock formations with his light.

Realizing that they had a definite goal, a certain distance to travel on their limited air supply, the divers did not delay on the way. Their course frequently took them through other subterranean rooms, where the walls stretched beyond the range of their lights. And at one place Benjamin stopped to show them a pair of tall, slender twin pillars formed by mineral-saturated water dripping from the ceiling of a dry cave. After taking a photograph of the unique formation, McKenney shined his light on his depth gauge. They were at a depth of 120 feet.

A few minutes later Benjamin led them into another large room. This one was filled with huge boulders and great angular slabs of rock. One such piece, measuring 20 to 30 feet across, had fallen from above and was supported by two others, forming a natural bridge.

By now they were ten minutes into their dive and had penetrated 800 feet into the cavern. McKenney was suddenly struck by the impression that the vaults and tunnels stretched on for miles. Never before, in all his years of diving, had he felt the sensation of flying. But here in this vaulted, sculptured amphitheater he felt as if he had suddenly sprouted wings and was soaring in slow motion past the spectacular ledges, gorges, canyons and ravines of the Grand Canyon.

Leaving this chamber, they made their way through a tunnel so narrow that their tanks clanged against the walls. It finally ended in a huge, cathedral-like room that seemed crowded with hundreds of stalagmites and stalactites, the all-white dripstones creating an eerie, sepulchral setting as the divers' lights wavered over Mother Nature's collection of strange statuary. They were now 1,200 feet inside the labyrinth. As McKenney took pictures, the giant 1,000-watt strobe periodically blasted the room with blinding light, momentarily etching the strange shapes and shadows on the divers' retinas; the glaring images remained split seconds after the room was again plunged into total darkness, except for the wavering, yellow beams of the divers' hand lights.

All too soon it seemed, Benjamin pointed at his watch and signaled that it was time to leave the grotto. They had been in the cavern for over 28 minutes.

The men checked their air gauges, knowing that even after they left the caverns they would have at least 30 minutes of decompression ahead of them before they could surface.

They had entered the cathedral room from a passageway near the ceiling, but now they dropped down 40 feet and squeezed through a narrow opening into another passageway at a depth of 190 feet. As they moved along it they felt the blue hole's current moving with them, making their swimming easier.

On the way out Benjamin paused to flash his light into a heavily silted side chamber, which was extremely dangerous for divers. What silt was not stirred up by their fins from the floor would surely descend upon them from the ceiling, dislodged by their bubbles. Divers have become lost in such conditions.

Five minutes later the group reached the entrance of the cave and passed through the swirling curtain of crevalle jacks in the basin.

They had entered the cave at sunset. Now as they hung on the vertical line, decompressing, it was dark outside and the sky was filled with stars.

Through the years Benjamin has been able to locate many new blue holes from the air. Most appear as a light blue spot against the surrounding light green ocean water. Some look like miniature atolls or blue-holed doughnuts due to an encircling dark ring of coral growth. Similar formations may lie just a few hundred yards away, yet the blue hole is missing. It has silted in and filled up with sand because for some reason its currents were not strong enough to keep the passageway clear. No one knows why the volume, rate of ebb and flow, and duration of slack time often varies from one blue hole to another, even those relatively close together. For example, a blue hole near Benjamin's Cave has a slack water period of about an hour, while Ben's Cave currents are slack for only ten minutes. Benjamin suspects that these variations may be caused by the size of the system and such current-altering factors as cave-ins and silting. But whatever the variables, Benjamin has found that the safest time to dive most blue holes is at the end of the slack in the ebb tide so that, by the time the divers are swimming out of the cave, they will have the outflowing currents assisting them.

Most Bahama blue holes are found from 10 to 50 feet underwater. Seen from the surface, they appear almost as a luminous blue patch against the surrounding water. Once, off No Name Cay near Great Abaco, I saw what appeared to be a blue hole in the reef. As our boat approached, the spot glowed turquoise blue in contrast to the surrounding dark eelgrass bottom. But when we looked closer we found merely a gleaming white patch of sand in a deep hole reflecting sunlight up through the clear blue depths. Were we looking at an expired blue hole, one that had simply run out of sufficient current to keep it clean and had filled with sand? Possibly.

Divers familiar with blue holes have found them already in the process of filling in, their diminishing currents growing too feeble to sweep them clean. Sometime in the future they will be completely gone, with hardly a scar on the bottom to show where they once were.

Benjamin has always been interested in caves, both wet and dry. In 1940 when he was spelunking in dry caves in England, he experimented with photographing some of the vast caverns he visited underground. One of the problems he experienced was getting enough light to illuminate the recesses of the cavern he wanted to photograph. Since flashbulbs were too weak to do the job, he opened his camera shutter and ignited quantities of magnesium flash powder. After each blinding flash, Benjamin was amazed to see the tips of the stalagmites, in the process of being formed from ceiling drippings, glow green for several additional seconds. Later he learned that this part of the dripstone consisted of crystalline calcium carbonate, a substance that would dissolve in water. What puzzled him in the Bahamas, then, was to find these same kind of dripstones up to 180 feet underwater, yet they had not dissolved. Why?

A possible explanation is that the water in the Bahamas is so highly saturated with lime that complex chemical changes may take place in the structure of the material in association with saltwater. While the stalactites and stalagmites may retain their general shape, Benjamin found that their outer surfaces became coated with a dirty gray covering that is less soluble. Experimenting with a small piece of dripstone that had been accidentally broken off from inside one of the blue holes, McKenney took it into a dark room and fired his electronic flash at it. For a second, the impacted crystalline calcium carbonate glowed bright green, substantiating the belief that it had been formed in a dry cave.

Interestingly, Andros Island is pock-marked with hundreds of inland blue holes, perfectly round sinks filled with fresh water often with saltwater bottoms. When a diver swims down through the fresh water and encounters the warm, denser salt water, the sensation is said to be similar to bouncing on a trampoline.

No matter how many years Benjamin spent exploring the Bahama blue holes, they never lost their attraction to him. One might think that one hole would look much like another—that if you've seen one you've seen them all. But, as any cave diver will tell you, this is not true. There is always something new and different, something unexpected to be seen or experienced. And as always, there is the constant search for the still undiscovered. Benjamin's fondest hope was to find two blue holes linked together by sunken subterranean passageways so that he could take his diving crew into one and come up in another. He never found this combination. But that in no way distracted him from the thrill of the hunt.

When people ask him what it is that fascinates him about blue holes, why he risks his life to explore them, he says he does it in "the hope of adding a bit to the world's sum of knowledge, the call of adventure, the indescribable sensation of putting one's foot or flipper where no man has gone before—all are part of the appeal to me of the blue holes."

To those divers who have shared that experience all they can add to the statement is a firm "Amen!"

13

DIVE INTO THE PAST
PART I

Of Florida's hundreds of springs and sinkholes, less than twenty are major tourist attractions. Others are just as crystal clear and sapphire blue as the Chamber of Commerce paints them, but since they are largely off the beaten track the crowds, fortunately, have not found them yet. Still others, however, are virtually unknown, undeveloped, unpublicized, unglamorous pools that missed getting Mother Nature's beauty treatment. Their shorelines are muck, their murky waters reek of sulfur and their underwater landscapes are often shrouded with thick layers of slime. Any one of them would have been a perfect setting for Hollywood's *Creature of the Black Lagoon*, which was actually filmed at Wakulla Springs.

One such water hole can be found in the undeveloped prairie-and-palm back country several miles inland from Port Charlotte in Sarasota County, on Florida's west coast. From the air, the circular, black pool enclosed in a collar of jungle growth looks disturbingly like an aerial view of the sacrificial cenote at Chichen Itza. This 250-foot-wide body of still, black water, with the malodorous aroma of rotten eggs, bears the innocent name of Little Salt Springs. In the early years the spring's remote location and rather spooky appearance discouraged widespread investigation by skin divers. But drawn by their curiosity to learn what lay below the surface of the mysterious pool, a few hearty souls braved it. One of the first to break through the murky barrier and swim down into its unknown depths was retired Air Force Lieutenant Colonel William R. Royal.

Royal is one of those people who seems to be more at home

in water than on land. His off-hours hobby in the Pacific during World War II was riding and killing sharks underwater. His friends considered him a superior diver, one who seemed to be able to dive to considerable depths and yet never be affected by nitrogen narcosis. As it had in so many other underwater adventures, curiosity brought Bill Royal to Little Salt Springs in January, 1959. Keeping a wary eye on the two alligators that shared the pool, Royal wallowed out through the muddy shallows in his single-tank Aqua-Lung, swam into the middle and finned down through the brown, brackish water to a depth of 70 feet. It was so murky his underwater flashlight barely illuminated the rock wall in front of him. Then, in the shadows, he saw the dark opening of a cave. Just inside, strange conical shapes thrust down from the ceiling. Royal drew closer, examining them with his flashlight. He could hardly believe his eyes. They were stalactites! He was 70 feet underwater, yet here were limestone formations that could only form in a dry cave!

Royal was so excited by his find that as soon as he could get to a telephone he called Dr. H. K. Brooks, a skin-diving geology professor at the University of Florida, to find out how long it had been since the sea level was low enough for stalactites to form in the cave. Dr. Brooks' answer: At least 6,000 years. Royal reasoned that if the caves were dry, then perhaps they had been inhabited. But 6,000 years ago? From what he could learn, the oldest evidence of man in Florida went back only 3,500 years. Nobody had found anything older.

He dived into the spring again in March. On a ledge just above the cave he found a partially fossilized human thighbone. This really excited him.

Royal promptly rounded up everyone he knew who might be interested in the discovery. Within a few days after his second dive, he had organized a modest expedition of sport divers, scholars and experts in various fields. This included a woman anthropologist, Dr. Luana Pettay, who was particularly interested in evidence of prehistoric Indians in Florida; geologist Brooks, who was anxious to see the stalactites; Professor Lackey, a microbiologist from the University of Florida; Dr. Eugenie Clark, an ichthyologist studying shark behavior at the Cape Haze Marine Laboratory near Sarasota; Dr. Marwin, a local dentist;

Iris Woolcock, a public-relations woman associated with the health spa at nearby Warm Mineral Springs; two accomplished skin divers, Norman Rack and Bob Chapman from Venice; and writer-photographer Bill Stephens, editor of the *Florida Outdoors* magazine.

Since the spring was on private property, the group had to get permission to dive there from the Mackle Company, which owned the land, and sign a paper absolving the company of re- sponsibility for any accidents that might occur.

The group drove as close as possible to the springs, then started across muddy pastures and fields, making their own track. When one car became stuck, they abandoned it and con- tinued in another. When it, too, bogged down in the mud, every- one pushed until it was out. When they came within 50 yards of the springs, they left the cars and carried their gear the rest of the way, crossing the muddiest places on planks Royal had laid down after his last trip to the site. At the water's edge they found a dry spot large enough for them to put on their equipment.

Leading the way into the water, Bill Royal, carrying an un- derwater light, swiftly disappeared like a shot, heading straight down toward the deepest part of the spring. The others, how- ever, worked their way around the edges in shallower water. Little Salt is shaped somewhat like an hourglass—the sides slope down to a depth of 35 feet, where they drop vertically for a short dis- tance through a 75-foot-wide hole, then begin a reverse slope and recede as the depth plunges to 210 feet. The bottom along the upper shoulders is velvet soft sediment about six inches deep. Feeling around in this ooze at the 30-foot depth, Marwin found several large fossil clam shells. Each time the divers picked up something, the bottom erupted in miniature mud explosions. Eugenie Clark spotted what appeared to be a golf ball standing out in sharp contrast against the grayish-brown bottom. She picked it up and turned it over in her hand. It was the socket ball from a human thighbone.

After investigating these depths, the divers rallied and be- gan swimming down into the hole, following the bursts of Bill Royal's bubbles coming up from below. They did not go far. Vis- ibility was so bad that they could hardly see each other a few feet away. Lacking any solid visual orientation, they gave up and swam back to the overhang.

Bill Stephens teamed up with Eugenie Clark and followed the vertical wall down until they came to an overhanging ledge. Beneath it they found a cave. Stephens worked his way into it, followed by Clark. She reached up to touch the slimy ceiling and felt stalactites. Not wishing to go any farther, Clark made her way out of the cave and started moving vertically along the rock wall. As she looked up toward the surface it appeared dark. Looking down, she saw a faint light from what she assumed was Royal's flashlight. But then she noticed air bubbles coming from the surface and heading down toward Royal's light. Suddenly she realized she had lost her sense of up and down. Instead of climbing up toward the surface, she was climbing deeper down into the hole. The dim light she saw in the other direction was daylight on the surface. Once properly oriented, with her eyes adjusted to the gloom, she saw Royal coming up from the bottom of the springs, swimming slowly just under the clusters of his bubbles. He was shining his light on something in his hand and passed Clark without seeing her clinging to the dark rock wall. It was an eerie sight—Royal rising slowly toward the surface while casually examining a handful of human bones in the pale yellow glow of his flashlight.

Waiting on the surface in a rubber raft, Dr. Pettay, the anthropologist, took the items Royal had picked up on the ledges and in the caves of the deeper part of the springs. The collection soon amounted to seven thighbones, part of a skull and various other human bone fragments. After examining the pieces, Pettay felt that they had come from prehistoric Indians who had once built large mounds found in various parts of Florida. But Royal thought they were older than the Mound Builders. He theorized that they came from prehistoric people who lived in the caves thousands of years before the Mound Builders.

Later, while they rested and warmed up, everyone speculated on the possibilities. The scientists generally held a conservative estimate of how old the bones were, pointing out that since several alligator vertebrae had also been found in the shallow depths of the springs, alligators might be responsible for taking the bodies back under the ledges into the caves. But Stephens, Royal and Clark doubted that alligators ever dived to the 70-foot depths where the human bones were found.

The following week most of the group, with the addition of Dr. Saunders, a veterinarian, and divers Charlie Corneal and Bud Kraft, returned to the springs for another dive. Since recent heavy rains had made a quagmire of the back country, everyone squeezed into two jeeps for the trip. It was a cold, bleak day, and its mood matched that of Little Salt Springs, with its macabre population of ancient skeletons. No one seemed overly jubilant about the undertaking.

Someone had mentioned one popular theory that the springs might have been used by ancient Indians as a sacrificial well, so while they all had full tanks they planned to dive directly to the bottom of the deepest part and search it for human bones.

They paddled a small boat out to the middle of the springs and dropped a weighted nylon rope to the bottom. Bill Royal, with a depth gauge on each arm, was to lead the way. Next would come Eugenie Clark, then Bill Stephens, the three intending to follow the line to the bottom 210 feet down. Charlie Corneal would remain in the boat with spare tanks; Bud Kraft would serve as safety diver, stationing himself on the line about 50 feet below the surface and remaining there to offer any assistance necessary.

Each of the three going down the line had double air tanks; Royal and Clark wore theirs, Bill Stephens wore a single tank and carried a spare tank equipped with a regulator under his arm.

They started down, sliding their hands along the thin, white line as they went. Daylight faded out completely at 50 feet. Royal and Stephens switched on their underwater lights. Clark, swimming between them, had none. Visibility was terrible. The beams of light could not penetrate the suspended particles in the water but only reflected back, creating a condition underwater photographers call "backscatter." Nobody saw the ledge at 60 feet as they passed it.

They were 100 feet down when Bill Royal's light went out. He came back up the line and passed the others as he headed for the surface. Clark and Stephens turned around and started up too, but at 80 feet they met Royal returning with a small flashlight. As they started back down again Stephens handed his stronger light to Clark who in turn kept it shining on Royal below her on the rope.

At 130 feet the trio paused to check their depth gauges. Although unaware of it at the time, Clark was feeling some of the effects of nitrogen narcosis. She remembered looking at her depth gauge and wondering why she could not tell what time it was. When the divers looked at each other they were all smiling broadly behind their masks.

"As we continued down the rope, Bill Royal leading with his little flashlight and me lighting him with the strong light," Clark reported, "I began to feel that I was breathing exceptionally fresh air. When we were deeper still, I suspected that someone had opened the window in our stuffy dark room and fresh air was coming in. The air seemed to be loaded with oxygen and I felt very light."

It seemed that the water around them was even muddier than before. Clark kept her dive light shining on Royal's hand, sliding down the rope just below her. Everything seemed to have a dreamlike quality to her now and she felt she was sinking very slowly into a velvet ooze. She struggled to see below her. Royal had disappeared. All she saw was his hand sticking up out of the mud, still clutching the rope. The thought drifted into her mind that poor Bill Royal was dead. It was not an upsetting conclusion, it simply left her with a sweet sadness. She reached down to touch his hand, but could not feel it. Her regulator seemed to be giving her sweet, rhythmical drafts of air all by itself. Then a voice was urging her to breathe deeply, saying it over and over. She thought she was in a hospital delivery room breathing anesthetic and about to give birth to her first child.

Then abruptly she realized that she was not in any hospital nor was she about to be anesthetized. She shook her head, trying to clear the fuzziness from her thoughts. Clutching the rope she turned her light upward, looking for Bill Stephens. He, too, had disappeared. This puzzled her. They had agreed before diving that under no circumstances would they let go of the safety rope. But Stephens had either turned it loose and wandered off into the darkness of the depths, or he had for some reason left them and gone up the rope toward the surface. She hoped it was the latter.

Clark knew now that she was feeling the effects of nitrogen narcosis. Instinctively she covered her mouthpiece with her hand, vaguely remembering she had once read that a person with nitrogen narcosis sometimes spits out the mouthpiece under the illusion that they can breathe water. She was taking no chances. All she could think of now was getting back to the surface. She started in that direction as fast as her fins would move her, clutching the rope and the light in her right hand as she ascended.

How long she continued upward she never knew. Her mind simply blotted out this detail. Somewhere along the way, however, reality came back to her, and she stopped and shined the light all around. There was no one nor nothing around her. She was suspended in a murky void that had no boundaries. Her only tangible link to life was the thin nylon rope on which she clung. She moved the beam of light along the single white strand in both directions, then stopped in complete confusion when she saw she was holding the rope horizontally. Which way should she go? She had never felt so alone in her entire life.

Suddenly she recalled something Royal had told her to do if she lost track of which way was up or down. "Take off your weight belt, hold it out in front of you," he said. "If it hangs upward, swim down to reach the surface."

Clark had wrapped her legs around the rope and was taking off her weight belt, when she decided to reach behind her and feel for her air bubbles to see which way they were going. The bubbles seemed to trail off to her left, so she followed them in a direction she felt was surely wrong but which logic told her had to be right. Then she remembered Royal, still down in the mud, and she knew she had to go back down after him to try and retrieve his body.

Hand over hand, she started back down the rope toward the bottom. She kept going until her mind again began to wander; the rhythmic drafts of air made her think she was drifting off to a relaxing sleep. Then, through the numb, dreamlike euphoria of nitrogen narcosis, reality pricked her mind into a fleeting awareness that she had to get out of the terrible dark depths as quickly as possible or she never would.

Feeling guilty about leaving Royal buried in the mud somewhere below her, she struck out toward the surface, sliding her hand up the rope as she moved, unmindful of the need to stop and decompress along the way, wanting only to reach sunlight and fresh air again.

As the dark water slowly turned a lighter shade of brown, she saw a figure on the rope above her. Just the sight of another human being sent a wave of tremendous relief through her. Was it Bill Stephens? No. As she approached the man she recognized their safety diver, Bud Kraft. She pointed down, trying to indicate to Kraft that Royal was still on the bottom, hoping that Kraft might be able to go down and help him. Then she signaled that she was continuing on up to the surface.

Moments later she felt her second great relief to see Bill Stephens on the surface beside their dive boat. As soon as she broke the surface, Clark hailed him with a joyful cry, explaining that she had been affected by nitrogen narcosis. Stephens replied that he had too. Clark noticed that there was frothy blood on his face and his mask.

Quickly she told the two men that Royal was in trouble on the bottom. Corneal was about to dive and see if he could help, when both Bill Royal and Bud Kraft appeared on the surface. The divers went ashore and warmed up by a fire. Royal was surprised to learn that Clark thought he was in trouble. He said when he reached bottom, he had simply let himself sink down into the ooze, while he held onto the rope with one hand and felt around the bottom for bones with his other. Unlike the others, he had not been bothered by nitrogen narcosis. The one who had the most trouble was Stephens. About the time he reached 200 feet his first tank of air ran out. He knew he had narcosis when he experienced difficulty performing the simple act of taking one mouthpiece out of his mouth and putting in the other. When this was finally accomplished, he was all right for a moment, then the tank slipped out of his grasp and for some reason he could not recover it. He started toward the surface, clutching his mouthpiece and its accordion hoses from which dangled his trailing air tank. Somewhere between the bottom and the top he knew something was badly wrong because great volumes of air bubbles rose around him. At first he thought this was the effect of nitrogen narcosis, but then he realized that he was indeed rising in a welter of bubbles and they were not all from his exhalations.

In his anxiousness to get to the surface he did not slow down when he passed the safety diver, Bud Kraft. By then it was a panic situation, and Stephens was in no condition to stop and see what was wrong.

Once he regained his composure on the surface he saw his problem. The night before the dive he had discovered a tear in one of his accordion air hoses and had patched it up with liquid neoprene cement. When the tank slipped out of his hands, its weight on the hose apparently tore it open again. Most of the air he was trying to breathe was bubbling up around him in the water.

After resting awhile, the divers returned to the springs. While Royal dived down to explore a cave 100 feet below the surface, the others searched the shallower depths. They had no trouble finding the scattered parts of human skeletons. Some of the bones were lighter in weight and color than others which were darker and heavier because they were highly mineralized.

Royal surfaced with the exciting news that 20 feet back into the cave he had been investigating, he found a human skeleton with a huge rock resting atop the leg bone as if it had fallen and pinned the man down. Wisely he did not disturb the bones, wishing instead to show them to the scientists in the group, then photograph them in place.

Pettay, Marwin and Clark decided to accompany Royal back down to look at the find. Swimming close together, they descended without a rope. Clark carried a light and kept shining it on the others to keep track of them and to be sure they were coming along all right in the darkness. Royal held Pettay 's hand since she was the least experienced of the divers.

When they reached the mouth of the cave, there were stalactites near the entrance. Pettay tugged anxiously on Royal and pointed toward the surface. The others checked her. She was wide-eyed but breathing normally. Royal took her back to the surface where she explained that she had become very apprehensive in front of the cave and was completely disoriented.

Leaving her with the others on shore, Royal returned to the divers awaiting him below at the mouth of the cave. He and Marwin entered first. Clark followed and very shortly she lost not only her sense of up and down, but she could not tell whether she was going in or out of the cave. The three of them seemed to her to be following a ledge along the wall. Royal later told her it was not a wall ledge but a groove along the cave floor. A moment later Marwin signaled her with a slashing motion of his index finger across his throat, indicating that he was running out of air. Clark was reaching out to signal Royal when he suddenly grabbed her and spun her around. With a firm grip on her he led Clark and Marwin out of the cave and up to the surface. Later he explained that they were within a few feet of the skeleton, when his regulator abruptly plugged up and he was unable to get any air. Still he calmly led the others back the way they had come and out of the cave.

Later that afternoon when they finished up the air in their spare tanks searching the shallows, Royal found part of a fossilized antler with the prongs carved off. It was the first evidence of Indian handicraft they had found in the springs.

If early man lived at Little Salt Springs during prehistoric times in dry caves 70 to 100 feet below the present water level, the group wondered if other springs in the area had been similarly inhabited. They now focused their attention on Warm Mineral Springs a couple of miles away. Instead of being cold, brackish water as was Little Salt, the water at Warm Mineral was over 80°F year around. Although it too was sulfurous and contained a high percentage of hydrogen sulfide, visibility was much better.

According to the commercial interests at the springs, Indians once came to Warm Mineral for its curative powers. For the same reason the springs attract people today, some afflicted with arthritis and similar ailments. They come to bathe in the spring's warm waters and to take mud baths near shore.

With Royal leading the way, Stephens, Pettay and Clark dived down to investigate one of the more promising areas at 40 feet below the surface. A large rock ledge along the side of the springs created a cavelike shelter beneath it. As the divers cautiously entered, they were amazed to find the floor of the cave composed of a layer of sediment six feet deep. But what really excited them was the discovery that it contained clearly defined sedimentary layers from one to three feet thick, each one different from another, the entire stratum probably accumulating over a period of thousands of years. The top and most modern layer, about three feet thick, mainly contained fine mud particles in which were embedded snail shells and alligator bones. A darker gray layer below it, about a foot thick and somewhat more compact, contained shells from two different species of snails, compacted leaves, broken stalactites, charcoal fragments, bones of deer, birds and humans.

After several dives Royal had picked from this layer two bone needles, a shaped piece of antler believed used as a spear thrower or atlatl weight, and several other bone artifacts. The bottom layer of light tan-colored sediment about one and one-half feet thick, contained wood and charcoal fragments, animal, bird and human bones. Beneath this was a layer of clay that embedded one end of a burned log three feet long, beside which were found several human finger bones. All this material rested on hard, limestone rock containing fossil starfish, shark's teeth and marine shells.

Since we know so little about primitive man in the Western Hemisphere, Royal and the others felt that the sedimentary deposit of animal, vegetable and human matter from the past was of enormous significance. It is generally believed that about 20,000 years ago, early man crossed from Asia to the North American continent on a land bridge that existed at the Bering Strait after the last ice age. Evidence of his occupation in New Mexico and Texas dates back to about 15,000 years ago. But these primitive nomadic hunters were not thought to have arrived in Florida until about 3,500 years ago. If the human bones and tools indicated that man was living in these caves when they were dry—that is, over 6,000 years ago, then Royal reasoned that these finds were possibly some of the oldest evidence of early man in North America.

They took their finds and their story to Dr. John M. Goggin, the head of the anthropology department at the University of Florida and the first professionally trained archaeologist to take up scuba diving and work actively in underwater archaeology. After telling him about their find, Royal and Clark thought he would be as excited about it as they. But according to Eugenie Clark in her popular autobiography, *The Lady and the Sharks*

(Harper & Row, 1969), "Dr. John Goggin—the noted ' Father of Florida Archaeology' at the Florida State Museum and the only archaeologist in Florida who was a scuba diver—disappointed us by being too busy to examine the site and did not think we knew what we were talking about."

In the 1962 newsletter of the Southeastern Archaeological Conference, however, Dr. Goggin reported, "Last spring I got word from the geologist at the University of Florida that a spring with many human bones in it had been found in the southern part of the state. Shortly thereafter I was contacted by Dr. Luana Pettay, a young physical anthropology graduate from Indiana who is now teaching at Ohio; she had been wintering in Venice, Florida, on the southwest coast. She called me up and told me that they had a spring in which a great quantity of human bones had been found. As a result we took our diving team down and looked at this spring and one other...." Dr. Goggin went on to describe the topography of Little Salt Springs, then added, "This area yielded a great quantity of heavily mineralized human bones. Miss Pettay and some local skin divers had recovered a great number, and when we went out we recovered a few more, although we were not interested in taking out any more than were necessary to absolutely determine the situation. But at the last count I believe there were enough femurs from one side to account for over 50 individuals, and apparently this bone bed is hardly scratched. The bulk of the bones are body bones. There are only a few skull fragments, although there is a large number of jaws compared to skulls. It has been postulated, by me at least, that these bones represent secondary burials thrown in from the bank and that the skulls on this steep slope simply went down to the bottom..." Dr. Goggin then discussed the finds at Warm Mineral Springs, an area, he said, that "is also being developed by people who are trying to sell lots around it...they are trying to convince the city that this is Ponce de Leon's fountain of youth..." Then, speaking of Royal and Clark's contentions, "Their argument, of course, is that these things were deposited when the stalactites were being formed. If stalactites were being formed it was a pretty wet period, and the idea of people being back in a little niche, presents a problem. According to Colonel Royal and Dr. Pettay these niches are six feet, maybe, but not much more. From what I saw [he accompanied Royal on one dive], six feet would be a pretty good measurement. It is a very fascinating problem but this business of ichthyologists and retired Air Force officers setting themselves up as archaeologists is a little discouraging."

And this was the crux of the matter. Egos and professionalism were involved, qualities that somehow seemed absurdly out of place in the field of science.

Disappointed but not deterred, the amateur archaeologists blundered on, Royal and the others certain that they had made an important discovery if someone would only listen. But what good was it if no one believed them?

Needing some indisputable proof, Dr. Clark went to work on her contacts in the scientific world until she persuaded the Scripps Institute of Oceanography to carbon date a piece of the burned log they found near the bones on the floor of the cave.

The reply from Scripps sent the divers into paroxysms of joy. The log was ten thousand years old!

Now if they could prove that the human bones found in the same stratum of sediment as the log had not been disturbed and were really an integral part of the stratum, they thought they could be the oldest human remains in the western hemisphere.

Again they appealed to the scientific community. Finally the curator of anthropology at the American Museum of Natural History asked a scuba-diving associate, a qualified New York anthropologist named Dr. Ford, to take a look at the underwater site. On his way to Warm Mineral Springs, Ford stopped off to see Dr. Goggin in Gainesville. Goggin told him he felt that the human bones had probably sifted down through the sediment instead of being in undisturbed chronological strata. However, he was interested in having Ford check to see if the sediment definitely was stratified in clearly defined layers as the divers had claimed.

Royal and Clark were sure that this was the break they had been waiting for and that Ford would have no trouble verifying their claim. However, misfortune struck in the form of a head cold that wiped out all of their hopes. Ford had only one day to dive, and on that day he developed a head cold that prevented him from diving any deeper than 20 feet. Beyond that depth he could not clear his ears, so he returned to the surface while the others waited beside their find 35 feet down, totally helpless. Ford was sorry about the situation, but there was nothing he could have done. He left without verifying the sedimentary layers and the bones within them. And no amount of explaining by the divers as to why he did not verify the find satisfied the critics. They promptly overlooked the fact that a head cold prevented Dr. Ford from diving down and doing so. All they remembered was that he had not verified the find, which, after the story was repeated a few times, acquired the implication that the find was not worth verifying.

The next stroke of bad luck was totally unexpected. It came in the summer of 1959, disguised as what they thought was the answer to their problem: national television wanted to film the find for the Huntley-Brinkley news program.

Royal and the others were delighted with this turn of events because now the entire country could see what they had found. Every archaeologist with a television set could witness it for himself. There was not the slightest doubt in their minds that after this exposure the archaeological world would beat a path down to Warm Mineral Springs to start investigating the find of the century. This time nothing could happen to spoil their plans. That was the trouble. Everything was too perfect.

The television crew arrived at Warm Mineral Springs and set up their equipment. Powerful underwater lights were readied to illuminate the underwater stage—the productive ledge at 35 feet. Finally, the big moment arrived. The diving television technicians were in their places; the actor-divers, with Bill Royal in the leading role, were waiting on the ledge stage. Everything was ready. All that was missing was the expert television diver-photographer, who was on the surface running a last check on his expensive 35mm movie camera enclosed in its massive, metal underwater housing.

The lights came on. The actors got ready. The photographer dropped down with his heavy underwater camera...and kept going. Everyone stared as he missed the ledge and disappeared into the black depths of the springs. When he failed to reappear, Royal and the others dived down after him. They caught up to him at 170 feet, still clinging doggedly to his overweight camera. After they dragged him back to the surface the photographer confessed that it was the first time he had ever "dived" below 30 feet.

Once again the stage was set, the lights went on, the camera man moved in to shoot the scene. He wanted Royal to point out some human bones in the sedimentary layer. While the camera whirred, Bill began removing some of the untouched middle layer of sediment. Suddenly he found a human skull, then the complete skeleton. Easing the skull out of the sediment, he held it up beside his head and grinned at the camera. As he turned it over in his hand, he saw through the hole in its bottom a light colored blob of something inside the cranium. He touched it and found it was soft.

On the surface the camera crew filmed Royal shaking out pieces of the "brain." But everyone knew that was impossible. Or was it? To Royal the mysterious blob did indeed look like human brain tissue. Putting the skull in a bucket of spring water, he drove quickly to Dr. Eugenie Clark's laboratory at Placida and excitedly announced that he had found a fresh brain thousands of years old from a skeleton in the middle layer.

The news promptly ended the dissection of triggerfish Dr. Clark and Dr. Lawrence Penner, from the University of Connecticut, were undertaking at the moment. After examining the find both scientists were equally astonished by the unique discovery. They recognized immediately the two convoluted cerebral hemispheres and the cerebellum of a human brain.

Clark telephoned her physician husband and other doctors in Sarasota for their opinions. None had ever heard of a brain existing in a natural state of preservation for any length of time, especially when it was in water.

After several hours the brain began to fall apart. Clark added formalin to the bucket of water to harden and preserve the tissue. The white matter turned gray. The next day her husband sawed a hole in the rear of the skull, removed the brain, and placed it in formalin. It was then taken to various medical experts for analysis. Sarasota neurosurgeon Dr. Benjamin H. Sullivan confirmed their opinion by identifying the pieces as part of the cerebrum and cerebellum of a human brain. Pathologist Dr. John Bracken examined a cross-section sample in a stained slide preparation by microscope and found no evidence of cellular structures remaining. But biochemist Dr. Isadore Chamelin found a test fragment contained 17.1% cholesterol.

Dr. Clark wrote a scientific report about it for publication, but the piece was turned down because the editor considered the findings far too improbable. What had hurt the discovery most was the television news coverage. No one could believe that such a discovery could be made "accidentally" before television cameras. It was too coincidental. Even the scientists who heard and were at least partially willing to believe in the discovery of ancient bones in Little Salt Springs, now laughed at the idea and thought the whole thing was a hoax.

For the next six months Eugenie Clark and the others tried to find some scientific evidence to substantiate their claim. Harvard University brain-fossil expert, Dr. Tilly Edinger, wrote that there were many cases of inferior Egyptian and Peruvian forms of mummification in which the brains had been left in the cadavers and were preserved intact. But she had never heard of a brain being preserved in water. When famous anthropologist Dr. K. P. Oakley of the British Museum wrote Dr. Clark that he had found a brain from the Roman period preserved in adipocere[*], she sent him photographs and fragments of the brain. Dr. Oakley ran tests to show that the brain had been impregnated by some mineral content.

But how old was it? That was the real question.

Since the human remains had come from the middle layer instead of the bottom layer with the burned log, it could indicate that they were probably less than 10,000 years old. A technique for the radiocarbon dating of bones was just then being perfected. Royal removed the entire skeleton from the layer and sent 52 of the bone samples to Monaco, where the complicated procedure of carbon dating was undertaken by Dr. J. Thommeret, head of the radiocarbon laboratory at the Monaco Scientific Center.

It took seven years to get all the results but the answer was worth waiting for. The brain had belonged to a human skeleton that carbon dated to between 7,140 and 7,580 years old!

---

[*] A waxy substance sometimes formed from dead bodies in moist burial places or underwater.

14

DIVE INTO THE PAST
PART II

D espite the carbon-dating evidence, in everyone's mind the word "hoax" was still too closely associated with the find. Besides, who could possibly believe in the existence of a 7,000 year old human brain? Mammoths maybe from thawing prehistoric Siberian glaciers, but not fragile, organic brain cells in a tepid water environment.

That left Bill Royal with some mineralized bones, a theory and the courage of his convictions to keep trying to attract attention to what he considered was a site of major archaeological importance. To his credit, Royal guarded the bony treasures against diver molestation for the next 12 years, before he finally succeeded in interesting the proper scientists. Meanwhile, Dr. John Goggin dived briefly at Little Salt and Warm Mineral Springs and drew his own conclusions on how the bones got there. He believed they had been cleaned, disjointed, and thrown in from the surface as an early form of burial. He also felt that there were other, more virginal sites to be considered. Since the science of underwater archaeology was still in its infancy, its practitioners were feeling their way. Dr. Goggin and his graduate students were pioneering the first recovery of evidence of early man in central Florida springs right up to the beginning of the terminal illness that took his life in 1962.

Two years later Florida hired one of his graduate students, Carl J. Clausen, as State Underwater Archaeologist. Clausen immediately had his hands full supervising Florida's treasure-salvage program involving the recovery of historically valuable artifacts from period shipwrecks off the Florida east coast. So it was not until March, 1971, 12 years after Bill Royal made the find, that his untiring efforts to have qualified people investigate the site resulted in the state sending Clausen down to see it.

As a student and an admirer of the late Dr. Goggin, Clausen came well fortified with his predecessor's appraisals and opinions of the situation at both Little Salt and Warm Mineral Springs. He knew the nature of the deposits at both springs and the radiocarbon date obtained by Royal and Clark at Warm Mineral.

On two separate occasions that March, Clausen dived into Warm Mineral Springs and Royal showed him human skeletal evidence that he said had been left undisturbed. Clausen, however, was not convinced. He thought the whole site looked as if it had been "massively damaged." Since any significant archaeological work depends on the materials remaining unmoved and in context, in Clausen's mind at least, Warm Mineral did not meet these criteria. He decided, instead, to see what possibilities existed at Little Salt Springs, a more isolated, less attractive spring where he thought it more likely the deposits would be undisturbed. Furthermore, Little Salt Springs was an area that Goggin had said deserved closer examination by a qualified archaeologist.

When the property owner, the General Development Corporation, learned that the state was interested in investigating the springs, the company offered to fund the program with a seven-thousand-dollar research grant. The state accepted and in May, 1971, a team moved in to begin Phase I of the Little Salt Springs exploration. A tent and trailer camp grew up outside the perimeter of jungle surrounding the sink; a truck and heavy crane from General Development brought in a 20 x 20-foot raft which was anchored in the springs; and the site was surveyed. Clausen took a human bone sample for radiocarbon 14 dating. The result indicated that the bones dated from 5000 B.P. (before present time), or about 3200 B.C.

In November other experts arrived for Phase II. Little Salt was given a thorough geological and limnological survey by Dr. H. Kelly Brooks, professor of geology at the University of Florida, and Dr. Edward Deevey, limnologist with the Florida State Museum. The results provided some intriguing information. Dr. Deevey found that the temperature of the springs remained constant to within one-hundredth of one degree, from just below the surface all the way down to its 210-foot-deep bottom. Moreover, six feet below the surface there was virtually no oxygen in the water. Both conditions created an ideal environment for the preservation of organic material.

By floating a sonar-type Fathometer across the surface of the pool along surveyed grid lines, Dr. Brooks determined the shape of Little Salt's upper basin; then by supporting the instrument's transducer at right angles from a core-drill pipe put down into the bottom, the scientists were able to determine the shape of the lower cavern itself, giving them an accurate underwater chart of the entire sinkhole. The tip of the core drill was 27 feet into the soft mud bottom. Deevey wanted a sample of the water-bottom interface, the last zone of clear water and the beginning of the soupy bottom. It was to go in a four-foot-long plastic tube with caps on each end. To get the sample, divers would have to go down, find a completely undisturbed area on the bottom, take the two caps off, ram the tube down into the bottom, put the top cap on, lift the tube out and then put on the bottom cap.

Clausen and his assistant, Robert Vickery, were to make the dive. The procedure was critical. In over 200 feet of water, in total darkness, they had to find an undisturbed area of the bottom, remain clear-headed enough to take the sample properly, then return to the surface. Each man wore double air tanks, a compass, knife, depth gauge, decompression meter and carried a dive light. Clausen also had a powerful strobe attached to his ankle, the pulsing flashes intended to help the divers keep track of each other. To stay oriented at that depth they planned to tie a line to the bottom of the core-drill pipe, follow it out 100 feet and take their sample. Since they lacked a proper cave-diving reel, Clausen would carry down a length of 100-foot-long, one-quarter-inch diameter polypropylene line coiled loosely around his left arm.

Following the core-drill pipe, they started their descent. Suffering from a mild head cold, Clausen had trouble clearing his ears. Repeatedly he stopped to painfully equalize the pressure before continuing on. The delays added up until it took them the remarkably long time of 14 minutes to get down 150 feet. With this much time already expended, their chances of getting nitrogen narcosis increased by leaps and bounds.

Finally on the bottom at 210 feet, immersed in swirling brown silt and lighted intermittently by the almost hypnotic flashes of dazzling brilliance from the strobe, Clausen tried to tie the end of his rope to the pipe. As long moments were spent fumbling to accomplish this seemingly simple task, he realized he was feeling the effects of nitrogen narcosis. Finally, however, the knot was tied. In the glow of his dive light he took a compass bearing and started paying out the line. As if in a dream he watched it fall off his arm in slow motion, the endless golden snake lying in loose suspended coils in the dark water around him. The next thing he knew his fins had stirred up the silt into a swirling curtain that choked out all light. Then somehow he got the coils of rope wrapped around both his arms and one leg. Very carefully he tried to untangle himself. The more he worked the worse it became. His mind was foggy, but he still knew he had to get himself out of that mess or he would never leave the bottom. Once, his regulator dropped out of his mouth. He managed to get it back in again. He had tunnel vision, he was disoriented, and he was getting a little frantic with all that line tied around him. He thought if he had to cut all the loops of that 100-foot line, he was still going to be there when his air ran out.

Vickery was no help. He had narcosis as bad as Clausen. At one point he found himself in a sitting position under the bottom, totally immersed in the soupy silt. When he struggled back up out of it, he found his companion still laboring with the coils of rope.

"He just sort of hung there in the water holding this capped tube and wondering what the hell I was doing," said Clausen. "I was getting it off me and I look over and I have gotten it on Vickery, and around both ends of the tube. Then, somehow, between the two of us we finally shucked it off. By now I decided it was time we got our tails out of there."

They followed what small amount of line they had back to the core-drill pipe. Momentarily, after they reached it in the darkness and in their disorientation, even that became lost. Twice

Clausen swam up to Vickery, whom he thought was holding onto it, but who in reality was only clutching the capped plastic tube. The third time this happened Clausen took the tube away from Vickery and hurled it laterally out into the darkness. At least he thought he had done so. The next day, however, when he repeated the dive, the capped tube was found sticking up vertically out of the bottom. Clausen surmised that rather than hurling it laterally, he had been swimming sideways and had actually jammed the tube down into the bottom when he thought he was throwing it away. After that he followed the rope back to the core-drill pipe, knowing that it was the core-drill pipe this time because he had thrown the tube away. He took hold of the pipe, but then he could not tell which way was up. Since a vertical line was attached to the core-drill with one end tied to its bottom, Clausen pulled it to see which end was tight. He could not tell. Finally, however, by common agreement, the two decided on the same direction and followed it up. Once they cleared 190 feet they began to lose their narcosis and were able to surface without any further difficulty.

The next day Clausen and two safety divers returned with a small cave-diving reel of line and easily got the sample they needed.

Phase III of the operation began just before Christmas. This was to be a full-scale underwater archaeological excavation involving scientists and diving teams from the underwater archaeological research section of Florida's Bureau of Historic Sites and Properties. Specially trained volunteer safety divers Bob and Sue Friedman, Earl Walden, Paul Therien, and Sheck Exley assumed the responsibility of accompanying, monitoring and recording all dives to insure the safety of the entire group. Bob Friedman would direct all diving operations and rigidly screen each diver in a Port Charlotte swimming pool before okaying them for dives in the springs. No one was exempt from his inscrutable examination.

During this phase Carl Clausen invited me to Little Salt to dive with the group and photograph the excavation. When I arrived the team was constructing a huge, segmented 12-inch-wide injection dredge made of 40-foot lengths of PVC pipe. The giant suction pipe was to be powered by a pump on shore. Reaching halfway across the springs, the long lengths were supported at strategic points by floating 55-gallon drums. As the excavation of a small section of the bottom took place, the device would operate like a vacuum cleaner, sucking up the mud, sand and silt that the archaeologist would be carefully fanning from the site. This would then be deposited elsewhere to prevent unnecessary roiling of the water in the test area.

A shore station was set up under the palms at the edge of the springs. Specialists installed highly sophisticated electronic equipment furnished by the Communications Science Laboratory of the University of Florida, for diver-to-surface, surface-to-diver verbal communication. It would be the first time such equipment was ever used in underwater archaeology.

During the work, Clausen would wear a Kirby-Morgan Clamshell helmet, enabling him to communicate with the shore station and dictate descriptions of the work in progress into a tape recorder for later reference.

In the morning of my second day at Little Salt, Clausen wanted to show me the area he would be working in the basin of the springs. Accompanying us were safety divers Bob Friedman and Sheck Exley. We donned our wet suits and single tanks that had been filled the night before from a temporary air-fill station, set up in a clearing a few steps from the shore station. All divers in the expedition were asked to wear buoyancy-compensating (BC) vests. By inflating or deflating the vest a diver could easily maintain neutral buoyancy, neither rising nor sinking, to prevent disturbance of the heavily silted bottom and its artifacts.

Pushing off from a small dock at the water's edge, we inflated our BC vests and swam slowly across the spring to the dive raft anchored near the site where Clausen had found a concentration of human and animal bones. The water reeked of hydrogen sulfide.

Near the raft we deflated our vests and started down. Clausen and Friedman led the way; Exley and I followed, clearing our ears as we went. Visibility was barely ten feet; the murky water was yellowish brown from millions of tiny sediment particles in suspension. About 20 feet down I was suddenly caught in what felt like a strong current forcing me to the right. Trying to counter

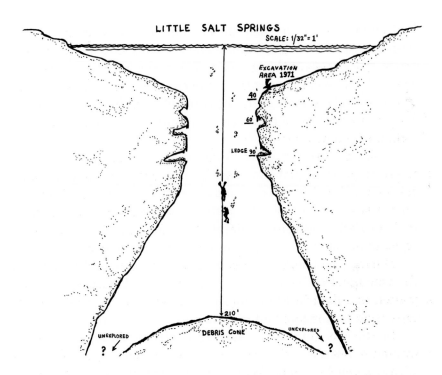

The hourglass shape of Little Salt Springs is typical of the formation created by the cave-in of the roof of an underground stream that has carved its way through the softer portions of limestone deposits. Percolation of surface waters assists this process of erosion.

it, I ended up settling backward in a vertical position. Nothing I did seemed to prevent me from turning to the right. Momentarily it flashed through my mind to get out of there, to pull my BC "rip cord" that would automatically inflate my vest and balloon me to the surface. But what puzzled me was that the "current" did not seem to be affecting my safety diver. Exley paused, looking at me. Still struggling to keep my balance, I signaled that I was spinning and shook my head.

He reached out and grasped my shoulders. We rose a few feet in the water and my spinning ceased. Then I knew what had happened, something I had only read about until then. I had had my first bout with vertigo. The condition sometimes afflicts divers who rupture an eardrum or in some other way have their sense of balance upset, sometimes simply by being visually disoriented in a water mass of tiny moving particles where there is no stable horizon. Whatever had caused it, the temporary imbalance had upset my equilibrium.

After that I was all right and continued on down to the bottom, guided by the sporadic bursts of bubbles from Clausen and Friedman's regulators.

They were waiting for us 35 feet below the surface, suspended in neutral buoyancy over a sloping bottom so obscure that, even in the dive lights, it was difficult to differentiate from the swirling brown water particles. As we drifted down toward them, Exley and I puffed a couple of breaths into our compensators, stopping our descent. Below, Clausen beckoned me with his dive light. Exhaling, I eased down beside him, careful to keep my fins away from the bottom. In the gloom he pointed and shined his light on something sticking up out of the thick, brown sediment. It looked like the upper half of a human femur. As my eyes grew accustomed to the gloom I saw other irregularities projecting from the powderlike sediment. Most were bones.

The next day, with the dredge in position, Clausen began excavating the test site, an area two meters square. Gradually, as he fanned away the detritus and it was sucked up the dredge, the bones became more prominent. Soon the entire site seemed to have sprouted mushroomlike sedimentary pedestals with each supporting a bone. After photographing them in place, Clausen carefully picked up each bone, tagged it and passed it back to safety diver Friedman, who placed it in a plastic bag for removal to the surface.

The next day, Clausen, wearing the Kirby-Morgan Clamshell helmet, had been excavating the site at 35 feet for over two hours when an accident occurred. I was on my knees beside him at the time, photographing the tagging of specimens. Just behind us a diver from the laboratory was manning the nozzle of the dredge. Apparently it was not sucking; earlier there had been a blockage. To clear it, the diver took the second stage of his regulator from his mouth, held it in front of the nozzle and pushed its purge button. A blast of high-pressure air shot into the pipe and rumbled upward, ever expanding, doubling its volume as it rushed through the narrow confines of the plugged pipe.

Next thing I knew the whole pipeline was writhing like a snake. The nozzle man held on until he was bucked off, and an excited voice boomed through the water from the underwater communications unit across the pool, "Hey you guys, get up out of there quick! Drums are busting loose all over the place!"

Bottom looked like an exploded smoke bomb. I headed for the surface. Clausen and the other diver were already there. Loose barrels bobbed across the springs. In hot pursuit, a diver in a dinghy tried to round them up. Clausen called him alongside, grabbed a rope and dived. A single, stubborn 55-gallon drum was supporting the weight of the entire dredge as it hovered over the spring's 210-foot-deep abyss. If that went, the whole works would be gone for good.

Moments later Clausen surfaced and passed the end of the rope to the boat. He had made a bounce dive down to the nozzle at 60 feet and secured it. Everything seemed fine. Then Clausen complained that his eyelids itched and his fingertips were tingling.

Safety officer Bob Friedman quickly checked Clausen's down time for the day and found that in making the bounce dive to 60 feet, Clausen had exceeded his no decompression limit. Now it appeared that he was feeling the first symptoms of the bends.

Friedman had him breathe 100 percent oxygen for three minutes to facilitate diffusion of the nitrogen in his system, then he got the archaeologist back into the water. Using spare tanks already secured for that purpose at decompression depths, Friedman and Sheck Exley took Clausen down the safety line to decompress for the next hour and 15 minutes. Because it was easiest to administer, Friedman used the British system of decompression tables and for safety's sake, he selected a decompression time that was longer than physiologically required for Clausen. When they finally came up, Clausen shivered from the cold water, but the other symptoms were gone. As luck would have it, the accident occurred during dive number 13!

In the following days the press and television people came to cover the dig. Bates Littlehales arrived with an array of camera equipment to record the event for a possible *National Geographic* magazine feature. Although some of the new arrivals had diving experience, none of the newspaper or television people passed safety officer Friedman's critical pool checkout. Consequently, a lot of frustrated reporters waited around the shore station for news developments.

During a lull in the excavation Sue Friedman took Littlehales and me down to the 60-foot ledge to see the large stalactites. Visibility was too poor for photographs, but we saw the dry-cave formations at close range with the dive lights.

As the work progressed, Clausen carefully removed layer after layer of sediment from the test area, verbally and photographically recording his every move, every detail of the stratigraphy, to assure himself of complete and accurate scientific documentation of the event for future reference. This was the first time anywhere that an important underwater archaeological site was being worked with techniques normally used in land archaeology. At the lower edge of the test site, just back from the edge of the drop-off through the central orifice of the springs, Clausen found two wooden pins or stakes that appeared to have been hammered into the bottom. Both were 35 feet underwater. "If they have shaped points we may have found something interesting," he said, speculating on their purpose. Had Paleo-man used the stakes to anchor a vine rope so he could climb down into the then dry cavern, lowering himself to the ledge below?

Clausen approached the possibilities of the pegs with the same slow, methodical precision he had employed through the entire dig. Painstakingly he pinpointed the exact location of the stakes by surface survey on a bottom-anchored marker floating directly over the find. Then he sought to determine what evidence, if any, lay below them on the 90-foot ledge.

That night, Clausen, Friedman, and University of Florida geologist George Cumming, descended down a modern line into the depths of the springs. In the stygian darkness, pierced only by the probing beams of their dive lights, they reached the rock ledge 90 feet down. According to the earlier side-scanning sonar readings, the irregular debris-laden shelf ringed the throat of the springs. Separating, the divers explored the area immediately below the stakes. The ledge fronted on a series of shallow caves, the upward sloping roof festooned with massive stalactites. As they carefully fanned away centuries of silt blanketing everything on the ledge, the divers were unprepared for the sight that met their eyes. Scattered before them were bones unlike anything they had seen in the upper pool. Specimens were bagged and brought to the surface for identification. Clausen and his team had found a veritable cemetery of fossil bones, later identified as those of prehistoric bison, mastodon or mammoth, giant land turtle and ground sloth. Had the animals fallen into the springs, or were they the leavings of some ancestral man's feast? So far, all the divers established was that early man could have climbed down a vine rope from the stakes to the 90-foot ledge.

The next day Clausen carefully fanned away the surrounding deposits and removed the 18-inch-long stakes. Both had shaped points. A sample of the wood sent for carbon-14 dating revealed that the stakes were between 9,325 and 9,965 years old.

The excavation at the 35-foot level exposed a three-layer profile, the uppermost layer about 40 centimeters thick and composed of loose, dark gray sediment containing contemporary leaves, twigs and sticks. The next layer consisted of freshwater marl, 15 to 40 centimeters thick, containing older but similar organic material mixed with clay, sand and small shells. In this area was found most of the human skeletal material, along with a large amount of charcoal. The third layer was mainly marine shell and gray sand with scattered organic material.

Until then most of the human skeletal remains had been unidentifiable bone fragments, and leg and arm bones. Then Clausen uncovered what appeared to be the front half of a human skull lying face down. He fanned away the surrounding deposit until the fragment was exposed and supported on a four-inch sedimentary pedestal. Being a stickler for authenticity, Clausen had no intention of repeating his recovery of this item for the photographers present. If we missed getting the picture the first time, we were out of luck. He intended picking up the piece only once. So after two days of fanning the debris aside and photographing the find in place, the big moment arrived. When it did, Littlehales and I were waiting patiently alongside him. Clausen carefully lifted the fragment and held it out to us in turn. The electronic flashes winked, briefly illuminating the diver in his strange-looking bright yellow clamshell helmet with his outstretched hand holding the front half of a human skull. In the gloom of the underwater cavern it was an eerie place to be looking at the bony features of a human who had died thousands of years ago.

Who was he? Why was he there? Why were all the other human skeletons there? The complete disorder of all the bones seemed to refute the idea that this was a burial site in the normal sense. It looked more like the site of some prehistoric massacre. Had one tribe caught another using their favorite water hole and this represented the result? Until all the evidence is in and the information analyzed, we can only guess at the answers. It is believed, however, that these early Floridians were hunters who killed game not with bow and arrow but with a spear-thrower, or atlatl, which hurled a lance with far greater velocity that if it had been thrown by hand. Preliminary examination of the skull and other bones indicate that Paleo-man's features resembled our own. While highly mineralized, the bones suggest that he lived primarily on a high-protein diet consisting largely of shellfish with enough grit in them to eventually wear down the crowns of his teeth. Based on skeletons found, the individuals ranged in age from six months to over forty years old. Nobody knows how they died, or how many perished at Little Salt Springs. On an exploratory dive with geologist George Cumming we spot-checked sites around the shallower part of the spring and found bones distributed practically everywhere. Someone estimated that there may be at least 200 human skeletons in the upper basin alone.

The work at Little Salt Springs came to a halt on January 12, 1972. The artifacts were packed and removed to the laboratory in Tallahassee for study. General Development Corporation encircled the entire area of the spring with an eight-foot-high, chain-link fence, topped with barbed wire to protect the site for future archaeological investigation.

Clausen then shifted the operation to Warm Mineral Springs for four days to make a test excavation at the state's expense. Underwater visibility and general working conditions at Warm Mineral were a welcome change. Clausen made several reconnaissance dives, searching for an area that had not been disturbed. "I had to really look hard for a place that had not been ruined by stripping off two of the original three layers of sediment in search for bones," he said. "Eventually, I did find an area that had been preserved from disturbance by a heavy cap of seven hundred to a thousand pounds of tufa, a form of porous limestone deposited by springs. We put in a small test and recovered the first bones that had ever been taken scientifically from the springs."

During this time Bill Royal took Clausen down and showed him a human jawbone. "It was under a heavy rock, very hard to get at," said Clausen. "The jawbone, I thought, had some of the lighter sediment under it where it should not have been." Thinking that the jaw and perhaps a skull that Royal said was behind it might have been moved, and realizing that it would be a long, difficult job of excavation and interpretation of what happened there, the archaeologist decided against recovering it. He felt that the bone material he already had was sufficient for carbon-14 dating.

It was about a year later that Clausen, who had gone on to become the state underwater archaeologist for Texas, learned the carbon date for his find at Warm Mineral Springs. Dr. A. B. Wesolowsky, University of Texas physical anthropologist, identified the bones as those of a human, possibly a six-year-old child. One is a nearly complete vertebra, the other a pelvis fragment. Carbon-14 dating showed them to be between 10,260 and 10,630 years old!

15

FINDING AMERICA'S
10,000-YEAR-OLD MAN

Once again Bill Royal must have had mixed feelings about his efforts to interest the proper scientists in the archaeological possibilities of Warm Mineral Springs. Over 12 years had elapsed since he started his crusade, and in the interim he had pretty much racked up a solid score of total rejection. Dr. John Goggin had shied away from the discovery because an amateur had found it, and the distinguished underwater archaeologist cared not to risk his reputation on something initiated by an amateur. Underwater archaeologist Carl Clausen, who shared many of Dr. Goggin's misgivings but was still willing to look, felt that Royal had already massively disturbed the site, ruining it for any future archaeological work. Despite the significance of the radiocarbon dating on the material Clausen sampled during his brief period there, he was no longer working for Florida but was already deeply involved in recovering treasure and artifacts from a 1554 Spanish shipwreck off Padre Island for the state of Texas.

That left Clausen's successor, Wilburn ("Sonny") Cockrell, in the position to decide where he wished to put the emphasis of his tenure as Florida State Underwater Archaeologist in charge of the Bureau of Historic Sites and Properties. Like his predecessor, Cockrell was confronted with the intricacies of managing Florida's treasure-salvage program, in which licensed salvagers worked for the state on a percentage basis in recovering treasure and artifacts from Florida's period shipwrecks. It was a complicated, time-consuming job for a man who was not particularly turned on by shipwreck archaeology. Nor was Cockrell particularly strong about what might be found at the bottom of a murky spring. He was more interested in finding early man sites on the continental shelf than in finding early burial sites inland.

"I declined an offer to involve myself with the Warm Mineral Springs site when I took this job in July, 1972, primarily because I felt it was Carl's [Clausen] research project and [he] expressed an interest in seeing the project continue," said Cockrell. "I thought it would be more efficient to let him run the project himself and for me to stay out of it."

Ironically, however, it was the new state archaeologist's decision to pursue his own interests that eventually led him to Warm Mineral Springs. Through the leadership of Professor Reynold Ruppe, then chairman of the anthropology department at Arizona State University and committee chairman for his Ph.D. studies, Cockrell had become involved in the theoretical search for early man sites on the continental shelf of the United States. And Florida's continental shelf is extensive, especially along the Gulf Coast where it goes out nearly 100 miles. Cockrell was so intrigued by this vast, unexplored area that when Sarasota County Historian, Doris Davis, invited him to join an informal group of interested people who were going out on a boat to dive in a submerged, freshwater spring several miles out in the Gulf of Mexico off the Florida west coast of Naples, Cockrell eagerly accepted. Included in the group were Bill Royal and his wife, Shirley.

The two-day diving excursion to the offshore springs was successful in more ways than one. Under a four-foot limestone ledge in 50 feet of water abounding with marine life, they dived to inspect the spring, with a freshwater temperature of 97°F. They had no digging equipment nor did they find any obvious evidence of human association with the spring, but Cockrell enjoyed the experience.

Before long the talk turned to other springs, specifically Warm Mineral Springs. And on that subject no one was more qualified to talk than Bill Royal.

"After being on the boat for a couple of days with Dottie Davis and Bill Royal, I got a completely different aspect of the one I had earlier," said Cockrell. "I was invited to come in and see a human mandible that Royal had found and taken out of the deposit to look at and placed back." Royal explained that about a year and a half earlier he had been removing the upper, modern layer of shallow sediment, looking for the older deposits. When he found the jawbone, he stopped digging. This was the reason for his original invitation to Carl Clausen, to show him the mandible. But Clausen, recognizing that the upper layer had been stripped off, was disinclined to spend his professional time and reputation with such deposits. He elected instead to seek out an undisturbed area for taking the samples he later had carbon dated. Then Clausen spent most of his effort working the nearby Little Salt Springs site.

Accepting Royal's invitation to dive at Warm Mineral Springs, Cockrell found it a totally unique opportunity. "Just diving with Royal is an experience in itself. Bill is one of the old-time divers who often dive alone, thereby breaking scuba diving's first cardinal rule. He dives deep and sometimes stays overly long. When he feels like it, he uses a decompression meter—a gauge that tells a diver how long he can remain at depth before he must make decompression stops on the way up or risk the bends—but it is hardly ever accurate, nor does it agree with anyone else's meter. Royal is an incredibly self-confident diver, who has survived accidents that would have killed ordinary men, always managing to escape with a minimum of scars from these ordeals. They include an armful of teeth marks, made by a reluctant alligator Royal once forcibly evicted from an underwater cave in the springs, and a platinum-capped thighbone, damaged by bone necrosis after a near fatal bout with the bends."

So Cockrell found himself embarking on a dive with a man who not only impressed him with his diving abilities, but also with the fact that he knew the location of every pebble and bone fragment in the upper 100 feet of the springs.

The other half of the experience had to do with the uniqueness of Warm Mineral Springs itself. On the surface it is a well-developed spa with snack bar, bath houses, bathing beach, and Muzak piped from palm trees beside a seemingly shallow water pond about 100 yards across. Enhancing the impression of a wading pool, a gently sloping shallow shelf has been dredged around the shoreline and a sandy beach put on it underwater. This goes out to a maximum depth of 5 feet, then, beyond a buoy line, it drops off straight down to a depth of over 200 feet.

Going off that shelf for the first time in cloudy water and sinking with no visual references for the next 30 feet, is something every diver should experience to appreciate. The underwater profile of Warm Mineral Springs is essentially the same hourglass configuration as Little Salt and similar sinks comprised of two limestone caverns atop each other joined by a chimney 70 yards across.

About 30 feet down, the descending diver sees massive stalactites and shallow caves along the walls of this chimney. So it was from here that Royal took Cockrell on a grand tour of the springs, the knowledgeable guide pointing out the sites of interest along the way, and the archaeologist justifiably impressed by everything he saw, including quite a few beautifully preserved collections of deer and extinct ground sloth bones. Royal continued on around the basin and showed him Clausen's excavation, which even after almost two years was just as clean a site as the day Carl left it, thanks to a lack of currents and only light siltation. With but a few special exceptions, scuba diving had not been allowed in the springs for the last 20 years.

Moving on to the north side of the pool, Royal took Cockrell down to a ledge filled with jumbled broken rock at a depth of 45 feet. The overhanging rock roof sloping up from the shallow cave before them contained stalactites. Royal had been fanning out a crevice under a rockfall involving three huge boulders weighing about 17 tons, when he uncovered the human jawbone. Now he pointed out his find to Cockrell, who photographed it and removed some of the associated sediments.

When Cockrell left Warm Mineral Springs that afternoon, he was more than a little impressed with everything he had seen. Now he wanted to learn more, to find out what lay beneath those huge broken rocks near the mandible, to see for himself if the deposits in that area had been disturbed.

In Tallahassee, Cockrell telephoned Clausen in Texas to learn if he planned to continue with his work at Warm Mineral. Clausen said he had no plans for the site and no objections to Cockrell working there.

Within days Cockrell was back at the springs accompanied

by two assistant divers. Anxious to satisfy himself about the stratigraphic nature of the deposits, he dived back down to the 45-foot ledge and began hand-fanning and examining the area behind the mandible, back on into the rocks behind the fallen ledge.

"I was immediately impressed by the fact that those deposits were intact, just as they were in any other portion of the springs," he said. "The leaf mold was compacted, there was preservation of roots and bark, and I recognized that the sediments were not moved in any way at all."

In the next few days Cockrell and his divers became totally absorbed in their search. Each morning Cockrell would dive down to his jumble of giant rocks, and hand-fan the narrow niches and crevices, following the sedimentary layer where it led, carefully removing it by degrees while he took samples of wood, bone, leaf mold and whatever else he turned up. The clues led him deeper into the rocks until he found himself working a small tunnel two feet high at its mouth, back to a point where it narrowed and the sediment layer continued around rocks. Still, he followed it. When the narrow tunnel proved too tight for both him and his tank, he returned to the mouth, propped the cylinder of air on rocks overhead and squirmed back onto the tunnel, clutching only the tank's hose and regulator. When at last the length of the hose proved too short to let him continue, his excitement and interest was running so high that he did something which, in retrospect, he realized was not the safest procedure: he proceeded to take a few breaths from his regulator, then leave it outside and crawl back into his tight hole and work until he needed another breath. Then he would crawl back out, hoping the rocks would not shift, to get another breath. Cockrell later recalls being so entranced with what he was doing that he had no thought for the chances he was taking. He finally ended up working entirely under the rocks, stopping only long enough to grab breaths of air from his regulator outside, while begrudging even that delay.

After a couple of days of this rather unorthodox working method, Bill Royal knew he had to come up with an answer to the problem before Cockrell or one of his relief divers worked himself so far from his air supply that something serious might happen. Royal partially solved the problem by equipping the diver with a pony bottle, a small cylinder of air that he could slide under his chest and take back in with him. Cockrell found that it beat holding their breaths. The real problem, however, was visibility. The divers had to push lights ahead of them into the narrow tunnel, then carefully hand-fan the sediments away and wait until the water cleared to record the nature of the deposit. They then collected the samples, some of which would be used for radiocarbon dating.

Working in the area of the jawbone, Cockrell and his men began finding long bones, several vertebrae, and pelvic fragments. Although somewhat scattered, they appeared to belong to the same skeleton. Could this have been a burial site? The farther he went, the more evidence Cockrell found to indicate it was.

"Finally, going on back in and removing the deposits, I eventually got to a place where I came in contact with a cranium," said Cockrell. "I was back in there around the corner, under the rocks doing this and I realized I had a lot more data than I was equipped to handle with the facilities I had. So I photographed the cranium in place and we stopped the excavation until we could come back better prepared to do the proper job that was required."

By then the news media people had descended on the group at the springs and were asking questions about the finds. All Cockrell could tell them was that there was an indication that the bones were 7,000 to 9,000 years B.C., based on the already known carbon-14 dates of the material gathered earlier by Royal and Clausen. Cockrell was assuming that the present deposits his crew was working, being at the same depth as the others, could possibly be just as old.

The news stories about the finds in Warm Mineral Springs attracted wide interest. Cockrell lacked both the staff and the funds to do a full-scale project—a fact he pointed out to the news people. Consequently, considerable interest was generated among various state politicians, historians and philanthropists eager to see the work continue. With assistance from the Sarasota County Historical Commission, the Mote Scientific Foundation and others, the state provided a fund of sixty-seven hundred dollars for at least the removal of what Cockrell was now calling a burial site.

Before the next phase commenced, however, Cockrell extended invitations to two individuals who were to make considerable scientific contributions to the project—Professor Reynold Ruppe of the Arizona State University and Dr. Vance Haynes of Southern Methodist University. Ruppe would closely assist Cockrell in the underwater excavation and recovery of artifacts, while Haynes was taken down to the site before the second major effort occurred to examine the deposits in place. Dr. Haynes, perhaps the country's leading authority on the relationship of Pleistocene megafauna (mastodon) and man, collected pollen samples at the underwater site. Cockrell knew that pollen was to be found in the spring's heavy deposits of vegetation, but as yet he had not taken any out for testing. Dr. Haynes ran the samples through his paleobotany laboratory at Southern Methodist University in Texas. The results showed fossil pollen in the springs that would help date the site. Hoaxers might be able to introduce fossil bones to the springs, but not the tons of datable vegetation. More importantly, Cockrell hoped that the fossil pollen would help establish what kind of climate existed in the area at the time the deposits were put down. Ruppe, who was strongly interested in the theoretical aspects of underwater archaeology, would remain through the entire excavation, alternating dives with Cockrell to avoid any loss of bottom time.

Two months after his initial work at the springs, Cockrell was back with more equipment, a larger staff of state divers and volunteer sport divers.

With the additional funds, the team solved some of their earlier problems. They bought two air compressors, one to power a four-inch PVC-pipe air lift to vacuum away sediments and keep the water from clouding, and another for a hookah rig. The latter is a diving apparatus employing a surface air compressor to pump air down to a diver through a length of hose. Now the excavator could work well up under the rocks with a constant air supply. A large raft was built near the site for a diver work station, and the management of the springs made a motor home available so the crew could stay close to their work.

With the operation finally in high gear the divers were working ten- to twelve-hour days. Sometimes they made night dives.

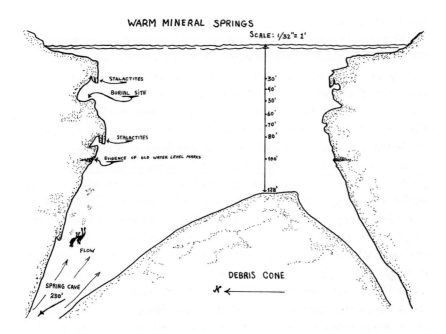

Future archaeological investigations at Florida's Warm Mineral Springs will include closer examination of the debris cone believed to contain everything ever thrown or fallen into the spring since its origin over 10,000 years ago.

While they were working at a depth of 45 feet, they had to figure 50 feet in computing their no-decompression time, which meant that only part of the time was spent diving and the rest was used on the surface, giving them time to breathe off the accumulated nitrogen in their systems. Therefore, at that depth, with no decompression, the divers could stay down only 100 minutes a day. This is not much bottom time for an archaeologist. And sometimes things happened to decrease it.

One day Cockrell was manning the nozzle of the airlift, wearing double weight belts for stability against the surge of the pipe and no swim fins to prevent him from disturbing deposits on the 45-foot deep ledge. As he laid down a tool, it fell off the ledge into the springs. Forgetting that he lacked fins and was overweighted, Cockrell plunged after it with the speed of a falling anchor. He was 90 feet down before he got his buoyancy compensating vest inflated to stop his fall. That trip cut heavily into his bottom time for the day and made him aware of the need for safety divers on the site at all times.

By the second phase, the archaeologists concluded that it would be impractical to continue tunneling back under the three huge broken rocks that blocked the site. Not only would they lose stratigraphic control over the sediment layers, but the rocks might shift or fall. The only alternative was to remove them.

Fifty-five gallon drums filled with air were to do the lifting. Ex-salvage diver Tiny Wir from Miami was on hand to help rig them. Figuring that each barrel would lift about 400 pounds, 6-8 barrels were chained around the rock to be moved first. Since it would require more lifting power to break the rock away from the sediment than to raise it the rest of the way, more barrels were attached to the chain just below the surface. If they used all the barrels at the rock, the whole conglomeration would rocket to the surface, spill air and drop the four-ton boulder back to the ledge again. Theoretically the upper barrels would do all the work of getting the rock off the bottom, while the lower ones buoyed it for disposal elsewhere.

"It was a well-planned operation," said Cockrell. "Our safety diver, the ex-salvage diver and Bill Royal were rigging the barrels. Dottie Davis, the county historian, and myself were to photograph the lifting. We were five people in the water. Everyone knew his station.

"I had gone down and was sitting on a lower ledge about 15 feet below the rock, focusing my camera, getting ready to take the picture. Visibility was so bad I could not see the rock, but I noticed when I swam down that everything was ready and all we needed was the final lifting from the barrels just below the surface. Suddenly, as I was sitting there, a fist-sized rock fell past my head. That had never happened here before and it occurred to me that it shouldn't be happening now. I left the camera where it was and kicked back to the middle of the springs to be out from under whatever was happening. As I did, the rock we were about to move came rushing down through the water onto the ledge where I was sitting, and almost crushed my camera. There was quite a bit of scurrying around after that. We were fortunate that no one was hurt. The whole thing happened when one of the divers decided that the lower barrels needed a few last squirts of air. He gave them one too many and the whole thing broke loose and shot for the surface. The people on top said it was quite a sight to see those upper two barrels shoot ten or fifteen feet out of the water, even with the rock attached. Of course, when they dumped their air, there wasn't enough lift left to hold the other barrels up and that's when the rock came sliding back down."

The next time they tried it they rigged a line all the way across the springs as a harness to control the direction of lift; then did the primary lifting from barrels in the center of that line. Moving the remaining two rocks and placing a mapping grid over the site took two weeks.

As each rock was removed, the other divers stayed away from the site to prevent any disturbance. Assuming that material directly underneath the rock would date the rockfall, Cockrell or Dr. Ruppe was the first to go in and examine the area.

Under one of the seven-ton boulders lay a broken stalactite. In the deposits beneath and around it were human skeletal remains. Below the 20-ton rock were found two more broken stalactites lying horizontal over the burial site. The stalactites had not come from the roof fall, and the scientists were at a loss as to how they got there. Had Paleo-man used them to cover the burial site? It was possible. From the samples taken there, radiocarbon tests dated them from 6000 to 8000 B.C., so the rockfall was at least that old.

The gradual fanning away of the deposits began again under less than ideal conditions. Even during the few periods when the water was clear, as soon as a diver went down to the site it rapidly clouded up. The cause was found to be the diver's own exhaust bubbles scrubbing algae off the overhanging ledge above and having it settle down over the site as sediment. Any finds were photographed in situ, with the movable mapping grid covering the area so that their exact location could be documented for later reference.

Dr. Haynes returned for the removal of the deposits. Considering the history of the site and the fact that there had been some question about the deposits being intact, it was of critical importance to Cockrell to have outside specialists there as wit-

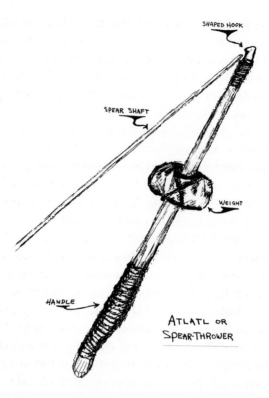

The atlatl, or spear-thrower, used by early man predated the bow and arrow. The spear or dart engaged a shaped hook of bone, wood or shell, attached to one end of the launcher and gripped by the same hand holding the weapon's butt. Serving as an extension of the arm, the atlatl was cast in an overhand or sidearm fashion. The spear was launched with greatly increased driving power while the launching stick remained in the hand. Stone weights added to the atlatl handle probably increased control and velocity.

nesses. So with archaeologist Dr. Ruppe, geologist Dr. Haynes, and U.S. Geological Survey hydrologist Dr. Francis Kohout, all on hand to verify the evidence, there would be no doubt.

Gradually the surrounding deposits were fanned away until nothing but the skull remained. Then, before movie and still photographers, it was finally removed, tagged, bagged, and brought to the surface to give the news media an opportunity to cover the event. Unfortunately the skull had been crushed when the roof of the cave collapsed thousands of years ago. The complete skeleton was not found, a result possibly, Cockrell believed, of the dispersal of the bones by rodents. However, they may still be found beyond the area excavated. At the other end of the rock-fall Royal recovered the skull of a young child, bringing to 15 the number of dismembered human skeletons recovered over the years from the same deposits.

After the major part of the removal work started, labora-tory analysis of associated organic material began. To compare results, 18 samples were sent to a New Jersey laboratory and 2 to Miami for radiocarbon dating. Four long, agonizingly slow months passed for Cockrell. He had nightmares about the samples returning with such an incongruously wide range of dates that there could be but one conclusion: the deposits were, as others had suspected, massively disturbed and completely use-less to the archaeologists. But, in fact, the results he received were far better than he had dared hope, not so much because of the age indicated, but because of the limited leeway given for each sample's date. The results showed an age range of speci-mens from early 6000 B.C. to 8360 B.C. Therefore, the oldest speci-men had a radiocarbon date of 10310 years B.P. (before present time) plus or minus 145 years, or about 11,000 actual calendar years. Cockrell had anticipated a 7000 to 9000 B.C. date, but he had also expected a standard deviation of 500 to 1,000 years for something that old. Not the tightness of plus or minus 145 years. That was almost unheard of. He sent back the Miami samples and asked for a rerun to be absolutely certain. The results were the same. Twenty samples and twenty tightly grouped dates. It signified that the radiocarbon dates obtained at different times by Royal, Clausen and, now, the team of Cockrell and Ruppe were all essentially the same for samples taken from the deposits at the same depth range in the springs. You couldn't ask for better age verification than that.

While this was an exciting, but not unexpected, revelation to the archaeologists, the test site on the 45-foot ledge did have one surprise still in store for them.

Several months after the recovery, Cockrell returned to Warm Mineral Springs for a pollen sample from the sealed site. From a small column of sediment back under the ledge, less than a foot from where the cranium was found, Cockrell fanned up a perfect atlatl, a shaped, shell spear-thrower hook. When attached to the end of a short stick or bone handle, the hook fitted the butt end of Paleo-man's spear, which he could apparently launch by atlatl much more efficiently than by hand. Cockrell recognized the artifact immediately. Only later, after closer examination of the beautifully carved hook, was he amazed to see that it still bore faint traces of the dark adhesive once used to attach it with lashing to the handle of the spear thrower. The artifact was so unexpected that Cockrell was more excited over finding it than he had been over the burial site. Under microscopic examination he found tiny shell and quartz fragments, indicating that it was probably of coastal manufacture. He was actually able to figure out the diameter and the indention of the cavity in the base of the spear, by studying the polished end of the spear-thrower spur. The artifact was so well preserved that Cockrell half expected to find the rest of the weapon intact. Was it a burial offering? Quite possibly. As nearly as can be ascertained, it is the earliest evidence of the use of a spear thrower found with an authentically dated burial site in North America.

Laymen are often puzzled by how an archaeologist can draw sweeping conclusions about the past from bits and pieces of evidence he has painstakingly recovered. What few people realize is that most such archaeological conclusions are based on a summation of information gathered from almost all other sciences: physics, especially atomic physics, with its capability of dating organic materials by measuring the decay products of certain radioactive isotopes; chemistry, with its various analytical techniques; biology, especially comparative anatomy, with its analysis of differences and similarities between organisms; botany, with its fossil pollen studies capable of indicating the kinds of vegetation and probable climate prevalent in the past; geology, of course, with its vast knowledge of the earth's history, its geologic time scale; and hydrology, dealing with the properties, distribution and effects of water on the earth's surface. With the help of these sciences the clues are analyzed, the information interpreted and the data assembled. And from this evidence the archaeologist draws his conclusions and writes his paper.

From data accumulated by Royal, Clausen, Cockrell, Ruppe and the results of the various scientific analyses, we begin to

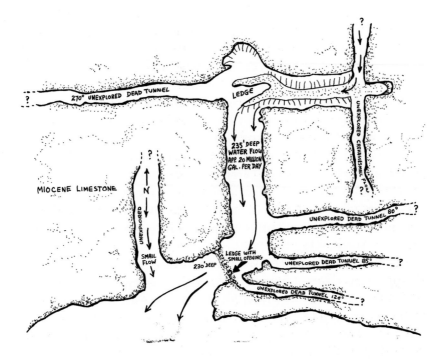

Bird's eye view of the 230-foot-deep subterranean maze from which flows the source of Warm Mineral Spring. Because of the depth, nitrogen narcosis is a primary hazard for the diving archaeologists exploring this system in their search for evidence of early man.

get a clearer picture of what life was probably like at Warm Mineral Springs over 10,000 years ago.

Geologically speaking, that time immediately follows a period of Pleistocene glaciation when the climate of southern Florida is cool and dry. Extensive grasslands and oak forests cover the terrain. A variety of wildlife abounds including the mammoth, mastodon, bison, giant ground sloth, cave bear, small horse and camel.

The sea level is 18 to 300 feet lower than it is today, exposing much more of the Florida peninsula, its surface occasionally pockmarked by the same kind of dissolved limestone pits later to be called karsts in Europe, cenotes in Yucatan and sinkholes in Florida. With the larger landmass exposed, Little Salt and Warm Mineral Springs are about 60 miles inland from the coast.

For the most part they are at this time essentially "dry" systems, with freshwater springs at their bottoms. Part of the year, when they are not living on the coast, small groups of people live around these freshwater sources. Entry and exit from the precipitously walled natural wells is by vine rope ladders and trees growing along the sinks' lower ledges. These primitive nut-gathering people hunt and protect themselves with spear throwers. On the ledges under the protective stalactite-festooned roof of shallow caves they sometimes bury their dead, covering the sites with broken stalactites. They may also practice another early form of "burial" by dismembering the body, cleaning the bones of flesh and consigning them to the depths of the spring.... The rest of the story has yet to be told.

From levels of destruction around the inside of the sink, it appears that the water level remained for some time at a point about 100 feet below ground level, leaving watermarks clearly etched in the walls of the sink. At some time the water rose rapidly enough to flood the caves and inundate great masses of vegetation. Instead of deteriorating, the organic material remained virtually intact for thousands of years. Scientists believe the reason for this is the lack of oxygen in the water below six feet.

There was no longer any doubt about the authenticity of the Warm Mineral finds or the fact that it was indeed a major archaeological site. But now it was also apparent that a larger effort needed to be made at the springs.

"The big project now is to assemble needed expertise for this department's project and continue to work there," said Cockrell. "I feel that we're probably going to find more human remains in that ledge. And I'm very intrigued with the bottom. That bottom is going to hold a record of everything that has fallen into it from the time (the sink) opened up until the time we dig it. There are hairpins and sunglasses up on top of the mound, and I suspect extinct megafauna [mastodon, mammoth, ground sloth, and so on], on the bottom of the mound, including, perhaps, burial offerings. I can't even predict...."

The apex of the debris cone in the bottom of the springs is presently 120 feet below the surface. The sides slope off to a depth of 210 feet, creating a 90-foot-high mound that undoubtedly contains the ultimate secrets of the springs. But for scuba divers on compressed air, depth will be a problem. For a diver to work a half-hour at 210 feet, he will be required to make four decompression stops totaling an hour and 20 minutes on the way up. And that half-hour is all the underwater work he will be allowed to do at that depth for the day.

Despite these problems the investigation at Warm Mineral Springs continued. Having already been granted increased financial assistance from contributing organizations, plus additional funding by the state of Florida to the amount of 97,000 dollars, Cockrell enlisted the aid of a wide range of scientific specialists in a full-scale year-long archaeological effort at Warm Mineral Springs.

This undoubtedly pleased the ever-persevering Bill Royal, who had been trying to bring this about for the last 15 years. In recognition of his efforts, on February 15, 1974, at a luncheon held in his honor, Florida's Secretary of State, Richard (Dick) Stone, presented Royal with an engraved plaque which read: *In grateful appreciation to Colonel William Royal for his contribution to our understanding of Man's past, and future, through his discovery and subsequent preservation of the early man remains at Warm Mineral Springs, Florida.*

It was a well-earned tribute to the man who had so long ago found the jawbone of a human skull and spent years trying to find a professional archaeologist to excavate the site. Carbon dating showed the jawbone and its skull to be over 10,000 years old—the oldest verified human remains, with 20 samples dated, recovered from a burial site in Southeastern United States.

Despite additional efforts made in subsequent years by underwater archaeologists, little more of significance has up to the present been learned about the age-old mysteries of early man that still remain hidden in the depths of Florida's Warm Mineral Springs and Little Salt Springs.

Bill Royal finally gave up waiting. He died in 1997 at the age of 92. In honor of his pioneering diving efforts to alert the scientific world to the importance of this site, Royal received one final tribute: His ashes were taken 235 feet down into Warm Mineral Springs and placed far back in a tight tunnel of the main spring source by *Deep Tech* publisher, Curt Bowen, wearing side-mount tanks. Bill would have appreciated that.

16

LOST

Ponce de Leon Springs, a few miles north of DeLand, Florida, is shaped like a huge bowl 150 feet across and 30 feet deep. From two openings on the bottom of the springs, some 20 million gallons of water flow each day, creating a boil on the surface. One opening is a foot wide; the other about three feet, surrounded by jagged rocks. Through the larger hole rushes the main flow of the springs.

According to local legend a party of Ponce de Leon's men was once attacked there by a band of marauding Indians. To lighten their load and protect their loot, the luckless Spaniards, so the story goes, shoved a heavy chest of gold coins into the springs and made a dash for freedom. All but one died in the attempt. Although he made it to Tampa and reported the whereabouts of the chest, continued Indian harassment prevented the Spaniards from ever recovering it.

Today, however, people still look for the treasure. Some say that on occasions when the spring's currents are extra strong, they push the chest near enough to the hole for divers to see, but they are unable to swim down through the strong outflowing currents to retrieve it.

This was the story that brought divers Charley Carneal, Ken Howe, Ken Henny, and Bill Royal to Ponce de Leon Springs several decades ago, hopeful of figuring a way to get through the hole to explore the underwater caves beyond.

Bill Royal, who already had several thousand hours of underwater diving experience in waters off both coasts of the United States, in the Caribbean, Central Pacific, Indian Ocean, Mediterranean and Black Sea, including countless descents into dozens of Florida springs, tells what happened next:

Wearing double-block Aqua-Lungs, we tried to go through this hole, but the force of the current tore our hands loose from the rocks and sent us tumbling to the surface. We tried a 25-pound weight with a line attached, but the water tossed the weight upward like a piece of cork.

Finally, we tied a rope to a 120-pound weight and worked it down the sloping sides of the springs to the opening. Getting the weight into the hole was a real job—it kept sinking into the soft sediment and clouding up the water. Finally, though, we made it. The weight fell into the hole and we let the rope slide through our hands. The weight stopped after falling only about 15 feet.

By this time we had used up about half of our air supply, so we went to the surface and discussed the next step. Before going far into the hole, we would need to drive into town and have our tanks refilled with air. Then we would take a long rope through the hole and tie it to the weight for a lifeline.

First, though, I was itching to see what was down that hole, so Charley Carneal and I decided to go down for a quick look around. Each of us had enough air for about 30 minutes, so there was little danger as long as we stayed near the opening.

Since I had the only waterproof flashlight, I led the way, pulling myself down the line against the fierce current which threw me back and forth against the rock walls and very nearly knocked the mouthpiece from my lips and the mask from my face. About six feet down, the shaft widened and the water pressure slackened off. I felt Charley grasp my flipper, and I knew he had made it too. Another six feet or so and I saw our weight lying on a limestone ledge. We were in an alcove seven or eight feet across. No treasure chest here.

The tunnel that fed the springs went off into darkness at a slight downward angle. I swam a short distance into the tunnel and saw that it opened into a bigger passage. Now there was practically no current. It was dark here, but I could look backward and see light streaming through the opening. I went a little farther and was about to turn back, when my light picked up a rectangular object on the floor ahead. My heart skipped a beat.

I had to see what it was.

When I drew near I saw that the object was a cement block with a rope tied to it and trailing off into the blackness. I pulled in the rope, which seemed to be about 60 feet long. I looked back for Charley, but couldn't see anything—not even the light from the hole. Evidently Charley had stayed near the bottom of the shaft since he had no light, and I must have gone around a curve in the tunnel, blocking my view of the shaft.

I wondered how the cement block had gotten there. Apparently other divers had been there and used the block and rope for a lifeline. I decided to do the same, and to swim about in a circle to get some idea of the size of the tunnel. I checked my depth gauge. Fifty-five feet.

Letting the rope slide through my hand, I swam deeper into the black hole, shining my flashlight on the floor. I passed a cave on my left, then an overhanging ledge. I was now in a larger chamber—my light barely reached the sides.

I came to the end of the rope and it slipped from my hand.

I reached back and felt for the rope. I turned in a circle, searching with my light. The rope should be on the floor. But where was the floor? I was suddenly totally disoriented.

There seemed to be no current, yet the rope was gone. I tried to visualize the way I had come and swam in what seemed to be the right direction until I came to a wall. Following it, I realized that another wall was close on the other side of me. I was in a narrow tunnel. Then I came to a dead-end.

Don't panic now, I told myself. *Take it easy.* I turned and swam the other way, hugging the floor. Or was it the ceiling? The floor dropped away, and I was suspended over a great shaft that dropped straight down. Or was it up? I could see the beam of my flashlight for at least 75 feet, where the light seemed to disappear into a black void. I checked my depth gauge and was surprised to see that I was 90 feet below the surface. My air would go fast at that depth.

I removed my weight belt and dropped it. The lead weights would obey the law of gravity and help to orient me. Also, with my body lighter by ten pounds I would be slightly buoyant. After the weights fell from my hand I started in the other direction, confident that I was going up. Soon I found myself in a narrow passage about six feet across. *How'd I get in here?* I turned to go back out the way I had come. *Damn. Here's another wall. Am I sealed in on all sides? No, here's a hole. Could that be the way out?*

I went through the hole and found myself in a large chamber. Now I tried to follow the direction of my exhaust bubbles. As I shined my light on them, they seemed to hang without motion. Then they drifted past my face toward my feet. *Is everything crazy? Could that be up?* I watched the bubbles as they collected in glistening pools, quivering like mercury. *That has to be the ceiling. But I can't dig my way through solid rock.*

My air began to suck hard, and I knew that I had less than ten minutes. *God, would I like to hold my babies once more. Stop that! Don't panic. Maybe this is the way out. No, no! This must be the tenth dead-end. Not much time left. There's that big hump of stone again. Third time I've passed it. Must get control of myself. Think. Look at the sediment my flippers have kicked up, hanging motionless in the water. No current here at all.*

Another dead-end. It's hopeless. I decided I must prepare to die. I'd steel myself to go like a man, not tearing my fingernails out trying to scratch my way out like a wild animal. No more than six or seven minutes. I hoped Charley was safe.

What's this? My light's going out. No. Just mud. I had gone head first into the floor up to my waist. *Must find a clean place to die. I've had a full 54 years. Why should I complain?*

But this is a hard way to die.

Is there an easy way?

Sure. Take the mouthpiece out.

Shut up! There's still hope.

My friends were standing somewhere above waiting for me. They wouldn't be worried yet. They'd know I still had air. In a few minutes they'd be plenty worried, but it'd be too late then. Maybe they'd look for me, but they'd be fools to go far from that opening. None of them had full tanks of air.

This is my tomb. Must hide my body in one of those blind holes. Or would the deep shaft be better? At least my family would be saved the expense of a funeral—that was one consolation. *I must go calmly and intelligently, not like that man Ken Howe told me about who panicked and died with help beside him, or*

*that poor kid who sucked his mouthpiece down his throat get-
ting that last cubic centimeter of air.*

*Watch that surge of panic. I must die with the dignity of a
man.*

My flashlight grew dim. I shut it off for a while as I continued to kick my flippers slowly, making each lungful of air last
as long as possible. After ten or twelve kicks I'd usually run into
a wall and follow it until it dead-ended. Then I'd turn around
and swim in another direction. Or I'd hold absolutely still, strain-
ing my eyes for a glimmer of light. My air was pulling harder. I
couldn't have much left. *Must decide on a place to die.*

Clank! The noise was startling as my tanks struck a rock—
the ceiling probably. I turned myself over and felt with my hands,
trying to seek the highest level, hoping there was some way out.
In every direction the ceiling seemed to slope downward. *It's
hopeless—why fight it?*

I turned the flashlight on again. *There's a dark hole. My coffin.* Then the light went out completely and finally.

*Where's the hole? I must find the hole. I've got to be closed in
when I die—and not just floating around like this forever.*

*I must think about my children. That will keep my mind from
snapping.* I ran into a wall and began feeling my way along it.
What's this! My God. A rope. It's the rope! Hope surged mightily
and I began pulling myself along the rope. Then I felt the block.

I'm near...so near. Which way is the shaft? I began paying out
the rope, swimming in a circle around the block, peering in every direction for a glint of that blessed light. I hit a wall and
started the other way. Another wall. I pulled myself back to the
block and started again in a different direction. Another wall.
My God, it is a tomb. I couldn't have more than a few minutes
left. Two hundred seconds, perhaps.

Finally I found a direction that permitted me to reach the
end of the rope and I lay absolutely still. *Wait, is that a current?*
It was a current, tugging at me gently, pulling me away from
the end of the rope. *This has to be the right way. The current can
only go to the surface.* I let go the rope and concentrated on not
moving a muscle. I could feel myself moving ever so slowly. When
I touched a wall or a rock, I could feel it go by me. Soon I was
moving faster. Where could the light be?

Then the current swept me upward. *Where's the light? It can't be night!* There was a surge of swift water, and I was jammed head first into an opening barely big enough for my head.

The wrong hole. I'm in the wrong hole! With all my strength I shoved against the rocks and pushed myself away from the hole. I kicked my flippers violently. The other hole was near. I had to stay away from the tiny ones.

Am I far enough away? Did I swim in the right direction? Wait. There's a current. Is it the same one? It seems to be going in a different direction.

My God! A light! The opening! There's the weight we dropped down the hole; and the blessed shaft. Swiftly I approached the stream of bright light pouring through the shaft. I twisted by the weight and started up. *Life—it's sweet.*

Something grabbed me behind the neck and held me tight while the water surged past. *Oh, no, no, no!* The limb of a dead tree was wedged between my tank and my back, holding me down. I was held at the bottom of the shaft, while the swift water pushed at me with such power that my mask was dislodged and flooded with water.

I can't do it. I can't get loose. So near and yet so far.

Desperately, frantically, I struggled. My last ounce of strength went into pushing myself down and under the limb; and when I finally succeeded and shot upward through the shaft and to the surface, I felt dazed, numb, and completely drained of energy and emotion. When my head broke the surface, brightness caused sharp pains to shoot through my eyes. I gasped and blinked and closed my eyes. When I opened them again, I thought I had never seen such a blue sky or such green trees. And the sound of kids laughing as they played on the edge of the springs was one of the most wonderful sounds I've ever heard.

My friends splashed in to help me ashore. They were amazed to see me alive. Charley Carneal had come out of the shaft 15 minutes before with his air gone and they had decided that my air was bound to be gone, too. When I appeared, they were deliberating over whether to call the sheriff and report my death or to telephone my wife.

Yes, I would dive in caves again. You don't stop doing what you love because of a close call. But it almost cost me my life to learn two important rules: never leave your buddy, and never go into a cave without a lifeline.

I also learned, to my satisfaction at least, that there isn't any treasure chest in Ponce de Leon Springs.

Several years later, Bill Royal had another near-fatal cave-diving accident. This time it was in Warm Mineral Springs, where he had been diving sporadically since 1960. By March 1970, he began in earnest, diving there seven days a week, trying to uncover sufficient material to work up interest in the scientific community for a full-scale archaeological study of the site. Royal made himself familiar with all areas of the springs. Leaving no corner unexplored, he dived to the very source of the springs itself—a cave 210 feet below the surface of the greenish, dark, silt-laden world at the bottom-most extremity of the sink. From a shallow opening beneath a ledge came a strong flow of water issuing from the boulder zone at a temperature of 97°F. He dived down to this deep fountainhead often, excavating around its entrance so he could enter the main shaft. He set up lifelines leading deep into its interior, rigged a 500-foot electric drop cord to a 1,000-watt bulb inside, measured the distance and direction of the cave's tunnels and made a rough survey of the system. It took him many dives over a period of several months to do these things, but once they were done he reached the point where he would be able to spend some time exploring the tunnels. Then, on March 18, 1972, the accident occured.

Royal had spent most of that day at the springs. In the morning he had joined his teenage daughter and a friend for a dive to 40 feet. Later he practiced free-diving down to 50 feet, hyperventilating to extend his underwater time. He did this from about eleven o'clock in the morning to three in the afternoon, while awaiting Dimitri Rebikoff and his wife who were to arrive in their airplane that afternoon. Rebikoff, a pioneer underwater photographer, inventor, and developer of manned vehicles, wanted to shoot some more underwater sequences for his movie, *The Earliest American*.

The party arrived at the springs about three o'clock. Since Royal had been taking photographs inside the deep cave with Rebikoff's Nikonos camera, which had a specially corrected 28-

mm lens, he decided to finish up the pictures there so he could return the camera to him that day.

While the others were taking photographs in the shallower waters of the springs, Royal prepared to make the deep dive alone, as he had so many times in the past. His normal procedure was to place extra scuba tanks at the 30-foot ledge in case they were needed for emergency decompression—a safety precaution he hadn't had to use in over a year. During his descent down the lifeline to the mouth of the cave, he wore a standard set of double tanks, both filled to 2,400 psi (pounds per square inch) pressure, with a small (20-cubic-foot) pony tank attached. In addition he carried a single (72-cubic-foot) tank also containing 2,400 psi of air. Normally he used this tank to go from the surface to the tunnel entrance, consuming half its air getting to the bottom. Leaving this tank outside the entrance, Royal would go in the cave on his doubles. At this depth and pressure he consumed his air at the rate of about ten pounds per breath, leaving him not more than ten or twelve minutes to work inside the cave. Then he had to leave, pick up his single tank at the entrance and use it to get him up to his decompression stop.

On this day, however, he changed his routine. Since his spare tanks were being used by the other divers, he had none to leave at the 30-foot shelf for a decompression emergency. Instead of carrying the single tank that usually got him to the bottom, he left it on the 10-foot ledge and decided to rely on the 20-cubic-foot pony tank to get him down to the tunnel entrance. Before leaving he plugged in the 500-foot extension cord to his 1,000-watt light awaiting him in the cave tunnel.

Then, wearing his double tanks, carrying his camera, flash, a hand light and the pony tank, he started down the guideline leading into the heart of the springs. As Royal rapidly descended through the darkening green depths he felt uneasy. He did not like the idea of making the deep dive so late in the afternoon.

Coming down the 35-degree wall slope, he stayed well above his guideline to avoid stirring up loose sediment which would roll down the steep incline and obscure the cave entrance. As luck would have it, however, he ran into sediment near the bottom. By the time he reached the end of his guideline at 210 feet down, visibility was so bad he could not see the cave entrance.

With his pony tank almost exhausted, he left it on a block of tufa and switched to his others. Breathing from the doubles, he started for the cave entrance instead of following his guideline. In the sediment he swam to the left of the entrance, missing it for the first time in over a year. Four minutes of precious air were wasted in trying to find the entrance. Again a feeling of uneasiness came over him. Things weren't right. He was tempted to abort the dive. But that thought, too, bothered him. "Abort" was a dirty word to an Air Force pilot. It meant a mission had to be canceled because of some failure, usually a human error.

Shrugging off his uneasiness, Royal decided to make a quick trip of it—go in, get his pictures, and get out. He followed the guideline to the 5-foot-high, 20-foot-wide cave entrance, feeling rather than seeing his way through the stirred up sediment. Fifteen feet in from the entrance the rope passed under a ledge and entered a small V-shaped hole barely big enough for a man and his tanks to get through. Royal swam on, squirming through the small opening, his tanks scraping rock. It was the only way in or out of the tunnel system.

Beyond the ledge the rope ran 15 feet due east, where it was tied off at a depth of 220 feet. Then it made a right-angle turn north along the tunnel's east wall, with markers and tie-offs every 30 feet.

Royal followed it swiftly, confident of his every move. Behind him the sediment closed in, but ahead the 97°F water was perfectly clear, flowing toward him from the spring's source. He went 110 feet into the narrow tunnel, knowing the distance because he had left his 1,000-watt light there on the west wall of the tunnel. Now he saw it was out, the bulb flooded.

He checked his pressure gauge. A thousand pounds left, the amount he usually had when he left the cave and was coming up. Talk about things not going right! To hell with this, he thought. I'm getting out of here.

He started back the way he had come, following the guideline along the east wall of the tunnel. Another line and the electric cable stretched along the west wall, but only the line he followed would lead him out through the small hole under the ledge.

Twenty feet from the right-angle turn that would take him there, the line suddenly went limp in his hands. Royal knew the trouble he was in the instant it happened. The rope had broken loose from its mooring. All he could do now was pull it taut and hope that it did not slide to the right and bury itself under the rock ledge.

He tightened up on it. Then he cautiously followed it into the swirling sediment. His light was of no use now, only his touch. He followed the line down under the ledge and ran into a solid rock wall. As he had feared, the rope was wedged in a narrow crevice. It was not the way out. He worked to his left, knowing that the hole was not more than 12 feet away. He felt along the rough barrier in front of him, but could not find the opening.

Disgusted, he turned and swam back, following his line into the tunnel until after about ten feet he came out into clear water again, the flow of the springs. Eventually it would wash the sediment out through the entrance so that he could see the opening. But by then, it would be too late. He was already so low on air that he would not take the time to look at his gauge. He was in the middle of the tunnel and could see his light cable and the other line along the west wall.

The hole was there someplace, he had just missed it. He followed the line back to the ledge and in the total darkness of swirling mud particles he tried again. But again he could not find it. He turned around and went back to the clear water. He knew he was in serious trouble now, even if he got out. His hand tightened on the rope. If he lost it there in the darkness he could easily go into a dead-end tunnel to the left of the ledge. And if that happened...

He went back to the ledge. His free hand groped along its base where the ledge met the mud. What a hell of a thing when you can't squeeze down in the sediment far enough to get under the ledge, he thought. Time is short. I'm letting everyone down who had faith in my ability to take care of myself down here. He thought about his other close escape 13 years earlier. There wasn't much hope on that one, but I made it and I've got to make this one too.

He swam back into clear water again. What now? Grab the other line and the light cord and drag them all to the left where the opening should be? Every breath was an effort now. He was running out of air. If he didn't make it this try, there would not be time for another. He swam to the west wall, scooped up the light cable and guideline and with all three together he followed them into the sediment...into the rock wall again. Wasting precious seconds he tightened the lines and pulled himself along them where they led to the left. Then he felt himself sliding through the unholy hole!

He wriggled from under the ledge, sucking hard to get the air from his tanks...now, just ten feet farther and he would be in the clear. As he went through the entrance, his air gave out. Outside the cave he grabbed up the nearly exhausted pony tank he had left there, remembering to blow the sediment out of its mouthpiece before sucking in so that he wouldn't choke. The next thing he knew he was not moving, his hand light was tangled in the rope. Slashing it free with his knife, Royal headed for the surface as fast as he could swim, hoping there was enough air left in his small cylinder for a dash to the ten-foot ledge and his spare tank before it ran out. It was too late now to wish he had left a 72-cubic-foot tank on the bottom so he could have come up slowly to let the nitrogen release itself normally. Now he would be lucky to get out of it alive.

As he rushed upward through the water toward the circle of light high overhead, he glanced at his decompression meter. It read close to 40 feet, the depth he would have had to stop at for his first decompression. At 65 feet, severe pain stabbed his back and under his rib cage. Pulling and swimming as fast as he could up the sloping line from the 60-foot tie-off, he hoped to see Rebikoff and the other divers in the water, but there was no sign of them. A picture came into his mind of his old friend Colonel Reynolds Moody sitting in a wheel chair for 14 years from an air embolism caused by a diving accident.

When he reached the ten-foot ledge and got the mouthpiece of the spare tank in place, the air in his pony tank was completely gone. Ten seconds more and it would have been too late.

He went back down to 30 feet, not daring to go deeper because he had to make the single tank of air last until help arrived. The other divers should have been in the water by now. His body pricked all over; his neck and chest ached severely. Every gasping breath was excruciating. Royal knew he was bent but good. It was decompression sickness: the bends. His long, fast rush up from the depths without slowing down or stopping to get rid of the nitrogen in his system was taking its toll. Nitrogen was bubbling in his system like soda water, the tiny gas globules trying to get out, jamming his joints, putting the pressure on his nerves with agonizing results.

After waiting a half hour without seeing any divers, Royal knew he had to go to the surface and tell his wife he was in serious trouble and needed double tanks for decompression.

He surfaced and shouted for help. Diver Phil Levine responded immediately by snatching up a set of doubles and hurrying to his aid. He helped Royal on with the tanks and accompanied him down one of the guidelines to 155 feet. Then Levine returned to the surface to get other tanks and divers.

On the way down, Royal was relieved to feel the pains begin to leave his body as he passed the 140-foot depth. After a prolonged wait at that depth he gradually worked his way up slowly, but the damage had already been done by his forced rapid ascent. As he rose this time, the pains returned. At about 130 feet he met Levine coming down to see how he was. Meanwhile, Royal's wife, Shirley, was telephoning the news to friends and professional diver Tiny Wir, who immediately called for medical and police assistance. Both were standing by when Royal finished out his decompression with Wir and Rebikoff, who helped him ashore a couple of hours later.

Rushed to the hospital, Royal was x-rayed to see if he had suffered an air embolism, a leakage of air bubbles directly from the lungs into the blood stream. After a clean report, there came a fast flight in Dimitri Rebikoff's airplane to the nearest available recompression chamber at the Naval Ordinance Laboratory in Fort Lauderdale. Then began an ordeal of another kind. For the next five hours Royal underwent decompression in a huge steel tank, resonating with the roar of compressed air building to pressures simulating a dive to 165 feet and subsequent ascent to the surface. He emerged with no feeling in his left arm, little in his right, and paralyzed from his waist down.

Following another long siege in the pressure chamber, the next day he was moved to the Veterans' Hospital in Miami. Specialists in Washington and Key West were consulted about the special treatment required to remove the nitrogen bubbles lodged in Royal's spine, causing the paralysis in his lower extremities. Two weeks later he was released, but it was months before he recovered the complete use of his legs and arms. But even before that, Royal was back at his favorite springs, helping himself into the water with his crutches so he could still enjoy his favorite sport.

Today, as a result of bone necrosis[*] from his near-fatal diving accident, he wears a platinum cap on the ball of his right femur.

Warm Mineral Springs cave missed getting its victim this time, but it was not the last time it would trap a diver.

The next time it happened was in March, 1973, after state archaeologist Sonny Cockrell and his team had completed the initial recoveries of the human skull and bone material from the burial site on the 43-foot ledge.

During the previous period of underwater work at the springs, Cockrell had dived down to the deep cave several times with Bill Royal. He had been in the tunnel beyond the ledge where Royal had been trapped, and now Royal wanted to take him down again to show him an area he had not seen before.

Charlie Patton, a reporter with the *St. Petersburg Times*, would accompany them as safety diver. Spare air tanks were left at the decompression depths. Royal and Patton wore 90-cubic foot tanks and carried dive lights, depth gauges, knives and compasses. Cockrell wore twin 72's with an octopus rig, a spare second stage regulator to use in case the main regulator malfunctions, or to pass to another diver who is out of air. In addition to the usual equipment he carried a decompression meter, two dive lights and an emergency flasher. The plan was to make a bounce dive (down and up with little delay), with Patton waiting outside the cave while Cockrell and Royal went inside briefly, then emerged to start back up.

This plan went awry from the beginning. The descent down through the warm, green water took longer than they had anticipated. By the time they reached the bottom, they were al-

---

[*]Medically termed "dysbaric necrosis," the disease often strikes divers going too deep and staying underwater too long. Tiny air bubbles block blood vessels in the bone, causing areas to eventually die and collapse. The damage to hips, shoulders or limbs requires plastic or metal replacements.

ready into a decompression dive. But since they had the spare tanks waiting on the ledge above them, it was no problem.

Patton took up his position outside the cave. The others entered on the guideline, Cockrell leading the way to the ledge where he had already been. He took a reading on his compass for an opening on the right where he thought Royal meant for him to go.

As he started swimming in that direction, however, Royal quickly flashed his light at him, signaling him back. "Apparently," thought Cockrell, "he wants me to go into the tunnel where we had already been."

They were at 210 feet, but Cockrell had no conscious sensation of feeling any narcosis yet. He was not the least apprehensive, but felt good about the dive, even a little elated about leading the way into the cave and seeing it all again, confident that, according to their agreement, Royal would be just five feet behind him.

Whether he was aware of it or not, narcosis probably accounted for Cockrell's failure to take a new compass bearing on the direction he was going, and for some of the events that followed.

He followed the guideline, sliding his hand along it with the standard finger-and-thumb loop; Royal was directly behind him. As Cockrell squeezed through the small opening under the ledge and came out of the sedimentation on the other side, he figured Royal meant another ledge further on, one which he could not see at that point. But ahead of him was a bend in the cave so he swam on, totally absorbed with what he was seeing.

"I swam into a tunnel with very low clearance, perhaps only a couple of feet," said Cockrell later. "I swam back into it and at this point the whole dive became confused. After that I could not remember whether I had been holding the safety line or not. But apparently I let go of it when I turned around because I was instantly engulfed in sediment. At that point I experienced my first real apprehension. Royal was no longer with me, and I had no idea where I was.

"My first reaction was to keep calm and stay where I was until the sediment cleared and Royal found me. But in the next five minutes neither happened. The sediment was so heavy that

I couldn't see my hand in front of my mask until I shined my light toward my mask, and barely made out its outline. I tried to remember Royal's sketch of the cave system so I might be able to recompute what the angle of this tunnel was compared to the one I had taken a compass angle on earlier, hoping to get a direction that I could start in if Bill didn't come. But I couldn't do it. I was too narced out.

"Finally I had to give up completely on the compass angle, thinking that anything I came up with would probably be wrong, and I'd be worse off than when I started. I then reached for my guaranteed-to-250-feet emergency flasher and it had collapsed under pressure. After that I turned on my secondary light and kept one pointing behind me and one in front so that I could get Bill in any direction he came. Then it dawned on me that I couldn't even see their beams unless they were at right angles, so I turned off my secondary light and just lay there waiting. When I finally realized that the lights weren't doing me any good and it was taking Bill a long time to find me, I began getting nervous. There was no panic yet. Not yet. But things I had heard from divers who had made body recoveries in caves kept creeping into my thoughts...stories that never made print, about divers in their last agonizing moments clawing at cave walls until their fingernails came off...." Cockrell fiddled with his equipment, did things to force his mind off his predicament.

Then suddenly from out of the silt came Bill Royal. Cockrell shined his light directly on him and was able to see him in the gradually clearing water. He had visualized their frantic search for him and now he did not want Royal to think he would react like a panicked diver, grabbing him in a death grip. So Cockrell reached out slowly and gently squeezed his hand to let him know that he was all right. Royal returned the squeeze, turned and swam away rapidly.

Cockrell was shocked. He didn't even have time to react, but struck out after Royal, trying to catch up to him. Frantically, he thought if he could just touch his foot he could follow him out. It did not even occur to him then to wonder why Royal was leaving him.

With the thick sediment swirling around him, all Cockrell managed to do was brush Royal's flipper as he swam off. Cockrell rushed on in blind frustration until something solid smashed into his back and chest. Bright lights seemed to explode before his eyes; sharp pain jabbed at his shoulders and chest. He had swum headfirst into a narrow crevice, wedging himself and his tank between the wall and the floor.

Total, unreasoning panic surged over him. He was trapped! The one man who could have saved him had left him to die! There was no question in his mind now. Others had died with much more going for them. But here he was 230 feet underwater and God knows how far back in a silted-up cave, caught tight, without anybody probably even looking for him anymore. *God, I've done it, I've really done it! I'm going to die!* He gasped breaths. Wild thoughts flashed through his mind. He remembered Royal saying he wanted to get in a hole where his body would not be found, and so did Cockrell. He was ashamed and embarrassed and did not want them to find his body there. He wondered who would find it, because there would be no one with any air left, and if Royal and Patton had already gone up, he was there alone now....

Ten minutes passed like hours before he forced his narcotized mind away from the morbid thoughts and tried to focus it on other things. He tried to breathe more slowly and normally, to try to push back the panic. He had to sharpen up and think.

There was no longer any need to stay in one place hoping to be found. Swimming around might get him completely out of range of any search effort—if one was still going on, which he doubted—but at least he would be trying something, keeping his mind off the other things.

Cockrell started squirming backward. Sharp limestone fragments that had gotten between his tanks and his back, cut and scratched him painfully. But finally he extricated himself. He still had air—not a great deal, but enough to go on a while longer. He swam away from the construction until he found himself in open water again. But he groped blindly, unable to see or touch anything recognizable. It puzzled him to find the sediment not clearing away, but always blanketing him like a suffocating shroud. At times he was sure his light had gone out, but when he pointed it at his mask he saw its dim, yellow glow.

He swam on and eventually reached clear water. To be able

to see something other than that enormous, all-enveloping murk was as overjoying to him as sight returning to a blind man. He swam further into the almost shockingly clear water and suddenly came upon a fixed line. One of Royal's guidelines!

His heart surged with renewed hope. He started following the guideline, then abruptly stopped, completely distressed by the realization that if he was swimming into clear water, then he had to be going deeper into the cave, instead of out of it. Back through the sediment was the way out. Or was it?

It took all the courage Cockrell could muster to make himself go back the way he had come, back into the blindness of heavy sediment...and maybe another dead-end rock crypt. But with his thumb and finger ringing the guideline, he followed it. How long it took or how far he swam, he never remembered. Sometime later he squeezed through the small V-shaped opening under the ledge and made his way out the entrance of the cave.

His first thought when he saw safety diver Charlie Patton squatting outside was, *I'll never go in the water again. Period. I can go back to land archaeology where this never happens.*

Patton was making rapid gestures with his thumb toward the surface. He had been sitting there, not moving, conserving his air. Since he was using only a single 90-cubic-foot tank, his air was getting low.

Cockrell pointed at him and put up one finger to indicate one diver. Patton pointed at Cockrell and held up two fingers, for the two of them. When Cockrell held up three fingers and made a question gesture with his hands, asking, "Where is Bill?" Patton pointed back at the cave.

Cockrell turned and started swimming back toward the entrance. He simply could not see leaving Royal in there as long as he still had any air left. Just as he started back into the cloud of sediment, he met Royal coming out. Everyone gave each other an OK sign and they started up for the surface, following the guideline to the first of their long decompression stops.

When they came out of the water sometime later, Royal asked Cockrell where he had been, saying that he had lost him. Cockrell looked at him in silence. When they compared experiences he learned that Royal had searched through the sediment for him and was under the impression that, when he ran into him and squeezed his hand, that he, Royal, was actually outside the cave and had encountered Charlie Patton. That was why Royal left so abruptly, to go back and find Cockrell.

Mistaken identity? Apparently. But Cockrell was wearing long hair, a full beard, prescription lenses in his mask, double tanks with an octopus rig, and had on a white shirt but no wet suit, while Patton had short hair, no beard, a single tank, no octopus rig and was wearing a black wet suit.

At depth, there is no accounting for the effects of nitrogen narcosis.

Could a similar accident have occurred under seemingly less dangerous circumstances, say at sea, in a relatively shallow water cave with many exits, no extreme sedimentation and no diver narcosis? The answer, of course, is an emphatic yes, as California diver Don K. Tooker found out one moonlit October night in a Laguna Beach cove.

Tooker and his companion had come to the cove to dive for the California spiny lobster that often came out at night to feed and prowl the bottom. The water was perfectly clear and averaged about 25 feet deep. Tooker, wearing a full wet suit and scuba tank, carried a ten-cell sealed Allen light for searching out lobster on the sand-and-rock bottom. He was using a new lightweight aluminum tank he had purchased the day before. Besides being more comfortable to wear, it held almost as much air as the big old heavy set of double steel tanks that he had left home for the first time in 16 years.

Snorkeling along the surface above him, carrying the game bag, Tooker's safety buddy would keep track of him by the glare of his light.

The two swam out from shore into the gentle Pacific swells. It was a perfect night, with a full moon and sparkling water. Tooker dived and moved along the bottom, playing his light beam over the rocks and marine growth. A rocky overhang loomed ahead. He angled down and went under it, surprised to find its eelgrass-covered wall receding into a large underwater cavern. Exotically beautiful niches opened up before him, resplendent in their colorful growths, tiny shimmering fish and an occasional lobster too small to be legal.

From one miniature aquarium to another, Tooker swam effortlessly in and out of the rocky corridors, fascinated by their beauty. Then he spotted what he had come after—a large six- to seven-pound lobster. But try as he might, he had trouble cornering the elusive, back-scuttling crayfish. Finally, after ten minutes of chasing it deeper into the cave, the struggling prize was his. Tooker turned to go up to his buddy on the surface, but found, instead of the open sea overhead, that he was enclosed in a rocky vault.

Backing out of the dead-end he started in the direction he thought he had come. Now, however, things were different. Wave action had picked up on the surface, and a strong surge swept through the cave, making swimming more difficult. To make matters even worse, it stirred up sand, drastically cutting down his visibility.

He glanced at his Sea-Vue gauge. About ten or fifteen minutes of air left. No serious problem yet. Ahead of him were three corridors to choose from. They all probably led back to the main cavern, but he did wish he knew which one he had come down.

Tooker swam into the largest one. An instant later the surge slammed him against the rock wall so savagely that it tore away his mask and mouthpiece, and knocked the light out of his hand. The only thing he retained a depth grip on was the lobster, which he promptly released.

Now, for the first time, the full impact of his predicament hit home. He was trapped in a cave and minutes away from drowning!

His flaying hand caught his mouthpiece. He jammed it between his jaws, thankful for the blast of cool air it still delivered. He found and cleared his mask, then recovered his light, still fortunately attached to his wrist by a nylon cord. If he lost or broke that one simple and now extremely precious piece of equipment, it was all over.

His breath came in short, rapid gasps. Panic edged in on him. Aware that it had to be kept back if he was ever going to get out of there alive, Tooker forced himself to stop gulping, to slow down, to keep his mind off the morbid thoughts trying to fill his head.

It was not easy, but he at last succeeded in controlling his breathing; then he concentrated on finding his way out.

He swam again toward the corridors, only to be knocked back again by the surge. There had to be other ways out of the cave. If it were daylight outside he could have seen them, but not at night with the sand swirling around him.

You haven't been diving for 20 years for nothing, he told himself. Think. There has to be another way out.

He turned around and swam some 20 yards back into the dead-end where he had been. Frantically he searched the rock wall looking for something he vaguely remembered seeing before. There it was, part way down, a small hole! It wasn't big enough for him to get through, but his light could. He pushed it through and shined it up. Above, he saw the beam reflecting on a foam-flecked, moving surface. So close, and yet so far.

He dropped down to the bottom of the wall, his light sweeping the darkness of every nook and cranny, then, between two huge boulders, he found what he was looking for, a V-shaped opening! It was his last chance.

He pushed himself into it. His head and shoulders were almost through, when his tank stuck. There was no time to waste. He was running out of air. It was this way or no way. He squirmed like an eel, slipping forward a few vital inches. Then he exhaled every last molecule of air in his lungs and tried again.

This time he scraped through the hole—home free! He surfaced in a narrow channel leading back to the sea. A few minutes more and he found his buddy waiting for him on the beach. Losing track of the light, he thought Tooker had come ashore.

It was only later that Tooker fully realized how close it had been. The only reason he got out of the small hole was because he was wearing a single tank. If he had been wearing his big set of doubles as he usually did...

On such slim threads of chance hangs the life of every unwary, untrained, unprepared diver who ever ventures into an underwater cave. No one knows how many have survived near-fatal accidents in these flooded catacombs. Most of the ones we know about are those who didn't.

17

LURE OF THE LABYRINTH

Morrison Spring in northwestern Florida is one of the more versatile springs in the state. The dish-shaped limestone basin features two caves and a strong flow of usually crystal clear water. Since the basin combines good visibility with unobstructed depths, scuba instructors often bring their classes there for checkout dives. Forty-five to fifty feet underwater, a well-lighted horizontal upper room with no currents appeals to the intermediate cave diver. A strong flow issues from the mouth of the second cave at about 65 feet. Once a diver fights his way through this current and penetrates the relatively narrow opening, he spirals down into a large room at 100 feet. Today, that's as far as a diver can go. But in the past before it was closed from this lower chamber, a tunnel led ever downward. Explored down to 290 feet, it continued on to unknown depths.

Morrison Springs not only attracts divers throughout Florida but also from surrounding states. So it was one early April in the late 1960's that four young Georgia divers, David Powell, Gordon Ayres, Vic Cranford and James Kelly, came there to dive. Cranford and Kelly met the other two boys for the first time at the springs.

Diving conditions were not as ideal as they had hoped; the water was somewhat murky from recent heavy rains. The manager of the air-fill station beside the springs warned the boys about diving under these conditions, but it was a bright April day, they had driven some distance for this outing and they intended to make the most of it.

Twenty-three year old James Kelly, recently discharged from

the army, and his companion, Vic Cranford, made a brief bounce-dive down to the mouth of the second chamber and found the water clear in the immediate vicinity of the lower cave. Feeling somewhat ill after the dive, Cranford decided against going back down. Instead, he returned to their car, where he put some medicine on an injured right hand and fell asleep around ten o'clock in the morning.

Finding himself without a diving buddy, Kelly joined forces with the only other divers preparing to enter the spring, 19-year-olds Powell and Ayres. Both boys were inexperienced divers; for one it was his first dive and for the other it was his second. But they felt no sense of danger or apprehension—after all, they were carrying with them a 300-foot length of red-and-white, floating polypropylene ski rope. How could they possibly get lost when all they had to do was follow this rope?

About two o'clock in the afternoon Cranford awakened, but could not find Kelly or the other boys. His diving gear was also missing. The manager of the air station was in town, but his wife, who had just returned 20 minutes earlier, said she had not seen the boys. A fisherman told Cranford that earlier in the morning he had seen a diver in a boat over the boil in the middle of the springs.

Fearing the worst, Cranford borrowed some diving gear and entered the springs. As he descended to the second chamber, he saw the body of one of the boys outside the mouth of the cave. It was entangled in the ski rope from the waist down and the currents were buffeting it against the rocks outside the cave. Lacking a knife, Cranford could not cut him loose.

Forcing his way down through the currents, following the taut line, Cranford entered the second chamber. Above him, being beaten against the rocks of the ceiling, was the other boy's body, completely entangled in the same length of ski rope. Pushed upward by the strong current, it anchored the other body outside the cave. On the floor of the chamber below, Cranford found the body of James Kelly, his face mask pushed forward on his regulator and several deep fingernail gouges in his forehead.

Eglin Air Force Base divers made the body recovery. Searching for clues to the cause of the tragedy, they found that the diver on the rope outside the cave had no knife, no weight belt, and his 72-cubic-foot air tank with a K valve (no air reserve) was empty.

The diver on the rope inside the cave also wore no wet suit. He wore a weight belt; his knife sheath was empty. His 72-cubic-foot tank had a J valve (air reserve), but since he had not pulled the rod that would have given him a few minutes more, his tank still contained 250 pounds of air. He had hemorrhaged in his mask.

Kelly, on the floor of the chamber, wore a weight belt and wet suit. His knife was still in its sheath. He, too, had neglected to pull the rod on the J valve of his 72-cubic-foot tank, which therefore still contained 250 pounds of air.

From the evidence, authorities concluded that this is what happened: While Kelly stayed behind on shore, Powell and Ayres descended to the second chamber, tying one end of their ski rope to a log outside the cave before descending with it into the cavern. On the surface the air in their single tanks would have lasted for over an hour. But now, at their depth of about 90 feet, they were under 4 times greater pressure and their air would last only a fourth as long. So, instead of the anticipated hour of leisure cave exploring, they had little more than 15 minutes. And few things will panic an inexperienced diver faster than running out of air unexpectedly.

After swimming around in the dark chamber, exploring it with his hand light, the boy wearing the tank with the J valve found it gradually more difficult to suck air from his regulator. Not realizing that he could pull down the rod on his J valve for the 250 pounds of reserve air that would have gotten him safely back to the surface, he made a panic ascent from the bottom of the second chamber, holding his breath. The rapidly expanding, high-pressure air ruptured his overexpanded lungs and caused him to suffer a spontaneous pneumothorax (air filled the space between the lungs and the lining of the chest wall on either side). This explains why he was later found floating near the ceiling of the vault even though wearing a weight belt.

It appears likely that his companion accompanied him in his panic ascent in an effort to help, and the two of them became entangled in their own unreeled buoyant lifeline. This would-be rescuer may have removed his buddy's knife to try and cut themselves free. But in the confusion, it slipped out of his hand and was lost.

Now the second diver began to run out of air. In an attempt to reach the surface, he swam out the cave mouth. But the rope, still tangled about his lower body, was abruptly jerked tight by the strong upsurging current. At its other end, his companion's entangled body jammed up against the ceiling to become a fatal anchor. Lacking a knife to cut himself free, he perished.

No one knows how many minutes elapsed before Kelly became alarmed about the missing boys, but it was probably well after the time it took for their air to be exhausted.

Apparently he borrowed a boat from the beach and paddled out to see what was wrong, and this was the person the fisherman reported seeing. Looking down through the boil of the springs, Kelly may have glimpsed the diver's body entangled outside the second chamber. Returning to shore, he borrowed his sleeping companion Cranford's diving gear and swam out to the springs. Although Kelly had dived before, he was not a certified diver and lacked any formal training in the use of scuba—an oversight that was now about to become costly.

As he approached the diver's body entangled outside the second chamber, for some unexplained reason, Kelly did not use the knife he carried to cut him loose. Instead, he fought his way down through the exit currents and successfully entered the second chamber. As he did so, he apparently suffered a massive sinus hemorrhage, or possibly a simultaneous ruptured eardrum, causing great pain and vertigo. The pain could easily explain his gouged forehead. It also seems likely that, either from this or from striking his head against the rock wall, he lost consciousness and sank to the floor below. When his air ran out he never awakened to pull the reserve rod on his J valve, or to drop his ten-pound weight belt. His knife was still in its sheath.

Powell, Ayres and Kelly died because they were completely unprepared to participate in a sport where the first mistake can be the last. Not only were they untrained, ill-equipped and inexperienced, but in trying to be safe by bringing a safety line along with them, Powell and Ayres were unwittingly providing themselves with the very thing that would lead to their deaths—a floating ski rope that would entangle them.

Over 100 divers have died in Florida's caves and sinkholes. In the 12 years between 1962 and 1974, fatalities averaged 6.6 cave-diving deaths a year in Florida alone. While other states have recorded diver fatalities in caves, quarries, pits and mines, national surveys showed that most occurred in Florida. Between 1946 and 1969 at least ten of the Florida cave and slough fatalities resulted from the use of ropes, usually the floating polypropylene type rather than the prescribed self-winding nylon line reel.

A diver's "safety" line figured in another fatality at Emerald Springs, also known as Mystery Sink, in Orlando, Florida. On August 13, 1970, 16-year-old certified scuba diver Fred Schmidt and diving instructor Hal Watts, thirty-two, planned to dive to 200 feet in the estimated 500-foot-deep sinkhole to search for an expensive safety vest lost there four days earlier. They intended to search half the area on the north side of the sinkhole at 200 feet, then the other half of the same area at the 150-foot level.

As they unpacked their diving gear at the sinkhole, Schmidt's face mask was shattered. Watts gave him the key to his dive shop in Orlando and told him to get a used mask. When the boy returned, he had an old mask that had lost its shape. Watts pointed this out to him, but Schmidt replied that he would dive with it anyway.

Watts checked him in it and found the mask sealed to Schmidt's face all right. When they entered the water they both carried lights, had depth gauges, decompression meters, wet suits, BC vests and double-tank rigs, each 72-cubic-foot tank filled to 2,400 pounds of air.

Following the fixed safety line down into the dark cavern to 200 feet, they searched the preplanned area, then ascended to 150 feet to make a sweep of that area. As Watts started swimming to his left, his foot tangled in a safety line, an old one that had been left there by the diver who had lost his safety vest. Stopping to untangle it, Watts noticed that Schmidt's foot was also tangled in the line.

They freed themselves and continued to swim to their left. About 30 or 40 feet from the line Watts turned to check his companion's air. Schmidt was not behind him. Watts swept his light around, searching for him in all directions. Then he saw Schmidt's light about 50 feet below him.

"I started down toward him, or his light," said Watts later. "I'm not sure the light was with him at the time—he may have dropped it. I had not swum down very far when the light disappeared."

Watts continued his descent and was suddenly surprised to see a large tree near the bottom. He had never seen any trees in the bottom area of the sink before and it startled him because he was not prepared to make a deep dive.

As he swung his light around looking for Schmidt, he saw the tree and two safety lines. Then he blacked out.

The next thing Watts remembered was bumping his head against the underside of a ledge sometimes called the upper wall. Regaining consciousness he found himself about 30 feet down. His pressure gauge indicated that he had only 400 psi of air left. His decompression meter showed that he had to stop at 30 feet and begin decompressing to avoid the bends. Instead of staying there, however, Watts surfaced and looked for Schmidt or his air bubbles. Seeing some bubbles breaking near the middle of the sink, he followed them down to a depth of 80 feet to find that they were the original bubbles from their 200-foot dive, finally working their way through the porous limestone ledge.

Watts returned to 30 feet and decompressed until he ran out of air, then he surfaced and scanned the sinkhole for any sign of the missing youth. Finding none, he drove to his shop, called the police and notified the boy's mother.

Rescue divers Bill Thompson and Wythe Simms tried to locate the body at 375 feet but the excessive depth limited their effort to no more than 40 seconds of bottom time. In the days that followed a call went out for special mixed-gas diving equipment that would enable a diver to work safely at these depths; however, none materialized.

Closed-circuit television cameras were lowered into the water to scan the depths of the spring, but they revealed nothing.

A couple of days later another attempt was made by scuba divers to find the body. The dive plan called for two safety divers at 150 feet, two more at 300 feet—all four staying near a vertical safety line that Hal Watts and John Gruner were to hold onto while making a sweeping search of the bottom at 350 feet.

As the dive commenced, the first two safety men descended to 150 feet to take the slack out of the line. Watts and Gruner followed, passing them on the way. As they reached bottom and began a ten-minute search, Watts looked up and saw the two safety divers above him at 300 feet.

Watts had hoped to have enough line to make a sweeping search, but there was no slack. His main light imploded, forcing him to use his secondary light. If he and his companion got in trouble, they were to flash a light at the safety divers above them who would come to their aid.

After ten minutes, Watts and Gruner started their ascent. They were to stop at 70 feet to begin decompressing. When they reached 250 feet, Watts saw the reason they had no slack. One of the safety divers, Bud Sims, had been keeping the line taut by hauling up the slack which had gathered in a mass above him. Then he apparently floated up high enough to become tangled in it.

"I saw Bud Sims completely wrapped up in the safety line," Watts reported later. "I also saw a light five or ten feet away. Bud was thrashing about and almost in a panic.

"I cut the line to the surface and put his hand on it and then I turned upside down and cut the line wrapped around his feet. I also blew two breaths of air into his safety vest."

They started rising quickly toward the surface, when something stopped them. Watts checked and found they were still held by line. He cut it and turned upright in time to see Sims take his regulator out of his mouth and put his safety-vest mouthpiece in. Watts, with an octopus rig on his double tanks, tried to get his spare mouthpiece into Sims's mouth but he would not take it. He suspected that Sims was too panicked to respond to his effort.

As they ascended through the murky water, they suddenly struck the underside of the projecting ledge. Watts felt some force from above trying to pull his regulator out of his mouth. Again he was entangled in a rope. Reaching up he slashed himself free.

The next thing he knew he was on the surface, thinking he had gotten Sims to the top where others could help him. Then Watts remembered that he was supposed to stop at 70 feet to start decompressing. He tried to go down, but he was entangled in a surface line. A fellow diver cut him loose and he descended to 45 or 50 feet, where he started breathing hard and having severe burning pains in his hips. Gruner joined him. At 30 feet Watts grew dizzy and nauseated and started to vomit. Another diver took him down and stayed with him for several hours of decompression. Then, after surfacing, Watts was hurried to a recompression chamber at the NASA Space Center at Cape Canaveral, where he underwent recompression treatment for the bends.

Not until he got out of the hospital several days later did he learn the full story of what happened to Sims. One of the other safety divers caught up to him at about 250 feet. He swam around to the back of his tank valve and tried to get him out of the tangled rope. Sims threw up his arms and knocked off the diver's mask. By the time the safety diver recovered and cleared his mask, Sims was gone.

At 150 feet another safety diver said he saw Sims coming up toward him very fast and tangled in line. Grabbing the line, he tried to stop his rapid ascent but failed.

Just after Watts surfaced, witnesses said, another diver hit the bottom of a boat hard and started back down. Since none of the other divers reported striking a boat, it must have been Bud Sims.

Observers concluded that Sims died due to a combination of nitrogen narcosis, panic and the blow to his head, which may have knocked him unconscious. The first victim, Fred Schmidt, may also have blacked out on his way up. Neither diver's body was ever recovered.

The hazards of deep diving, along with the failure to stay within arm's reach of a diving buddy, failure to understand or follow an original dive plan and failure to keep calm—all contributed to these diver deaths, one of the accidents complicated further by the ominous specter of a hazardous "safety" line.

Experienced cave divers are fond of pointing out to the public that caves do not kill divers, divers do. This is true. They kill themselves through ignorance of the sport they are trying to participate in, ignorance of their equipment and its proper use, ignorance of the specialized cave-diving techniques, ignorance of the caves themselves and the hazardous conditions that can trap them, and ignorance of how to cope with the unexpected.

Let a newsman write an article about the "Killer Caves," and cave divers bristle. They love those deep, dark water-filled holes in the ground and are ready to do battle whenever outsiders malign them. But the caves themselves are not always the benign pictures of serene innocence that their surface charms suggest. Take Ponce de Leon Springs near DeLand, Florida, for instance. Seen from the surface, De Leon is a blue-green paradise surrounded by statuesque palms and shady moss-festooned oaks. Bathers frolic in the clear, 72-degree water while others bask in the sun on the manicured green lawn on shore. Summertime strollers amble around parklike grounds enjoying the placid scene. A dance area with a jukebox overlooks the blue water. An underwater glass-walled room gives spectators a fish-eye view of bathers.

In the middle of the springs the surface boils with the force of 19 million gallons a day of fresh water that surges up out of the two- by four-foot opening in the limestone bottom of the springs' basin. Beyond this point the bright picture of serenity vanishes.

A diver, entering the hole against the strong outflow of the springs, pulls himself along by means of rock projections at the entrance. Once inside, the current subsides as he swims down, following the cavern's narrow, 40-degree sloping passageway where filtered surface light is gradually replaced by an all-encompassing gray gloom. At 50 feet below the surface the tunnel widens into a murky cavern called the Mud Room because walls, floor and ceiling are thick with silt. A man can push his arm full length into the ooze without reaching bedrock. An expert knows how to avoid stirring up the silt with his movements, but not even he can prevent his exhaled bubbles from scrubbing silt off the ceiling and creating just as much zero visibility as if he had come in like a novice and disturbed the bottom with his fins. The difference is that a trained cave diver knows how to cope with such situations—how to find his way by compass bearing or guideline without being able to see. But the novice, not expecting to be silted in, may soon lose his way and end up panicking, feverishly seeking the room's entrance with such vigor-

In the mid-1950s, University of Florida professor Dr. John M. Goggin, who received his Ph.D. in anthropology at Yale in 1948, was possibly the only fully accredited anthropologist in the world who scuba dived, and was first to recognize the archaeological value of underwater sites. Yet he was skeptical that the Florida Little Salt and Warm Mineral Springs finds were, as Bill Royal believed, from the Ice Ages. But, over a decade later, Florida State Underwater Archaeologist, Carl Clausen, one of Goggin's former students, proved Royal correct. Photo courtesy of Carl Clausen.

Bill Royal and Bill Stephens examine some of the human remains they recovered from Little Salt Springs during an exploratory dive with Dr. Eugenie Clark and others in 1956. Photo by Bill Stephens.

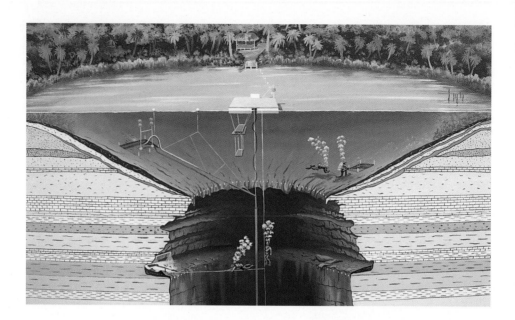

An artist's perspective of the efforts made by Carl Clausen and his group of Florida underwater archaeologists at Little Salt Springs during excavations on the 40-foot deep ledge. Photo courtesy of Carl Clausen.

On Little Salt Springs' 40-foot ledge, Clausen photographs large land turtle remains uncovered in an ancient fire site. Photo by Robert Burgess.

Wearing a Kirby-Morgan Clam-shell helmet with a communica-tions link to the surface, Clausen describes his excavation of early man remains during Phase III of the work at Little Salt Springs. Photo courtesy of Carl Clausen.

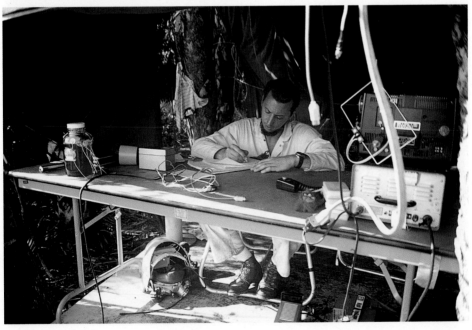

The Little Salt Springs effort began with an operations center covered with a tarp at the edge of the remote spring. Trained cave diving experts were welcome volunteers to the operation. Photo by Robert Burgess.

Called "Gadget Man" for obvious reasons, volunteer cave diving expert, Safety Diver Bob Friedman scrupulously screened every diver's ability who entered Little Salt Springs, then kept detailed records of all dives. Photo by Robert Burgess.

During the 1972 Phase III Little Salt Springs project, divers test an underwater video system made available to them by its inventor (center), diving pioneer Dimitri Rebinkoff. Photo by Robert Burgess.

With plenty on his mind, Florida Underwater Archaeologist Carl J. Clausen has the double responsibility of the Little Salt Springs Project and archaeologically documenting artifacts recovered by state contracted divers salvaging the Spanish Treasure Fleet of 1715 along Florida's southeast coast. Photo by Robert Burgess.

Thirty feet underwater, the author and Bill Royal examine underwater stalactites around the perimeter of Warm Mineral Springs. When Royal first found them, he knew the water level had to have been lower for these dry cave formations to form, possibly during the last Ice Age. Photo courtesy of Robert Burgess.

At the Warm Mineral Springs site, Bill Royal holds a bone needle made from a piece of deer bone carefully shaped, he believes, by an early man using the fossil shark tooth fragment he found with the artifact. Photo by Robert Burgess.

Florida State Underwater Archaeologist, Wilburn "Sonny" Cockrell examines the carved bone atlatl spear thrower tip he recovered from the burial site in Warm Mineral Springs. Photo courtesy of Sonny Cockrell.

SPRING WAS ONCE A CAVE

Lieut. Col. William Royal, underwater explorer and author, while diving in Warm Mineral Springs in 1958 discovered stalactites and stalagmites well below the water line which provided evidence this spring was a dry cave over a very long period of years, possibly during the last ice age. Other dives resulted in the finding of ancient human skulls, bones and animal remains which gave indications of the presence of human and animal life in this part of Florida long before the beginning of written history. In 1977 the national significance of Warm Mineral Springs was recognized when it was placed on the National Register of Historic Places.

SARASOTA COUNTY HISTORICAL COMMISSION

Bill Royal beside the Warm Mineral Springs historical marker acknowledging his contribution which put the site on the National Register of Historic Places. Photo courtesy of Bill Royal.

Dr. Eugenie Clark and Bill Royal watch as Dr. Ilias Konstantinu saws open the controversial skull Royal recovered from Warm Mineral Springs in 1959 that contained human brain material later verified as being over 10,000 years old. Photo by Bill Stephens.

Contrary to popular belief, it is rare to find early man potsherds in underwater caves. Most ended up in land deposits or were washed from those sites into open waterways. Photo by Robert Burgess.

In 1976 diver Charles Harnage looks over some of the fossils and artifacts we found in and around Florida springs. The mastodon tooth (left) came from the sand slope leading into Peacock III cave near Luraville, Florida. So did my find of a Dire Wolf jaw bone in a fire site with a 2,900-year-old Lafayette point. Photo by Robert Burgess.

During a 1976 look into Marianna, Florida's Blue Springs, the author's extension flashes illuminate a companion and rock features near the entrance at 55 feet. Note the cluster of "Peanut Bulbs" held by holes in a piece of rubber innertube, to the right of my head. Photo by Robert Burgess.

Early warning signs placed by members of the Florida Skin Diver Association and the National Association for Cave Diving clearly state their concern that more diver fatalities in underwater caves could lead to the systems being closed to all divers whether properly trained or not. Photo by Robert Burgess.

THIS CAVE IS VERY DANGEROUS
AND REQUIRES SPECIAL
PROCEDURES AND EQUIPMENT
DIVERS DIED HERE
YOUR DEATH MAY CAUSE
ALL SPRINGS TO BE CLOSED
FSDA THINK! NACD

Thirty feet underwater, in the roof of the central passage leading into Twin Wells Sink near Marianna Blue Springs, this pocket of air was six inches deep in 1978. Water level lines on the air pocket's walls show where 10 years of divers' exhalations finally lowered the water level. The reddish color is due to a color correction filter on my lens. Photo by Robert Burgess.

Surface view of rock formations in the clear water near the entrance of Peacock I cave system. The site now has a convenient dive deck and steps for divers visiting Peacock Springs State Park near Luraville. Photo by Robert Burgess.

Forty feet down, divers are framed by the keyhole opening to the dead-end cavern at northwest Florida's Morrison Spring. Photo by Robert Burgess.

Bird's eye view of the Devil's Eye and Ear, popular cave diving sites at north Florida's Ginnie Springs on the Santa Fe River near High Springs. Photo by Wes Skiles.

In the mid-1970s, using extension bulb flashes fired when triggered by a solenoid in my housed camera, my dive buddy, Charles Harnage is framed in the throat of Ginnie Springs' main cavern long before today's grill was put there to prevent fatalities beyond this point. Photo by Robert Burgess.

On the deck at Ginnie Springs, professional underwater photographer and videographer, Wes Skiles of Karst Productions Inc., shows some of the equipment it takes to be a successful underwater cave photographer today. Photo by Paul Smith.

Using the side mount technique he developed for negotiating extremely tight tunnel constrictions, Woody Jasper works his way along a 16-inch high passage in Bluebird Spring, Georgia. Photo by Wes Skiles.

Mark Long and Woody Jasper explore a tunnel in Sweetwater Spring, Florida. Photo by Wes Skiles.

Woody Jasper checks out some of the underwater beauty that marks Florida's Hart Spring on the Suwannee River six miles north of Franning Springs. Photo by Wes Skiles.

In 1989 carrying six tanks, Sheck Exley prepares to break his previous record at Mante by diving to 867 feet on open circuit scuba. Photo by Sergio Zambrano. Courtesy of Sheck Exley.

These root-gnarled, water-loving cypress trees ring the crystal clear waters of northwest Florida's Morrison Springs basin, providing cover for fish and a spectacular view for divers. Photo by Robert Burgess.

Lalo Fiorelli and Lee Racicot returning from a triple-stage penetration of over a mile into the Yucatan's Sac-Actun cave system in 1993. Photo by Lalo Fiorelli.

Mike Madden, a pioneer of cave exploration in Mexico's Yucatan Peninsula, explores Chac's Room in Naharon Cave in 1987, nearly 1,500 feet from the cave's mouth. Photo by Lalo Fiorelli.

The Cuzen-ah passage of the Yucatan's Sac-Actun is one of the most detailed and highly decorated in the system. Photo by Lalo Fiorelli.

Opposite: Evy Cambridge traversing the Corral Cenote on the way up-cave at the Ponderosa in the Yucatan. The Ponderosa was discovered and named by resident divers Tony and Nancy DeRosa. Photo by Lalo Fiorelli.

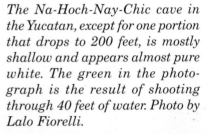

The Na-Hoch-Nay-Chic cave in the Yucatan, except for one portion that drops to 200 feet, is mostly shallow and appears almost pure white. The green in the photograph is the result of shooting through 40 feet of water. Photo by Lalo Fiorelli.

This portion of the full-column speleothem in the Yucatan's Na-Hoch-Nay-Chic cave is more than 20 feet high and 5 feet across. Photo by Lalo Fiorelli.

ous movements that conditions worsen, he becomes more disoriented and, unless he is one of the few fortunate victims to escape such circumstances, he becomes another cave-diving statistic.

In the end, such a diver brings about his own untimely end, of course. But such easily accessible caverns as the Mud Room are too hazardous to be left available to the general diving public. They are extremely hazardous high-risk areas and as such should be closed to scuba divers.

Getting lost in caves rates high on the list of cave diving fatalities. It is a common affliction of the untrained, unequipped, inexperienced cave diver who goes where he does not belong. Scuba diving is itself a hazardous sport. To do it without any training is tantamount to playing Russian roulette with a loaded revolver. Basic scuba certification does not prepare a diver for the problems he can have in the closed environment of an underwater cave. Not even full cave diver certification training carries with it any fail-safe guarantees. Even the best sometimes lose. Caves play no favorites. One of the most tragic losses involved a tremendously talented young marine biologist considered one of the best divers in the country, until he made a mistake in a cave.

Blond, blue-eyed, supple Conrad Limbaugh had dived since he was 12 years old. In 1949, as chief of diving operations, he was first to introduce free diving to the Scripps Institute of Oceanography at La Jolla, California. In his early compressed-air dives he used one of the first two Aqua-Lungs brought into the United States from France by Commander Douglas Fane of the Navy Underwater Demolition Team.

Realizing that one day scuba diving would be a valuable tool to the underwater researcher, Limbaugh's enthusiasm rubbed off on a whole new generation of scientists. He started a scuba diving course at Scripps that launched a long procession of noted academicians into and under the sea. The talented Limbaugh went on to distinguish himself in the fields of oceanography and marine biology, completing among others, an outstanding study of shark behavior along the California coast. Then, on a field trip to the Mediterranean on March 20, 1960, he decided to investigate an underwater cave near Cassis, France.

A few years earlier French divers had established that the subterranean system was a freshwater river flowing into the sea. Limbaugh and a French acquaintance decided to investigate the cavern. Limbaugh filmed their entry with an underwater movie camera. Then the two divers swam into the strong, outflowing currents. About 150 feet along the jagged passageway from the cave mouth, their lights illuminated a high pile of rubble. Squeezing through the small opening at the top of the rock pile, they saw daylight overhead. Investigating, they found a rock shelf leading to the surface. The rubble had fallen from the sinkhole to the cavern floor in ages past. The passageway continued underground, traveling horizontally an average of 30 feet below the water's surface. The tunnel was rugged going, with great rock barriers, vaulted ceilings and wall-to-wall water. At one point the divers discovered ancient stalagmites on the floor, indicating that the cave was once dry. Then, several hundred feet inside the dark cavern, the two divers somehow became separated. The Frenchman searched for Limbaugh as long as his air lasted, then swam back to the sea entrance. Limbaugh did not come out. The Frenchman telephoned the French Office of Underwater Research in Marseilles, and requested divers; then he called Paris to notify Jacques Cousteau, who was attending an oceanographic meeting with Limbaugh's chief of staff at Scripps.

Cousteau immediately ordered all his diving teams in the Mediterranean to help. Dozens of France's finest divers, including two US Navy divers summoned from London, converged on the cavern at Cassis. Then began a mammoth all-out effort to find Limbaugh. Working on the slim hope that he had found an air pocket and was still alive, the chain-diving teams probed every nook and cranny of the cave in relays, around the clock. After two days of this massive, dangerous effort, it became apparent that Limbaugh was no longer alive. Sadly, the search was now reduced to the routine task of body recovery.

Two weeks later, two professional divers found Limbaugh's body in a ceiling pocket 450 feet inside the tunnel. On the floor of the cave lay his movie camera. Despite some leakage, part of the film was still good. When processed it dimly showed some of the daylight scenes at the start of the ill-fated cave-diving trip.

A year later, 70 French and American dignitaries held a me-

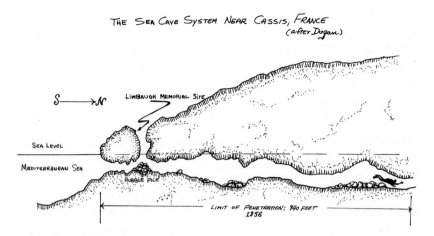

THE SEA CAVE SYSTEM NEAR CASSIS, FRANCE
(after Dugan)

The cavern created by the underground river at Cassis claimed the life of one of America's most promising scuba diving pioneers.

morial service at Cassis for the young American scientist. Solemnly, they removed an American flag from a rock beside the sinkhole leading down to the river. Inset in it, a bronze plaque read: *In memory of the American scholar Conrad Limbaugh, who lost his life in a daring dive in the underground river of Cassis, 20 March 1960. Club Alpine Francais, Section de Provence. Federation Francaise d'Etudes et des Sports Sous-Marin.*

No matter where a cave-diving accident occurs, someone is always responsible for going in and recovering the body. In Florida, that task falls to a dedicated dive team made up of volunteers from the National Association for Cave Diving (NACD) based at Gainesville, Florida. Whenever a cave-diving fatality occurs anywhere in the state, these men are immediately notified by the sheriff' s office and they come at once.

In an effort to learn everything about the accident, the body-recovery team spares no effort to get at the facts. Each of the expert cave divers is as thorough as a detective. Once found by the team, the victims are not moved until they are closely observed and sometimes photographed in the positions found. The recovery divers then check to see if any air is left in the victim's tank by looking at his submersible pressure gauge; they also try to determine whether his equipment has malfunctioned by trying to breathe from his regulator. Everything is carefully noted: the position of the body; whether or not it was tangled in a safety rope; what equipment the victim had; whether or not he jettisoned some of it; his position in relation to other victims; how deep the water; how far the victim was in the cave; and whatever other information will provide as accurate a picture as possible of what occurred and why.

This data then becomes part of a continuing statistical file on Florida cave-diving fatalities. The more popular dive sites are the ones which appear the most safe, yet the ones which sometimes claim the most lives.

One such popular diving site is Ginnie Springs near Trenton, Florida. Today it is probably one of the best and safest cave-diving sites in the world, but once it had a record of having the third largest number of cave-diving fatalities in the state. By 1975, 18 divers had lost their lives there. Five days before Christmas of 1967, this "benign" spring was the site of one of the worst accidents in cave-diving history—the drowning of four University of Georgia students, 300 feet back in a cave.

There were five young men in the group but only four wet suits, so they drew straws to see who was the "unlucky" one to stay ashore while the others dived into the cave.

Another diver took the first two down to a point well within the tunnel, where they tied off their ski rope. Then he returned to the surface, and about five minutes later he took the other two divers down and showed them where the ski rope was tied. Again he returned to the surface and spent the next 45 minutes snorkeling. When his wife became alarmed because the four men had not returned, he went down into the cave with only a quarter tank of air to see if he could find them. He followed the shaft as far as he dared and thought he saw a light in the distance. But since visibility was bad because of stirred up silt and he was running out of air, he surfaced and had his wife telephone the sheriff.

The NACD recovery team was notified, and four of its divers hurried to the scene. Questioning witnesses at the spring, they learned what had happened. Then the quartet geared up, made their dive plan and entered the cave.

Quickly they descended to the floor of the main tunnel, where they found the ski rope tied off some distance in. Following it by unreeling their own safety line along the right branch of the tunnel, the group's leader suddenly indicated that he had spotted the first body. These excerpts from the detailed accident report tell what happened:

"I quickly moved up beside [the leader] and gave him a signal to stop and not to move anything until we had a chance to look over the whole scene and form a good mental picture of it," wrote one of the team members. "Then, after a minute or two, I moved closer to the victim for a better look, because we could see only two bodies from where we were. As I moved up and over them, I could see a third body lying between the two huge boulders which form a restriction in the small tunnel. I was baffled about the absence of the fourth body. We thought the fourth diver might be further back in the tunnel...."

While two of the divers took the first two bodies to the surface, the other men manipulated the third body out of the way so that they could pass over a pile of boulders and search beyond them.

"Passing this point, we went on along the small tunnel for about 50 feet, where we encountered a clay bank which bore finger and knee marks along the floor. Small pockets of air trapped on the ceiling of the tunnel at this point indicated that the divers had come this far back. These signs (air and finger marks) continued back for another 100 feet where we encountered several more clay banks which appeared undisturbed...."

The divers continued searching another 50 feet without finding any trace of the fourth diver's body. They were then about 500 feet from the entrance, the distance the divers probably penetrated before turning around and trying to find their way back. "It is reasonable to believe that they must have stirred up a great deal of silt along these clay banks, greatly obscuring the visibility for their exit....

"When we reached the restricting boulders from behind them, we realized what must have happened to the three victims. With visibility in the six-inch range, I got myself wedged between the boulders three times in trying to fit through the small crevice where the safety line went. These two large rocks in the narrow tunnel completely obstruct the passageway except for a very small squeeze over them which is easy to find going in, when the visibility is excellent, but which is a lot more difficult to find in coming back out, when the visibility is next to zero. Crossing over the boulders through this squeeze took us several minutes of careful, patient effort with only six-inch visibility; the three victims had not been able to manage it."

After six separate dives searching every possible place in the passageway, the team was still unable to find the fourth victim. Two days later the team made another exhaustive search, and on their ninth dive two of the divers took a last look into the left branch of the tunnel.

"After poking in and about many little holes and crevices along the left tunnel, we found ourselves about 275 feet from the cave entrance. At this point the left tunnel makes a sharp bend to the right, and straight ahead is a small side passage (about half the size of the windshield of a car), which I realized I hadn't examined before. As I stuck my head into the small opening, something caught my eye. I turned and saw a camera lying in a tiny crevice in the floor to my left. We knew that the fourth diver had had a camera with him when he went down, so I knew I was finally on the right track. I squeezed myself through the small, tight tunnel which extended about 15 feet to a little grotto. There to the left of the tunnel on the floor of the grotto was the body of the fourth diver wedged fairly tightly into a horizontal crevice on the opposite side of the tiny room. In this position he could not be seen from the main left tunnel. He held a light in his hand and his mask was pushed up on top of his head. After much maneuvering, I was finally able to free the body from the crevice and push it ahead of me through the narrow passage...."

Some of the reasons for this multiple tragedy were lack of experience and lack of equipment. Two of the victims had never dived before. None had ever been diving in a cave. None had cave-diver training. All victims wore single tanks. No diver, even a trained cave-diver, should make this kind of deep penetration on a single tank. It allows no air reserve for emergency, as do double tanks used properly, that is, one-third of the air to get into the cave, one-third to get out, and one-third always kept in reserve for an emergency.

None of the divers were using submersible air gauges. Without knowing how much air he had, a diver could easily run out of it before he exited from a cave. This single omission probably killed more untrained cave divers than anything else. When an innocent swam down into a cave's complex passageways thinking that a full tank of air would last him just as long at depth as it did on the surface, he was often doomed. When an open-water diver made that mistake, at least he could come immediately to the surface when he ran out of air. The cave diver could not.

The three divers in the right branch of the cave had a single light with them; the fourth diver in the left tunnel also had but one. The four divers had only two lights between them. No party of divers should ever enter a cave without at least three lights per diver.

The victims were using polypropylene ski rope for their safety line, with no spool or reel for rolling it up. Although strong and tough, this kind of rope is less dense than water and tends to float on the ceiling of a tunnel. Divers moving under it are rather easily entangled. Currents can also move it easily into tight rock crevices where a diver cannot pass, and it therefore does not guide him out the same course he came in. Nylon line on a jam-proof cave-diving reel is best.

Instead of tying their safety line at or outside the entrance of the cave, the victims tied theirs too far inside—at least 100 feet in from the entrance. Even if they had managed to squeeze through over the pile of rocks, in trying to find their way out through the silt, they could easily get lost between the point at which they tied off their line and the entrance of the cave. This is possibly what happened to the fourth diver.

Ginnie Springs eventually became totally "safe" by the placing of a grill over one end of a passageway, preventing divers from entering more dangerous areas.

Today, of course, we realize that proper cave diver training programs are the absolute prerequisite before any diver even thinks about succumbing to the lure of the labyrith.

18

CAVE DIVING:
EVOLUTION OF THE SPORT

Cave diving in the United States has gone through a fascinating evolution. At first the concept of going into underwater caves, even though basically the same as now, was approached in a very piecemeal fashion. All the rules had to be invented from the beginning. No one knew what the rules were, but gradually figured them out. The basics were: We've got to take a line. We've got to stay up off the floor. We have to have enough light to see. And we have to save enough air to get out.

The problems that plagued diving then was that there were no buoyancy compensators, no pressure gauges, no underwater lights, no line reels. Cave diving was totally primitive when compared to techniques and equipment available in the sport today. In the beginning—during the 1950's and 1960's—we approached the exploration of underwater caves very crudely. But it was the best we knew to do.

The early innovators of the sport, people like Dr. George Benjamin who began inventing things from the beginning, then Tom Mount and Sheck Exley, were three of many who pioneered the sport. The solutions to their basic problems were often crude but effective.

For example, since there was no such thing as a means to control your buoyancy, the earliest buoyancy compensators were plastic milk jugs. To keep themselves out of the silt that obscured visibility, cave divers took the regulators out of their mouths, shot air into the jugs, and clung to them or clipped them off on their belts to give themselves more buoyancy. After that they started using jerry cans. First they tied them to their arms but found it tiring to have their arms lifted, but nothing else. So they put them back on their waist. Then they decided to use two for balance, attaching them to a military style cartridge web belt. About the time cave divers were saying there had to be a better way, the dive industry came out with what was to be called a "buoyancy compensator."

One of the earliest was a cloth-covered horse-collar-shaped rubber bladder that fitted around the diver's neck and chest. It was inflated by the diver blowing into an air valve tube near his mouth. This evolved into an automatic method of inflating with a manual method for dumping air, and led to the many different styles of BC's popular over the years.

More than any other pioneering cave diver, Jacksonville, Florida-born Sheck Exley approached cave diving from a problem-solving manner of thinking. He was very systematic about everything he did from exploration to note-keeping, always trying to improve his efforts. He emerged early as a leader wanting to establish rules.

"Look," he said, "too many divers are dying in caves. Things are killing us in the dark. We have to start looking more closely at what's happening to these people in caves, and analyzing the accidents for the reasons."

This was the beginning of the analytical method called "accident analysis" used today. The idea was to look at what happened, try to figure out what went wrong, and develop a rule that kept divers from doing that wrong thing. A simple approach, but from that came Sheck 's safety concept which he wrote for a small group of cave diving enthusiasts calling their organization the Dixie Cavern Kings. This pamphlet was the first ever published on the basic rules of cave diving.

Exley was attending the University of Georgia, when he started coming down to Florida during the weekends to cave dive. From that pamphlet came the sport's first life-preserving principles—take a line, take three lights apiece, save air to come out on. These were the first basic rules that started giving the sport of cave diving structure and shape.

Soon, enough people were interested in cave diving that it was time for organization. The first official organization in the United States was the NACD, the National Association for Cave

Diving. It formed around 1968. Within this group were the first safety guidelines and concepts of training, although there was no formal training until the 1970's.

The actual teaching of cave diving techniques became a reality as equipment improved. Some of the more important things that evolved was the idea of having more than one second stage, a second hose and regulator to breathe off the same tank in the event of having to provide air for a diver in distress. This idea originated from the sport of cave diving. It was what divers later called the octopus or safe second, one of the most standard pieces of equipment used in scuba diving today.

Eventually, the automatic inflator for buoyancy compensators was born from the same basic need. Such items came about because of obvious problems—cave divers were unable to be buoyant enough to stay up off the silty floor.

The idea of a safe second originated from observations made by Sheck Exley. He realized divers lacked a satisfactory way to share air. Repeatedly, he tried to work out ways in which when a problem arose, it was possible to share air with a dive buddy and get out of a cave without dying. Using the single hose and regulator to buddy breathe, Sheck wrote that this way was too difficult in the confines of a dark underwater cave under highly stressful conditions. Inevitably the two divers ended up stopping and struggling just to share air. "You can't make any more progress," he said. "We must have a better way to do it."

From that came the idea of two second stages, a second regulator on an extension hose enabling a companion to share your air supply while the two of you exited the cave. Though the idea was easy enough to come by, actually doing it was difficult because the first stage regulator from which the spare was to be attached, lacked a low pressure port for attachment.

Exley took this problem to Joseph Califano in Jacksonville. Califano was a machine shop genius who designed underwater equipment. The name of his business was titled, "Underwater Designers."

The senior Joseph said, "No problem. We'll take this part of the first stage off, spin a new one, drill extra holes in it, and you can have as many things on the end of this regulator as you want."

Early caving enthusiast Wes Skiles recalls seeing one of those first ones: "Sheck had it on his regulator and I used to go down to Underwater Designers as a kid and just explore all of those things with great fascination. Yep, sure enough, here was this brass end to a chrome regulator—a Calypso regulator which was the first that this was done to—and here was this port, this end to a regulator that only had one hole out of it. Now it had five! You could stick five hoses into it. That was the birth of multiports. Inflator hoses and second stage hoses could now be added in different positions on it. For this reason it was called an 'octopus.' From that point on, cave diving got a lot safer."

Almost on a simultaneous course, Dr. George Benjamin of Canada, invented the Benjamin Manifold. He said, "This is the weak link to the system. Two tanks going into one regulator you have three major O-rings—one from each tank, and one where the air passes from the valve to the regulator. You're betting your entire life on this one regulator.

"If one regulator fails at an O-ring point, neither the pressure gauge, the inflator hose, or either one of the second stage mouthpieces will be any good, and you will certainly die."

Benjamin's solution: "You must have two of everything, so if one fails completely, then you have a secondary system you can fall back on independent from the first system." Thus was born the Benjamin Manifold. Today, it is called the Ideal manifold.

Similarly, other developments in use today by the general diving community, came originally from the sport of cave diving. This included specialized lights, Y valves, the concept of having a longer second stage hose so you can move more freely. When you are out of air, who wants to feel restricted? It's a horrible feeling to barely survive an out-of-air ordeal only to get air from a person who has this little hose that's jerking you around, holding you close to a person you do not want to be near. You want freedom. You want to go to the surface.

Cave divers wanted something in which the divers sharing air could do it while swimming single file. Their answer was to make the backup regulator's hose long enough to do this.

Even the smallest things became important in an emergency. One of the weak links was how divers were using their second stage. It seemed to take years before Skiles and others figured out how to make that spare easily accessible. Before that divers just let it drag, or used some crude attachment that didn't let them get to it easily.

So they invented the second stage holder—a rubber strap that you could jerk loose to either hand it to a companion or use yourself.

Over the years, all manner of equipment evolved to make the sport safer. To this day, cave diving continues to lead the dive industry in the development of safe diving systems, right down to the design of the buoyancy compensators, stabilizer jackets, etc. This came about because cave divers needed more compact, more balanced equipment. Thin designs, thermal designs resulted.

Now into the 90's comes mixed gases. When this concept of technical diving arrived and people started talking about mixed gases, it brought on heated debate in the general diving community. Experienced cave divers wondered why. This system of using advance life support diving equipment, mixed gases, and oxygen for decompression was what cave divers had been using quietly and regularly for 15 years. Now it is much more widely used by the general diving community in its application to deep diving whether under ice or on shipwrecks, or by divers just wanting to stay longer and do more.

Cave diver training has similarly evolved. Nobody wanted to train a diver to cave dive and then have him turn around and die in a cave. There were strict rules and regulations. There was an elite crew at the head of cave diving that decided how the National Association of Cave Diving would be ruled and run. Those who finished the course, the first two became instructors. That was the method. Rules became structured and what you did became outlined. A handful more became instructors.

All during this process, divers were drowning in caves. We still hadn't come to the point where the rules were clearly understood.

"The biggest downfall of the cave divers in the 60's and early 7 0's was deep diving," said Wes Skiles. "We'd figured out all the other things about the dangers of incorrectly using lines and lights, the air rules, and we now had pressure gauges. We had no excuse. When I came into the sport in 1973, there was really no reason not to operate safely. But deep diving they hadn't figured out. A number of trained cave divers—all in a short period of time—lost their lives in caves."

When trained, experienced cave divers perished as easily as untrained inexperienced divers, the very foundation of this new sport was threatened. Many of those who pioneered it thought it best to keep what they had learned to themselves. If outsiders learned even a little bit of what they knew, they might add to the increasing death rate and so incite the public that it would simply put all caves off limits and do away with the sport as being simply too dangerous to do.

In time, however, it was realized that this was an improper approach. Not all divers wanted to be deep-penetration cave divers. But it was certainly essential that divers in the general diving community who desired diving in an enclosed overhead environment, such as under a ledge, or into a cavern, have some basic training on the subject.

Thus evolved the programs in effect today. The introductory course is called Cavern Diving. This course and those that follow are sanctioned by today's national organizations specializing in this kind of diving. They are the National Speleological Society - Cave Diving Section (NSS-CDS), and the National Association of Cave Diving (NACD). Training is also available through PADI Cavern, and NAUI Cavern and Cave programs. Fully qualified instructors run periodic training sessions at Florida's Ginnie Springs, probably one of the most ideal systems available to U.S. divers. Here's a brief overview of all the courses as they exist today:

CAVERN DIVER: Introductory course on how to dive in a submerged underground, or overhead environment normally reached by daylight. This two-day course provides divers with the necessary knowledge and skills to dive within these enclosed daylight zones. Topics cover cavern environment, accident analysis, stress, equipment modification, communication, planning and preparation, emergencies, swimming techniques, and guideline handling. Four dives are made. Students must be at least 16 years old, in good physical shape, and have an Open Water Level or equivalent diver certification.

INTRODUCTION TO CAVE DIVING: This course is designed

for divers wishing to dive beyond the daylight zone, safely making limited penetrations into caves on a single air tank. This two- or three-day course requiring the student to have certain specialized equipment, enables divers to perfect skills learned in Cavern Diving, and to learn more advanced techniques and procedures required for elementary cave dives. Special emergency procedures, setting proper limits, and navigation with guidelines are among the topics taught. Four limited penetration cave dives are made in at least two different locations. Divers learn how to share air, use touch-contact communication, air-sharing in simulated out-of-air cave exiting scenarios, use of guide lines, techniques for trimming buoyancy, and conservation-minded propulsion techniques. The minimum age is 18; and a NACD Cavern Diver course or equivalent is required.

APPRENTICE CAVE DIVER: This is the third step in cave diver training courses. Emphasis here is on dive planning and skill perfection through actual cave dives. Techniques learned earlier are expanded. This two-day course includes four cave dives including air-sharing in a lights out, eyes-closed situation in a minor constriction using single-file swimming method; line-jumping and techniques for maintaining continual line to the surface. Special equipment is required along with prior preliminary courses in introduction to cave diving. Minimum age is 18.

FULL CAVE DIVER: This is the fourth level in cave diving course designed for divers wishing the most advanced and comprehensive training in the sport. It includes decompression theory and practice, advanced navigation, cave survey, and discussions on various cave diving situations. At least four cave dives are made using three dive sites during the two-day session. Training includes a stage dive, side-mounted equipment use, diver propulsion vehicle use, or techniques for sump dives. One dive to a depth of 90 feet but no more than 130 feet; complex mazes; surveying. The minimum age is 18 and preliminary cave diving courses are required.

In summary: The total cave diving training program, including dives, lectures and training, takes in at least 15 cavern or cave dives in a minimum of at least six days for the entire course from Cavern Diver to Full Cave Diver. For further information, divers can contact the agencies listed in the appendix.

19

INTO THE CAVES WITH GUN AND CAMERA

Anyone who has ever tried to take a photograph in the total darkness of an underwater cave has tales to tell. Mostly tales of woe. Since I've been poking around inside sunken caves with flash gun and camera off and on for almost a quarter century, I know a tale or two about woe.

In the beginning, no matter how often you try, even with today's hi-tech point-and-shoot-cameras, results are usually disappointing. If misery enjoys company, take solace in the fact that you're not alone; scores of photographers before you, and scores to follow have all shared the same experience sometime in their careers.

After that initial disappointment, you either go back to photographing daisies and butterflies on grassy knolls, or like me, you stubbornly keep clicking away in caves until one day it dawns on you that to take good cave-diving photographs, you have to learn techniques different from those of land photographers.

Once you accept this, the rest falls into place. Eventually, you actually begin to get underwater photographs in caves that stand head-and-shoulders above anything you ever shot in the beginning. Believe me, however, that transition from bad to better is not easy to come by. It took me almost a quarter of a century, and I'm a fast learner. Moreover, I'm still learning new tricks.

In this brief discussion, however, I'll try to give you an overview of how it was, and how we learned to improve techniques in the fine art of wet cave photography.

Years ago, our most pressing problem was how to get a regular camera and flash into an underwater cave and back out again without flooding the works.

When I started, we were having to fabricate our own underwater camera housings and flash guns. My first serious unit was a nicely crafted Plexiglas housing large enough to include my 35mm camera, light meter, and a power pack for firing an underwater flash. The latter consumed peanut-sized flash bulbs, clear for black-and white film, blue for color.

Four wing-nutted bolts and a large O-ring kept the back of my underwater camera housing closed. External controls adjusted the lens aperture, advanced the film, and triggered the camera which was a 35mm Edixa equipped with a 28mm lens. A custom-made lead weight screwed to the bottom of the housing gave it slightly negative buoyancy.

The main reason I chose this combination of land camera in a plastic box was because at the time I couldn't afford investing in both a 35mm French-made Calypso underwater camera (which was later acquired by the Japanese and marketed as the Nikonos) and the then brand-new innovative wide-angle lens soon to appear on the market as the Nikonos 28mm.

Having tested the Calypso underwater with its standard 35mm lens, I found it so lacking in depth of field, it was impractical. But by converting my land camera to underwater use, the 28mm wide-angle on it worked satisfactorily when everything went well. Unfortunately, those moments were rare. In the cold, wet, total darkness of an underwater cave, things photographically almost always had a way of going wrong. There, Murphy's Law reigned supreme. What could go wrong not only did, but what couldn't go wrong usually did too.

Consequently, picturing underwater caves was often a study in chaos. Bone-chilling cold chaos, if I remember correctly because in those days we wore no wet suits. Photographs of us in that 68-degree water always showed us looking exactly the way we were—a paler shade of blue. And it couldn't be blamed on our color film, because that was before the early version of Ektachrome was born, which gave everything a strong blue cast. Great for tropical sea backgrounds but not much else.

We used the fastest color film we had. But trying to get good results by shooting Kodachrome 25 as compared to today 's zippy emulsions was like trying to race a turtle against a hare. But in those days we were barely out of the Dark Ages of the Brownie box camera. The mere mention to outsiders that we were taking a land camera underwater inside a totally black cave to try and photograph God knows what, if and when it was illuminated by a split-second burst of light, revealing a scene completely obscured by muddy water, was to instantly certify ourselves as nuts.

The point is, we kept trying. We were driven by the desire to capture on film some of the mystery and beauty we saw in sunken caves, if only to show less fortunate landlubbers what they were missing. Our only trouble was that technology hadn't caught up to our lofty hopes and expectations. It was about a decade or two behind. Consequently, our early achievements were seldom much to cheer about, but we persisted.

Fortunately, our frustration tolerances were exceedingly high. After all, how could we possibly capture a fraction of that experience on a piece of film the size of a postage stamp, let alone expect someone totally unfamiliar with that alien world to be impressed with our efforts?

That's why the whole cave-shooting scene became more of an "in house" operation. Those in the know, those companions who had been there at our side and knew the frustration of the undertaking, they alone appreciated what pictorial achievements occurred. Dive shop shows became popular. So too did annual show-and-tell programs featuring guest underwater photographers regaling audiences of other divers. Soon, amateur underwater photographers were getting properly certified to enter caves and were trying to take photographs the way the pros were doing it. If they had watched and learned their lessons well, they began to achieve appropriate results. But most successes evolved through many trials and errors.

Trial and error was what I was doing in trying to photograph just inside the easiest caverns from 1972 on. We were definitely not deep-penetration cave divers and had no interest in going much further than where available light penetrated. But even there, quite quickly we realized the danger of stirring up silt. This often had us putting aside our fins and churning around inside caverns like fish without tails. It also taught us how to achieve an inverted positive buoyancy and to walk through silt on our fingertips. Not a particularly easy feat for models who often had to carry coils of electrical extension cables, multiple flash units, and clusters of flash-bulbs in net bags.

The reason for the off-camera flash attempts was to avoid the backscatter effect of light bouncing back into the lens from the finest colloidal particles of silt suspended in the water between us and our subject.

This effect spelled disaster no matter how clear the water seemed at the time. But by letting companions carry hand-held flash guns some 15 to 30 feet from the camera, one might begin to overcome the back-scatter problem.

Like everyone else, I started with the flash at the camera. Then I found I got better results the further the flash was away from it, sometimes even at high, right angles. Before my long extension wire attempts, the forerunner of that idea was a six-foot-long, slightly arched bamboo pole held at arm's length high overhead. Atop the pole was fastened the flash gun. The linking electrical cable was taped to the pole and ran back to thumb-screw terminals on my camera housing. They connected to a 22-volt battery and a capacitor inside the housing that produced enough of a jolt to fire extension flashes.

Right from the beginning two major problems arose. One had to do with communicating with my companions holding the flash guns, the other with keeping the flashes properly functioning. Underwater, electrical contacts failed more often than they fired. Despite all efforts to keep contacts soldered and pristine, their decision to fire, or not to fire, we decided, was entirely up to the whims of the aquatic leprechauns in underwater caves that controlled such events.

When a model is poised in midwater blackness with his back to you holding flash guns in each of his outstretched arms pointing toward a wall formation you want to photograph, it is a set-up fraught with frustrations difficult to imagine.

If just one flash fires, only half a picture gets lit. Moreover, the model may not have realized it and not know he has to ditch both bulbs and reload to try again. You put down everything carefully, swim over and motion him to reload.

If on the second try, only one bulb fires again, then he needs to give it immediate first aid. Like wiggle the bulb, pushing it harder against contacts, or whatever.

Or maybe the trouble is at the camera end and you pause to fidget with the connections there. By the time you are ready to shoot again, your model has become so tired his arms have tilted far enough forward so that now instead of pointing them at the wall, the flash guns are pointed at the floor.

In the rumble of exhaled air inside a cave, no amount of shouting into your regulator will snap the diver out of his reverie and get him to raise his arms. Once more you must place your camera on the floor oh so gently lest you stir up a tornado of mud, then just as carefully you must float up like a feather into the water mass and wiggle over to the fellow who is still deep in reverie.

Pulling his arms back upright and pointing with stabbing gestures at the wall to emphasize the problem while shouting instructions through your regulator, you again retreat light as a feather to your camera and oh so gently pick it up to shoot.

This time neither flash fires. You shout and curse into your regulator, but nobody hears you. So you start all over again.

Failure to be able to communicate in this environment is the curse of our sport. Early on when I read that Jacques Cousteau once captured a pocket of air in the hood of his wetsuit and talked underwater through it, I used the principle for a gadget I called, "The Great Underwater Communicator."

I made the thing from a half-gallon plastic Clorox jug, a circle of rubber innertube and a crude one-way valve. Cutting off the jug's neck, I carved an opening for my mouth. Then I removed the jug's bottom and stretched the rubber diaphragm over it. The one-way valve went on the underside.

My idea was to exhale into the jug, pushing water out the side valve. Shouting into the air pocket vibrated the rubber diaphragm sending the sound waves through the water to my companions.

Theoretically, that was it. Instant communication. Unfortunately, my bid for fame ended abruptly when I found that after I exhaled into the jug, I had no breath left to talk. By the time I regained my regulator and cleared it for a breath, the "Great Communicator" was flooded.

I went back to shouting, waving and flashing my light.

Most lessons were learned the hard way, lessons no dry land photographer ever wrestles with. For instance, after making a cave dive once, I surfaced to change film, then descended to the cave again. The brief exchange from cold water to hot air back to cold water again left a layer of fog on the inside of my Plexiglas housing.

Not to worry, I signaled my companion. We would just swim into an air pocket just inside the bottom of the cave, stand up in waist-deep water, take off the back of the housing and wipe away the fog.

Again, flawless theory. It was the principle of the thing that got us. In the dry chamber we were 30 feet underwater. I unscrewed the wingnuts but couldn't pry the back off of the housing. While I was gripping and grunting trying to break that seal, it suddenly dawned on me what was wrong.

As I wing-nutted things back together again, I grinned sheepishly at my companion and murmured, "I think we just had a lesson in physics."

Fortunately, plenty of pressure was holding that back on the housing. Had I forced it off, filling the housing with the chamber's high pressure air, the camera housing might have exploded when I surfaced. At the very least, the back of the housing would have come off a lot easier.

What finally brought on my transition from housed camera to Nikonos camera made solely for underwater photography, was an event that occurred just as we were about to enter a cave for a major shoot. Moments before, I had surfaced from another cavern downriver and loaded a fresh roll of film in the camera. After securing everything, we motored upriver, parked the boat, then made a long up-river swim to reach the mouth of the cavern.

Just as we were about to enter, I glanced at the camera housing to make sure everything was cocked and okay. Everything was cocked but not okay. What called my attention to that was the air bubble inside the housing. The whole thing had flooded!

Night and day for the next week I labored over the sad results of that accident. I managed to oven dry the camera so that it still worked, but the lens was another thing.

Figuring that if I was particularly careful to draw a picture of each and every element in that lens as I carefully disassembled it, there was no way I could incorrectly put it all back together again. That idea was as full of holes as my "Great Underwater Communicator."

After a dozen tries, I was still getting only center sharpness, the edges were out of focus. Experts said there was something about having the elements "out of column", meaning turned in ways they weren't supposed to be turned, that might be causing it. After a dozen more attempts at reconstruction, I discovered that one element was in backwards. When it was turned around, the lens performed almost as good as new. Only trouble was, I never trusted its accuracy after that.

I graduated to the Nikonos system and have been content ever since. What boosted the quality of my photographs considerably was the 15mm ultra wide-angle lens. It enabled a coverage of subject matter in tight areas that was unobtainable in any other way. When electronic strobes came on the scene, they opened up even wider vistas of possibilities. In the hands of assistants, these strobes could be set on slave so that they fired automatically from the bounce of a primary light. By holding a slave strobe off to one side of cave formations or a cave diving model, setting the main light source on a purposely lower intensity, the multiple strobed formation began to take on a third dimensional effect one never could achieve with a completely flat lighted scene.

We began to discover other tricks too. For example, if a dome of air occurred in a ceiling pocket, scenes strobed beneath it are mirrored in its surface. Using this technique to its fullest advantage, we would instruct a model not to exhale directly under the dome, but move up close to it and look up. By positioning the light out of the scene so that it bounced downward into the model's mask, it created an excellent mirror image.

We were always experimenting with different ways to use lights, even in the early days with my Plexiglas housed camera. The earliest open shutter attempts were made around the mid-70's in the Twin Wells Sink near Marianna, Florida. Since the back of this cave contained interesting limestone formations, we taped a large sash weight to a tripod's center post, screwed the housing atop it, and set the camera where it took in the entire back wall of the cave.

I then swam to a point ten feet from the wall, stayed low, and snapped off my small hand light. At this signal, my dive buddy opened the camera shutter that had been preset on the B (Bulb) setting. I then fired off a self-contained flash gun rigged with a button switch. In the darkness I changed bulbs, moved ten feet to my right and fired the flash again. I did this four times and after the last flash, my companion closed the shutter.

The resulting color shot showed the back wall of the cave fully illuminated with four silhouettes of me aiming the flashes. Called "painting the walls with light," this technique has been around ever since cameras were invented, but few had ever used it in underwater caves.

Today, using the powerful strobes that are available, we can easily use this same technique to illuminate the entire under-water cavern providing that the diver with the wall-painting light strobe doesn't mind swimming around in the dark, and can do so without banging into too many unseen obstacles. Surprisingly, even the lowest amount of available light lets your eyes adjust to the darkness so that you can see where you are going. One of my more recent variations on that technique with which you can do the entire operation yourself—trigger the camera as well as light the scene with multiple flashes—involves nothing more complex than a large plastic clip that ties off to the camera. Here's how it works:

The weighted tripod and Nikonos V with a 15mm lens is set up where, by sighting and sweeping a handlight over the dis-tant scene, you can establish the area you intend to cover. Once properly positioned the camera is locked in place. You are shoot-ing with Fuji 100 color film. You set the lens on its widest aper-ture, f2.8, and "B" for open shutter. This means that once the camera button is pressed down and *held down* throughout the duration of the open shutter shot, the shutter will remain open. It will close only when that button pressure is released.

So you can quickly relocate the camera tripod in the dark chamber after the last strobe is fired, you have previously taped a small penlight to one leg with the lens pointed down toward the cave floor. Turned on, it will emit less light than a shielded candle but it will be enough to enable you to locate it quickly.

To illuminate the cave walls, you will be carrying another underwater camera connected to a strobe but without any film in it. All you want is a fast system for firing the strobe repeatedly after each recycling period. Plan to work from the cave floor, each shot bringing you back closer to your mounted camera.

Once everything is ready for action, and your eyes have nicely adjusted to the low ambient light so you can see where you are going in the cavern, switch on the tiny target light on the tripod leg. Then reach up and securely push down and wedge the large plastic clip onto the Nikonos V button mount so that it holds down the button opening the lens and will keep it that way until you return to unclip it.

Then carefully ease directly up to the domed ceiling, move across it into camera range to the opposite wall and commence repeatedly strobing the light toward the wall about ten feet from it. Never fire the strobe on an angle that will shoot light back toward the open lens. Where possible keep yourself low and fire with the light overhead.

You may take five or ten minutes working your way around the cave back toward your camera set-up, but once you have fired enough strobes to do the job, ease back to the camera and release the clip. Advance the film, reset the aperture to a smaller f-stop, perhaps an f5.6 this time, and repeat the process. After that close down one more time with an f8 and go again. Probably all of the shots will turn out all right, but one or more may be better exposed that the others. Learn to experiment, and bracket whatever you are uncertain about. The final results will repay all your efforts. The same technique works in a totally black cave if you use a shielded pen light to find your way and never point it toward the camera position.

Another related technique is to back up a fellow strobe photographer with a hand-held camera without a strobe. The hand-held camera that is to take the picture is set on open shutter. With a previously arranged light signal, such as the wagging of the front photographer's strobe with a modeling light attached, the second photographer opens his shutter. The first or front photographer then fires his flash at a formation or model or whatever. As soon as the flash fires, the backup cameraman releases his finger and closes the shutter.

The kind of picture you get resembles the third dimensional shots we achieved with our first housed camera trailing electrical cables and power-pack firing mechanism. The difference is that this technique simplifies the whole thing for the same results.

Wes Skiles is one of today's most accomplished underwater photographers whether he shoots stills, movies or videos. He has done this innovational work and achieved such a high degree of professional ability strictly because he was willing to try new and creative photographic techniques.

Skiles got started early in his career by cleaning yards and doing odd jobs as a teenager so that he could purchase a used Nikonos II with a bulb flashgun.

He and his buddies would take bags full of flashbulbs into caves and be lucky if part of them ever worked. If a bulb failed he shoved it back into the bag with the others. Eventually he learned to wear an arm band that held the bulbs, putting the fired ones in a different bag.

"I started to get some pretty wild images back in underwater caves of friends and I going where we shouldn't be because we didn't have the training nor the equipment to be there and taking pictures of it. Proof that we were out of our minds," said Skiles.

As Skiles got more proficient with cave photography, he began showing his slides. He knew there was lots of room for improvement, realizing he needed better knowledge of how to light up the dark places.

"When you work photographically in a world devoid of light, you have to come to truly understand in a 30,000th of a second what your strobe did," he said. "And there is no real way to know what kind of pattern of light you've emitted."

It was a long, exasperating self-learning period for Skiles and his assistants. He readily admits that none of his popular photographs would be what they are without the help of team members.

"When I take a photograph, it's a collective effort of the person pushing the camera button and having these other divers in the passageway holding strobes and knowing what their strobe is going to do. I direct them, but it is only through a long period of evolution that they know how to work with me. They know what my patterns are and the formulas for making pictures and that's how we do it."

Skiles, like others of this period, progressed from using the Nikonos II with bulb flash, to single electronic strobe photography which was better than bulbs because of its consistency.

Then he discovered the concept of slave sensors and slaving strobes. These are strobes possessing a sensor which, when activated by the light of another strobe, are themselves fired. It's remote control light. Fire strobe one from here, and the sensor picks up the light signal to automatically fire a second or third strobe over there.

Early on, Skiles was motivated by real life hero, Dr. George Benjamin, whose explorations and remarkable cave diving photographs using flash extensions in Bahamian blue holes, inspired many novice photographers. In the 60's and 70's, Benjamin pioneered cave diving by inventing such things as the Benjamin manifold, the concept of manifolds we use in cave diving today. He was an explorer, mapper, writer, and he really laid the foundation for what he was doing. But over everything, he was an underwater photographer. That was his lifelong pursuit, and he was doing innovative things that no one else had ever tried before.

"His imagery set a precedent for me," said Skiles. "I looked at his images and thought, 'That's what underwater cave photography can be if you really know what you are doing.' His work was a combination of wonderfully composed art and perfect use of lighting. You really felt that you were in a cave when you looked at Benjamin's photos. That's what I strived for and it gave me a goal. When I got into the sport of cave diving, there were only about 52 certified cave divers. The community was pretty young. Nobody said they wanted to do photography in caves in 1975. Today there are probably more than 10,000 certified cave divers. And a large percentage of those want to take good photographs in caves."

Skiles wanted to get photographs that were better lighted than those taken with a strobe. Those with frontal lighting were always too flat and uninteresting to him. So the first thing he did to solve the problem was to try and convince manufacturers that they needed a sensor he could point one way and a strobe he could point any way he wanted to.

"Everyone wanted the sensor on the strobe, but that was not the way we needed it. We wanted to do our own thing and we needed that sensor to read the source of light coming from the camera."

Skiles's photo crew went through a long developmental stage trying to find manufacturers with the proper slave sensors that fire with strobes. That was the beginning of taking the kind of photographs he visualized. He would describe what he wanted to the photo team, and the positions of each diver, and where he wanted the light to fall. They would shoot that scene, then critique it and try to improve it later.

It was not easy to create a pictorial illusion of a cave with depth to it when you are dealing with only a two-dimensional photograph.

"A cave is a place of black infinity," said Skiles. "You want to express that feeling of a tunnel passing through the earth. If you fire a flash, you paint brightly with light the things closest to you. That overexposes the foreground, and the elongated tunnel to the back is lost in darkness. This kind of treatment is avoided when you use staged slave strobes in the hands of people placed behind the dive model in the foreground."

After some success with this method, Skiles went from one strobe to three strobes. Then he began painting with light.

"We would set a camera on a tripod either upside down on a ceiling using a milk jug full of air to hold it to the ceiling, or on the floor using a regular weighted tripod."

This was the technique I described earlier involving open shutter exposures and strobes that are fired in different areas of a cavern to paint the walls with light.

From these techniques, Skiles moved into the area of underwater cave cinematography.

"When I started doing motion picture imagery inside underwater caves, I could turn on powerful cinema lights and see what I was doing. For the first time I could see the results of our lighting and correct it on sight. It was as if the strobes stayed on."

And from that, Skiles could really see what everyone was doing. The filming lights were putting out a huge quantity of light in an even 1,200-beam pattern so that the photographer had the same visual coverage as a strobe. Not as bright as that peak at 5600°K, but very effective when one is able to see his lighting setup.

These were battery powered lights. Each diver carried a battery pack about six pounds negative and about two feet long. It was worn alongside his dive tank, between his tanks or like a stage bottle in front. A cord linked it to the light. Now his divers were carrying real lights that looked pictorially proper to have in their hands.

The ability to see what he was shooting with motion picture lights carried over to how Skiles wanted to light his scenes with strobes for still photography. So he soon began combining cinema lighting and high-speed films to be able to photograph stills with flood lights. Now, his photo team did not have to worry about extension cords or strobes or slave sensors. They could move through the cave corridors and do creative photography.

Today, Wes Skiles and his film company, Karst Productions of High Springs, Florida, travel worldwide on photo assignments. He does underwater film productions for the *Discovery Channel*, *Arts and Entertainment*, *911*, and *Travel Quest*. And when he has a chance, he works on still another progressive concept of cave photography. This time he plans to combine two techniques—using 3200°K incandescent lighting with 5600°K electronic strobes.

"One of the things that never has been done photographically," he feels, "is to capture the sense of power of the water flow, the speed of the current, and the movement of vehicles going through caves." To remedy this, Skiles plans to shoot a series of motion photographs using what is called "rear curtain sync" on modern cameras to capture movements while freezing the diver's image on the leading edge with a strobe's burst of light at the end of the image.

By doing this, he feels he will be able to achieve still photographs with motion. Coupled with the third-dimensional effect of creative lighting, such scenes should appear totally realistic to viewers.

"They should lend themselves well to multi-projector shows," said Skiles. "That's what we're exploring visually now. I think one of the future goals of photography will be to truly capture the feel of cave diving, with all the impact of its motion and power. These are things that are still missing in today 's cave photographs."

20

No Picnic at Otter

To Woody Jasper on that hot summer afternoon, his decision as to what to do if it rained or didn't rain, certainly did not seem like a matter of life or death. At least not at the time. That day was his company's big picnic at Florida's Otter Spring on the Suwannee River, and whether or not it rained was insignificant. If it rained, Woody and his family would take the car; if it didn't rain, he and his wife, Kathy, would pile the kids into the back with his dive gear, and drive the truck.

Since the rain never came, Woody and his merry crew rattled off to the company picnic in his dusty pickup truck. It might not have rained, but it was close. He felt it in his bones.

Woody was the kind of guy who took no joy in knowing that he could unerringly predict weather by the subtle aches and pains in his joints. Considering the years he had been mistreating them, he figured he was largely to blame. After all, he was no fan of spectator sports. Woody always wanted to be out there doing it, doing the action stuff, maybe like an explorer, always pushing his way into new places.

That's why he had been so gung-ho about motorcycle endurance stuff in the woods. He liked to lay out trails through the roughest country, then see if he could make it. He liked challenges. He liked plotting a trail through the river swamp and trying to beat his way through it on the cycle.

But he ended up so bent and bruised from these efforts that he moved out of endurance motorcycling into something milder. He and Kathy took up trash canoeing. The challenge here was to pick out the trashiest overgrown waterway you could find, then try to beat your way up that tributary until either you or it gave out. Woody's wife, Kathy, was as nutty about this kind of thing as he was. Maybe even more. Her nickname in the sport was "buzz-saw." She could paddle her way through the trashiest place imaginable. All Woody had to do was set her in the bow of the canoe, push that bow into a log-jam and she'd tear through it, paddling until you dropped.

In the long run, however, all that activity didn't do much to alleviate Woody's arthritic joints. So he got out of trash canoeing and eventually ended up as a certified cave diver.

Not that this wasn't a rigorous sport, but there was something about the water that eased his joints. Even though when he walked down to the water's edge to gear up he had to use his air tank like a crutch to keep from wobbling, once Woody Jasper eased into the water, he was pure fluid motion. Amazingly, as soon as he was water borne, the aches and pains faded away.

But what could he really do in this sport, he wondered. Physically he was incapable of making any of those long-range deep penetrations his cave diving buddies always talked about. Woody was practically a cripple in a sport made for none but the fittest. Nobody wanted to buddy up with somebody who might not be able to cut it when the going got tough. Still, Woody had this explorer instinct nibbling at him.

"I sort of consciously tried to figure out if there was a niche left for me," he said. "About the only one was this exploring thing in the little places. It seemed the little places were where people hadn't really tried to explore too much, particularly people that were oriented to going 300 feet deep and a mile back. They weren't overly inspired to go to the shallow caves...like why go there when I can go in and bore a hole to China?"

So he ended up at one of those shallow spring caves. It was only 12 feet deep, but Woody liked it. It was wide and low, so low in places that while in one of his exploratory moods, Woody got himself thoroughly stuck in the passageway. It took him several minutes to extricate himself, but when he emerged from that experience, he came out with ideas that changed the way many cave divers did their diving in the early 1980's.

Woody said, "Why do we always wear our tanks on our backs and get stuck in the tight places when it would be easier to clip them off at our waists and not get stuck?"

The caving community thought this new upstart was out of his mind wanting to change such formal rules as that. But Woody didn't mind. He never cared much for rules. He just did what worked best. And in time some of the others began to see the sense of what he was doing. His technique called "side mounting" became common practice in the sport.

Wes Skiles and Woody Jasper "found" each other in a total silt-out of a cave one day. Skiles went diving with this rather strange fellow he wasn't too sure about, a guy with off-beat ideas, who used his air tank for a crutch and wobbled when he walked. The two got into a silt-out that was a humdinger. Skiles described it later as "grim, grim, grim." He said he was just sitting there trying to figure out a tiny window of visibility when along came Woody and the two had a "quiet conversation" checking out their situation. Woody was cool and totally collected. In fact, Skiles realized this crazy guy was actually relishing the experience. Together they worked through the problem.

From then on they teamed up and started diving together. Along with their buddy, Lamar Hires, the trio was soon taking on whatever challenges came along. And always, Woody was developing new ways to do things—a better way to carry a light pack in a butt mount position, for example, or a simpler way to clip on equipment. He was an innovator. In a cave crisis, Woody could always be relied upon to figure out things while remaining totally calm, which was one of the most desirable traits cave divers sought in their tightly bonded cave diving buddies. It could, and often did, mean the difference between life or death.

As the Jasper family made its way to the company picnic, four scuba divers entered Otter Spring cave system to look around. Totally untrained for what they were about to encounter, just going in there was the biggest mistake of their lives.

When the Jaspers arrived at the park, the picnic was in full swing. The food was great, the socializing typically job oriented, and everyone was having a fine time.

Then, one of their members noticed a commotion near the edge of the spring. Investigating, he learned that something serious had happened to the divers in the cave. Only one had managed to find his way out. The other three had now been in there long after they should have returned. Someone phoned 911 for help. The police were on their way.

Knowing that Woody was a cave diver, his co-worker told him about the accident.

Woody hurried to see what was wrong. A small crowd stood on shore. One was a dive instructor. With him was the excited diver who had made it out of the cave.

"He said they were some distance inside the cave when the place suddenly silted up," said Woody. "Being the last one in, this guy turned around and tried to find his way out. After banging around in a panic, he finally found his way out. The other three didn't make it. They had been in there long enough that I knew there was no hope of finding them alive.

"By the time I grabbed my dive gear out of the truck, some of the silt had settled," said Woody. He didn't bother putting on his wet suit—just slipped on his tank, took a light, and went.

As he submerged and moved into the murky mouth of the cave, the spring water had already numbed him to any discomfort. He followed a fixed line that started just inside the entrance. His only thought now was how bad it was going to be getting three bodies out by himself on only one tank of air.

Woody moved into the muddied water of the passageway, sweeping his light back and forth in front of him. He had made body recoveries before. He knew what he would probably find first: cast-off equipment—things divers jerk off in their final frenzied fight to get one more gasp of air.

The silty condition increased the deeper Woody penetrated the cave passage. The silt limited the range of his light. It illuminated only a short way in front of him. He braced for whatever might suddenly appear out of that brown murk.

When he was about 100 feet in, his light picked out a diver's face mask and snorkel lying on the floor of the cave.

Woody stopped and looked around more carefully. As the yellow beam crawled across the cave floor, searching for the familiar huddled forms, he failed to find them.

"Where are they?" he wondered. "It has to have happened near here."

Woody moved his light beam higher in the cave. Suddenly, he saw first their fins, then their legs. Two of the bodies were wedged in a tight ceiling crevice overhead.

Rather than go on, looking for the third body, Woody eased up to the bodies above him. On the chance that there might still be some spark of life left, he took the Calypso regulator out of his mouth, stuck it up between the divers, and pushed the purge button.

A huge volume of air erupted in the domed ceiling.

"I figured nothing would get anyone's attention faster that a blast of air if they weren't dead," said Woody.

But neither body responded. Woody grabbed the leg of the closest diver and pulled the body down off the ceiling. With a quick sweep of his light he glimpsed the pasty face. The mask was gone.

Woody towed the diver's body out of the cave.

On shore, Kathy Jasper had taken charge of the situation, knowing what was about to come next.

"Everybody, get back now," she said. "Take the kids. Give 'e m some room, there's going to be dead bodies coming out here soon."

As helping hands dragged the limp form out of the water and began customary CPR (cardio-pulmonary resuscitation) efforts, Woody went back into the cave to recover the other body.

As he put his light on it and was moving up to get it, a cold, clammy hand suddenly shot out of the gloom and grabbed him!

Woody jerked back, his heart pumping wildly! Suddenly he realized that the diver in the air pocket overhead was still alive! Squeezing up beside him in the ceiling crevice, Woody quickly gave the diver his reserve regulator. All he could think was, if the guy was alive, why hadn't he responded when Woody took his buddy's body?

Moments later, once the diver was able to talk in the tight air bubble, Woody learned what had happened. When the divers stirred up the silt, they thrashed around in a panic trying to find their way out. If they had been ten feet away in either direction, they'd have missed the slightly indented place in the cave roof that had trapped enough exhaled air for them to survive a while longer. They stayed in this air pocket until eventually using up all of the trapped oxygen, then one after the other they both lost consciousness. Their inflated buoyancy compensators kept them wedged in the ceiling crevice. The diver who regained consciousness after Woody's shot of air, had no way of knowing that Woody's quick-thinking saved his life. But when he came to, he was shocked to find his dive buddy gone.

The glare of Woody's light and the movement beneath him made him grab frantically, thinking he was grabbing his friend, not his rescuer.

The surviving diver still had his mask on. Once he felt ready to make the trip, breathing off Woody's spare regulator, the pair started out of the cave. Woody was a bit apprehensive about how it would go, but the rescued diver performed fine, following Woody along the fixed line to just before the cave entrance where the line ended. From there they had to swim a short distance to the cave mouth. Woody thought, "If he's going to panic, that's where it'll be."

Just before reaching the end of the line, Woody felt the diver stop. "Oh, oh," he thought. "Here's where the fighting starts."

But the diver had only caught his watch on the guideline. Once he freed himself, he nodded, ready to go.

"He was perfectly calm," said Woody. "We went out without a bit of trouble."

The crowd on shore was amazed to learn that the second diver was still alive. And Woody was equally amazed to learn that their efforts had revived the first diver.

The third diver, however, had not been so lucky. They found his body about 75 feet further along the tunnel.

The events put a damper on the picnic. As he and the family drove their truck home, Woody thought how lucky it had been that it hadn't rained. Insignificant as it seemed at the time, his taking the truck with its dive gear in back had meant the difference between life or death for those two divers in the cave.

⭢ 21 ⭢

THE ORDEAL AT BLUEBIRD

Not all cave diving is done for the sole purpose of exploring underwater caves. Sometimes, cave explorers find their subterranean passageways blocked by bodies of water. These sumps may continue indefinitely, or may simply be narrow, watery barricades to dry caves further in the system.

Ever since French cave explorer Norbert Casteret breached a sump in the French Pyrenees in 1922, discovering a dry cave once used by prehistoric members of the Clan of the Cave Bear 20,000 years ago, modern cavers always hope the next sump they conquer will reveal a similar secret cave containing Ice-Age artifacts.

The thought of being able to swim through a water lock and emerge in a subterranean world of striking beauty seen only by those skilled enough to breach the barrier, is enough to entice explorers into a sometimes subtle death trap.

In Tennessee, Alabama and Georgia, several large water-filled cave systems are rumored to turn into dry caves. Some are believed connected to other cave systems; others are believed to be separate self-contained systems. But what all had in common was a secret dry cave whose entrance was guarded by water.

Three accomplished Florida cave divers—Woody Jasper, Lamar Hires, and Wes Skiles—began searching for such a system in Bluebird Spring near LaFayette, Georgia. They believed that Bluebird was part of one of the deepest cave systems in the southeastern United States. If they could find that hidden connection through a wet or dry cave and link up to the bottom of this larger system, it would be an important geological discovery.

Earlier, however, after an exhaustive search by a British team of cave divers led by a well-known British explorer, this expert concluded that no link existed; there was absolutely no way to reach the big cave system through Bluebird Spring.

This assessment only spurred the Florida divers to search harder. They knew the link existed because dye they released in Bluebird Spring was found later in the large cave system.

Finally, after many dives, the team found a water-filled sump leading to a hitherto undiscovered dry cave inside the mountain. The reason they had found it when no one else could was because one of their members—Woody Jasper—devised a new cave diving technique that paid off. Working their way through tight, constricting passageways that had blocked others, they reached the long-hidden cave at Bluebird, but were unable to explore it carefully for a possible link to the larger system.

Weeks later, however, a larger team of experienced Florida cave divers joined forces for another try. This time Jeff Stillo, Paul Smith, Luis Menoyo, Woody Jasper, Lamar Hires, and Wes Skiles, returned to Bluebird Spring for a major exploration of the secret cave.

Once the divers entered the constrictions of the sunken sump, things got tighter and tighter. The limestone corridor started out as a body-sized tube about one-and-a-half feet wide, two feet high and 300 feet long. It passed through a series of low passageways with many radiating tunnels off both sides. Then it entered a small chamber with three tunnels, and a fourth, very small, low bedding plane leading out of it. It was through this bedding plane that diver Woody Jasper originally took his tanks off and pushed them ahead of himself through this passageway. It was understandable why this had blocked earlier explorers. The passageway was far too small to allow a diver to enter with his air tank conventionally carried on his back. So narrow was the passageway such places were called "body tubes." A diver had to take off his tank and push it ahead of him through the opening.

Now, all six team members did similarly, pushing their tanks and squirming themselves one by one through the narrow body space. It was what these cavers called "a tanks off, side mount body squeeze." You even had to turn your head sideways to get through one spot. This particular constriction was only about as long as a person's body, but it was impossibly tight—just large enough to pass through as long as your arms were ahead of you.

Once you pushed through this extreme constriction for six feet, you were confronted by a low, flat ceiling-and-floor body squeeze continuing for another 30 feet. This bedding plane opened into a shaft where the divers rose up and soon surfaced in a lake containing a small waterfall. Once they climbed up the waterfall, they were in a dry cave—Bluebird's secret cavern created in its long-forgotten geological past.

From this point, the cave led into a beautiful big canyon off which was a series of different sized passageways, all containing striking stalagmite and stalactite formations.

On this particular day, the divers stayed inside the dry cave exploring for about six hours. While there they performed various experiments. One of their goals was to see if they could pick up dye traces released by another caving team in the big cave to which they hoped to find the link.

The dye came through successfully, 12 minutes after its scheduled release in the big cave. Those in Bluebird were thrilled to see it appear. After that, three of the team members, Jeff Stillo, Luis Menoyo, and Paul Smith decided to exit the cave. Woody Jasper, Lamar Hires, and Wes Skiles chose to stay behind and continue exploring.

The plan was for these team members to leave in advance to avoid diver congestion while getting through the constricted areas of the sump.

An hour later, Woody Jasper and Lamar Hires decided to leave the cave as well. Skiles, having just found a new tunnel, decided to stay in the cave alone and explore this side passage further.

As his two companions left, Skiles went deeper into the cave passageway and did a series of digs, widening constrictions in order to squeeze himself through several tight places.

Progressing to a point some 900 feet from the main cave, Skiles decided he had gone far enough, and decided it was time to return.

As he headed back, he thought how great it was to be in the

cave completely alone, and that he would be able to return to the quiet lake room, put on his gear, slip into the cold water of Bluebird Spring, and have a nice unimpeded exit out of the cave.

But when he arrived at the lake he was surprised to find Jasper and Hires there, looking dejected. Knowing these individuals well, Skiles couldn't understand why they should still be there, both of them looking at each other the way they were.

The two were discussing an entanglement. Both divers were clearly upset. Jasper said he would go back down and try one more time.

Skiles suddenly realized that the group's exit out of the cave was blocked for some reason. "I wasn't sure what was going on," he said. "I tried to get information out of Lamar, but he was really caught up in the seriousness of our situation, a seriousness that I hadn't fully grasped yet."

Apparently, the guideline they had used to come into the cave, was broken. Jasper and Hires had stayed underwater for quite a while with no solution to the problem. They failed to find the continuous line that led out.

Hires and Skiles sat there awhile while Skiles got his dive gear together.

When Jasper surfaced, Skiles thought to himself, Woody will come through. He'll find the way. He always gets us out of predicaments like this. Now that he's back it's just a matter of gearing up, getting in the water and getting the hell out of Dodge.

But Woody came up shaking his head no.

Skiles's hope vanished. Over the years of diving dangerous caves with his close friend, Wes had come to respect Woody Jasper's innate cave diving ability even more than his own. But now, if even he had found no solution, things were bad. Woody's response shook Skiles.

The worst of it was that no one had any idea what had happened, or why the line was broken. But Jasper and Hires now had only enough air to go straight out. Each of them had only the remnants of a single tank of air. Jasper and Hires had already done a 50-minute dive on their tanks, exploring and mapping the cave coming in. They never dreamed they would need lots of air to get out again. The water was extremely cold and murky, but it was shallow, which meant their air consumption would be relatively low under normal circumstances. They had both reserved 1,000 pounds of air to get out of the cave. This would have been more than adequate for two or three exits. But now, Jasper and Hires were down to below 500 pounds in their tanks, the bare minimum a diver ever wants for surfacing. And here they were hundreds of feet back underwater inside of a cave passageway without a way out.

Wes geared up and slid underwater to see what he could do. In the darkness of the passageway he bumped around trying to think out their problem. It occurred to him that he had some resources available that he could use. Since he had been mapping the cave earlier, and had thought about a way out by referencing where he was according to his survey, he wondered now if that was the solution. As he checked his slate, he oriented himself to where he had surveyed.

"I knew where that point was and was able to go find it because the line was still intact to this one tunnel," he said. "It didn't lead out, but by knowing which way that tunnel lay, I was able to approximate the angle in which the other tunnel should be. I set my compass that way, descended to the depth where this passageway should be, and proceeded to push myself into little coffin-shaped tunnels.

"I did this two or three times, would get stuck, and couldn't go anywhere. Then I'd back out and try again, each time tying off a line to the primary one so I could follow it back again if the passage didn't go. About the third try, I pushed my body into this passageway and was able to go further. I kept going. I was laying a line even though it was not leading out of the cave. At least I had a line so that I could get back up to the lake.

"I was going through this tube tunnel and I ran into an object. As I bumped it, I thought it was a body. I pulled on the object, knowing that I would feel the weight of the corpse behind it as I had so many times before, but it moved more freely.

"As I pulled it up close to my mask I realized that it was the life support pack of caving gear—underwear, water and food— that Paul Smith carries with him regularly.

"Immediately, I had the sinking feeling that Paul, although not attached to the bag, must be there nearby and certainly dead somewhere underwater."

Pushing the pack out of the way, Skiles went on further, finding first a mask, then a light, then dive tables. Now, he was more certain than ever that there had been a drowning. On all the body recoveries he had ever made, finding jettisoned gear before finding the corpse was common. This was typical. He knew that one of his friends was dead somewhere ahead of him in the passageway.

"I pushed on, knowing that we had to get out of the cave," said Skiles. "At that point I pushed through the tight body tube and broke into an open area, groping in zero visibility around the room. Suddenly, my hand touched the broken line!"

Adrenalin surged through him like a shock wave. His thoughts raced, but he forced himself to think methodically, the way he had trained himself to think out difficult situations in the past.

"I was getting very low on air and I was very cold," he said. "But I couldn't make any mistakes now because it could cost us our lives. Even if we were to survive at this point, which was not a sure thing yet, I now painstakingly took precious time to tie bowline knots as opposed to some granny knot, tying the lines together. Also, the reel of dive line that I was now through with and had no further need for because the lines were joined, I went ahead and tied a proper loop and bowline knot to the end of that line, secured it properly to the reel, locked it all down and reclipped it to me. My first thought was to discard it, but decided I might need it again. Even though I was dangerously low on air, it was extremely important to pay attention to that kind of detail. Not that it would save my life now, but that's the kind of attention it takes to survive in cave diving."

At this point Skiles was faced with two decisions. Either he went back through the constrictions and murky maze of passageways to tell Jasper and Hires he had found the way out, or he went out of the cave. Skiles knew he had little more than enough air to maybe get himself out. But he also knew he had to let Jasper and Hires know something. The question was: what was the right thing to do at this highly critical moment?

Skiles turned and swam back into the passageway. He had to let his friends know that it was likely that they would be dealing with one or more bodies jammed in the narrow cave passageway he had not yet investigated. Certainly it looked as if Paul, if not also Luis and Jeff, would all be found drowned in that passageway.

Breathing shallowly, Skiles hurried back to the lake room. As he surfaced with Paul's pack in his hand, the pack came up first with Skiles behind it. When Jasper and Hires saw it, they knew immediately that one of their friends was dead. They recognized the pack as belonging to Paul Smith.

Skiles quickly explained that he had found the way, but it didn't look good. It was possible that they would have to try getting around the bodies that would physically be blocking the passageway they were trying to get through. With the low amount of air they all had now, it was going to be tough, getting around them and out of the cave. As far as waiting for help to arrive, that was out of the question. The technique of side-mount tanks was so new at the time that the six divers who had now been trapped or drowned in Bluebird, were about the only ones in the cave diving community practicing this new concept. This terrifying realization meant that absolutely no one could come to their rescue because no one else knew how to get into the cave! If they were going to be saved, they had to do it themselves, under their own power. And it had to be done right away.

By now, all three were shaking uncontrollably from being cold and wet. They had been in the cave now almost eight hours. This was an unusually cold cave with 52-degree water temperature. From the way they felt, it might just as well have been ice water.

Skiles started out. He went back through the body-sized passageway with his tank off, pushing it ahead of him, careful not to break the line again.

He got almost all of the way through the squeeze when suddenly a very cold hand came out of the darkness and a face was thrust up into his, almost scaring the life out of him. As soon as it was there, it was gone again.

Somehow or another, one of the divers—it looked like Luis Menoyo but Skiles wasn't sure—was still underwater in the cave. Wes couldn't understand how this was possible. Breathing his air as slowly and as shallowly as possible, he made his way out of the cave.

Miraculously, he found no bodies blocking his way. But there were so many passageways in the cave he knew they might be someplace else.

Surfacing, Skiles was overjoyed to find that their missing friends had made it through the passageway and were safely outside. In due course, Hires, and then Jasper made their way along the repaired line and emerged from the cave.

Only later did the survivors hear about the most traumatic part of the experience. It had occurred earlier when the first ones to leave were trying to make their way out. Luis Menoyo actually got out without any problem whatsoever. He was in front and he followed the line out of the cave. Behind him, in the low tanks-off squeeze area, Jeff Stillo got hopelessly entangled in the line. He tried to free himself but couldn't. His mask was flooding, he was running out of air, and he was desperately using all of his strength to get free.

Finally, he broke the line. In doing so he also kicked off Paul Smith's mask who was directly behind him in the squeeze, leaving Paul with a broken line, no mask and in zero visibility, completely lost.

Stillo frantically fought his way out of the cave somehow, making it to the surface on his last breath of air.

Paul Smith, an amazing individual, managed somehow to remain calm. Unable to see, extremely cold, and completely lost, he pulled his way through the low squeeze into a room with a labyrinth of tunnels. But which one went out?

He groped blindly. There is no way to feel your way out of this kind of situation. Cave divers have tried it as a controlled test to see if they can reason their way out without light, doing it by feel alone while a safety diver hovers overhead watching what they do. But no one ever succeeds.

So one can imagine the horror Smith felt as he groped through this room with multiple options of ways out, but only one was the right way. Fighting to keep from breathing hard on the little air he had left, he had to make the right choice, or die for his mistake.

Suddenly Smith's hand touched a wisp of line. It was one end of the broken guide line, but was it running back into the cave, or out of it? Only one thing was certain, he had to follow it.

As he fumbled through the darkness, keeping an index finger and thumb tightly looped around this frail cord, he came to other lines intersecting the one he followed. Smith had to know whether he was going in or out of the cave to make the right decision.

Each intersection was a life or death decision—Russian roulette with both air and time quickly running out on him. Quietly praying that he was headed out of the cave, Smith made his decisions accordingly.

He guessed right. The line led him out of the cave.

The divers outside knew that their friends were now trapped inside the cave. With the line broken in that murky maze, Skiles, Hires and Jasper had no way out whatsoever. Moreover, those outside knew how much air everyone had expended before they went into the cave, and how little all of them now had to figure their way past the broken line. In that muddy maze, there wasn't even a hope that they could make it.

As far as the group getting more air and making any concerted rescue attempt, that too seemed hopeless. Bluebird Spring was in a remote enough mountain area that a round-trip to an air fill station would take eight hours. By then, their comrades would probably have used up what little air they had trying to find their way through the break area.

Someone from outside had to go back into the cave and try to repair the broken line. If it wasn't repaired, the divers inside would probably not make it out.

Since Luis Menoyo had experienced the least traumatic exit, he volunteered to use his remaining air to make one quick attempt to repair the broken line.

Which explained why it was Luis who suddenly appeared out of the murk in the cave as Skiles came out. His urgency and failure to stay longer with Skiles was due to his having hardly any air left himself; he had to exit the cave quickly.

After Skiles came Lamar Hires without mishap. Woody Jasper was the last to work his way through the passageway. During that time his light failed, and since by then it was night outside, there was no light whatsoever. He followed the line by feel alone, and exited in the dark of night, a night that was suddenly bright with search lights.

As each of the three came out of the cave, they were startled to see over a hundred people around the spring basin concerned over the outcome. Blue lights on rescue vehicles flashed, car headlights and powerful hand lights swept the pool, campfires burned brightly. As the divers waded ashore, worried spectators stared at the survivors in disbelief. They thought all three divers had died inside the cave. Now, to their stunned delight, they realized that everyone had survived the nearly tragic ordeal at Bluebird Spring. Slowly, but with growing intensity, the crowd began applauding.

22

Lost, but to God

Near the small town of Curimagua, Venezuela, a centuries old stone road built by the Spanish snakes up through the sultry tropical jungle into the remote San Luis Mountains. This trail ends at a rocky grotto, a small cave named Acarite formed by fallen rocks. To some, the place looks like a religious shrine. Bizarre offerings are often left there, which has led to speculation that Acarite is associated with devil worship and witchcraft. Locals speak in hushed tones of people who entered the shrine in the past, and were never seen again. But outwardly, the small cave looks harmless, its presence in this verdant landscape marked only by the dung-colored stream that flows sluggishly out of its stony orifice from some hidden source deep within the bowels of the brooding mountain.

One sultry day in July 1991, it was this source that interested two adventuresome 30-year-old Venezuelan divers named Gustavo Badillo and Eduardo Wallis. Both believed that the brownish dark water flowing from this opening in the side of the mountain actually leads to the largest subterranean lake in South America.

This was not just wishful thinking. During the dry season, people could wade up the shallow stream and pass from one domed room to another, going deeper and deeper into the heart of the mountain. In 1973, a British expedition without scuba equipment had penetrated the cave during a low-water period and explored its passageway for about 600 feet. The Brits drew a map of the system showing a long, slightly curved single passageway at the end of which they had drawn a question mark.

Doing some research on the cave, Gustavo and Eduardo obtained a copy of the British map from a man who had accompanied the expedition.

"If we pick up on their lead and explore the system past the question mark, what a prize to prove that Acarite is bigger than anything the British found in 1973, that it is indeed South America's largest subterranean lake!" they thought.

Both men were scuba divers but not trained in cave diving. Gustavo had been trained as a cavern diver and both had explored different caves before, some of them dry caves with underwater passages consisting of a single passageway. Having talked with the former expedition member of the British team, Eduardo and Gustavo believed they could easily find their way into the underground lake and return again. After all, they planned to lay a single line which they would follow in and out. No problem.

Which was what Gustavo told his girlfriend, Maria Helena Mendoza, when the two divers and their buddy, Ricardo, drove from Caracas to Coro to pick her up. There, they also obtained the proper passes to enter the cave, and met their guide, Asmel, who knew the mountain well.

Despite Gustavo's assurance that the cave offered no threat to them, Maria Helena worried. She knew that when he had told his employers, the Indriagos, at the dive shop where he worked that he wanted to complete the map of Acarite, they tried repeatedly to talk him out of going. They even refused him the use of a line reel and other equipment, hoping that by doing so they would dissuade him from making this extremely dangerous attempt. His employer's wife, Vivian Indriago, knew what she was talking about; she had taken a cave diving course in Florida. She urged Gustavo to wait until he could accompany experienced cave divers from Florida into the cave.

But Gustavo was determined to do it himself, to map the system and be the first Venezuelan diver to do it. If his dive shop employers would not furnish him a proper cave diving reel and line, he would put a coil of rope in a nylon mesh bag and feed it out as they needed it. Once they got 150 feet inside of the underwater cave, they would tie on a smaller line and go further.

It was a long, scary drive up the steep, winding trail through the jungle. When they finally reached the cave, darkness had fallen. The group unloaded their jeep and set up camp. So excited were Gustavo and Eduardo to finally be within reach of their goal, they decided to dive at once. It made no difference that it was night—the blackness inside or outside the cave was all alike. The divers would each carry three lights.

As they geared up, Maria Helena was more apprehensive than ever. She did not like the look of the cave. The water flowing out of it was high and extremely muddy. Gustavo assured her that it was all right, that they would go in and be back out in 20 minutes.

"But what if you aren't?" she asked. "What should I do if something goes wrong?"

Gustavo shrugged. "Go for help," he said. "Phone my bosses, Vivian and Fernando Indriago."

Maria Helena pressed a small laminated picture of the Virgin Del Carmen printed with a prayer into Gustavo's hand. "Take this with you," she urged. "As long as you have this, nothing will happen to you."

They said their goodbyes as the divers entered the cave, tied the end of their rope to a buoy and started swimming into the outflow. It was 8 o'clock Saturday evening, July 13. Their friend, Ricardo, lit a candle in a water glass and floated it near the buoy so the divers would have a marker in the darkness when they came out.

As the men went underwater, Eduardo was leading and Gustavo was paying out the rope behind him. The water was extremely cold and muddy. Visibility was reduced to inches. The two progressed largely by feeling the walls around them, Eduardo staying to what he thought was the main passageway.

Not long into the dive, Eduardo realized that the map they had reproduced on their slate was not accurate. The passageway had too many alternate passageways. Each one took the diver underwater briefly, then he was able to surface in a dome of air. There were so many different domed chambers, it was confusing. On one occasion, Eduardo surfaced in one chamber and heard Gustavo surface in another, but neither diver could see each other. By calling, however, Gustavo responded to the sound and was able to find the domed chamber where Eduardo was waiting.

They were about a half hour into their dive when both realized things were not going well. Gustavo had been marking "X"s on the walls of the chambers so they could recognize any they had already visited.

"We better go back to the entrance and start over again," Eduardo suggested. "Our map's just not right."

"Good idea," said Gustavo. He was having trouble with the rope. It was tangled around his legs. As he untangled himself and pulled it, he realized the rope was slack. "You better go back and tie it off again," he told Eduardo.

"Okay." Eduardo slid underwater and started off in the direction they had come. Moments later he ran into a solid wall of rock. Perplexed, he back-tracked, again working down what he figured was the main tunnel shaft. But again, it was a dead end. Moreover, in whatever direction he went, he neither found the main corridor, nor Gustavo or the rope.

In a near panic he bounced from wall to wall, eagerly searching passageways that might lead out. Suddenly he squeezed through a narrow slot between the bottom and a boulder and found himself in a large chamber with an air surface. At first he thought it was just another dome, until he saw the tiny flickering light that Ricardo had left in a glass floating on the water. Eduardo had found his way out, but failed to recognize it because of the darkness.

Quickly he swam across the pool to where the others were waiting. He asked if Gustavo had come out of the cave yet.

"No," exclaimed Maria, suddenly frightened. "He was supposed to be with you!"

Eduardo explained that they got separated and he thought maybe Gustavo had already come out.

The anxious group waited 45 minutes, hoping that Gustavo would find his way out. But it was soon apparent that this was not going to happen. When their dive line came loose from its buoy, their eagerness to tighten it up left them with no line through the maze of chambers.

Eduardo decided he had to go back into the cave and find Gustavo. He had a short line left, and by tying on pieces of clothing and various bits of rope he fashioned a crude lifeline. Tying it securely outside and trailing it behind him, he swam back into the labyrinth of domed underwater rooms.

In the depths of the cave as far as he could go with this make-shift line, Eduardo again surfaced in the chamber where he had left his friend. Gustavo was gone. Eduardo repeatedly called his name and banged his tank with his dive knife. But when the echoes died, all he heard was a deathly silence.

Tying the make-shift line off to a small rock in case Gustavo came back to the chamber and could follow it out of the cavern, Eduardo swam back out and joined the others for an all night vigil.

At daylight, Gustavo's friends suspected the worst had happened. Somehow they had to get help. Maria told Eduardo and Ricardo to drive back to the nearest village and phone for help. She would wait at the cave in case Gustavo was able to find his way out.

Hurriedly, the men drove back the way they had come. At the first phone they called everyone who might be able to provide help.

At 7 A.M. as he was about to board his small jet at the Caracas airport, Fernandez Indriago, Gustavo's boss from the dive shop, received Eduardo's call and learned what had happened. He immediately phoned his wife, Vivian. The only qualified person she could think of for a search in that dangerous system, was a Florida cave diving instructor named Steve Gerrard.

It was Sunday morning when the call reached Gerrard. Vivian knew that Steve could probably be found at a small north Florida dive shop from which he often taught cave diving courses. In fact, Steve was just preparing to take a group of divers to a nearby popular spring when the urgent plea for help reached him.

Calls of this kind were not unusual for experienced cave diver Steve Gerrard. They might be unexpected and come at the most inconvenient times, but they were usually all alike. Someone had failed to come back from a cave dive and Steve was asked to make the body recovery. In the seven previous times he had responded, the results were always the same: seven lifeless casualties, due usually to their inexperience and carelessness.

Vivian's call was different in that she was asking Steve to come rescue a lost diver, basing her belief that he was still alive on the possibility that he might have made it to an air pocket and still be clinging to life.

Steve told Vivian that he would try to contact other experienced body recovery divers and see what could be done. But frankly, considering the length of time the diver had been in the cave, there was little hope of him surviving, especially after she told him the water temperature was around 50 degrees. That factor alone ruled out his survival. Even if Gustavo was in an air pocket, he would die from hypothermia, the rapid loss of body heat. And by now, he had been in that underwater cave for 13 hours!

But Gerrard tried to find help. He phoned several body recovery divers in south Florida. None was willing to go. After all, Steve was asking them to fly 1,500 miles to Venezuela just to crawl into a muddy underwater maze to bring out a corpse. Understandably, no one was eager for that kind of thankless experience. There were enough of those tragic scenarios going on in the underwater spring caves right at home.

Steve took his class to the spring as scheduled. There, he mentioned it to one of his fellow instructors, John Orlowski, a former student Gerrard had trained as a cave diver several months earlier. Orlowski hailed originally from Pennsylvania and wasn't the least disturbed about diving cold, muddy waters emanating from complex cave systems. Indeed, when Steve asked him if he was interested in flying to Venezuela with him on a body recovery, Orlowski found the idea appealing from the standpoint of an opportunity to explore a new system in an area he had never dived before. But hey, there was no rush. Orlowski went back to the dive shop and was there when Vivian's husband, Fernando, called again at 10 o'clock. After talking with Orlowski, Fernando voiced his irritation on hearing that the rescue team was not already on its way to Venezuela. Not that the dive shop owner believed there was much chance of finding Gustavo alive, but he was getting pressure from inexperienced Venezuelan divers eager to attempt a body recovery. Fernando feared that if more went into the cave, more lives would be lost.

Another day would be wasted waiting on a commercial flight.

The only other hope was to charter a private jet at a cost of $10,000. Fernando contacted Gustav o's parents to see what they thought of the idea. They urged him to do whatever was necessary to get the American divers there so they could get started.

Fernando phoned the dive shop with his plan. He would pick the divers up at the Gainesville airport at 10 o'clock that night. With his wife and another pilot, Fernando took off from Caracas in a chartered nine-seat Cessna jet. Ahead lay a grueling nine-hour round-trip flight, with scant chance of doing anything more than recovering the body of his friend, Gustavo.... Were they crazy to try? The family, already burdened by the tragedy, was now faced with the $10,000 expense that might mean only that they could bring out the body a day early. Was it really worth it? Fernando and Vivian felt it was the only right thing to do.

On the return flight to Venezuela, Steve and John discussed recovery procedures they would use. Orlowski had never been on a body recovery before. Gerrard tried to prepare him for the ordeal ahead.

The small jet landed at Coro which was the closest airport to the cave. From there they took a jeep the rest of the way along the precipitous, little used mountain trail to the site. There, the Venezuelans had laid out numerous air tanks and equipment for the effort. Gerrard looked at the slow moving muddy water and shook his head. He was glad Orlowski didn't mind diving in that kind of sludge.

"So you want to be a cave diver?" he murmured to his friend. Orlowski rolled his eyes. It was the question Steve always asked new divers wanting to start cave diving classes with him. John reached down and felt the water.

He looked up surprised. "Hey, it's not even close to 50 degrees! More like the mid-60's is my guess."

If he had made it to an air pocket, could a diver in a wet suit possibly avoid hypothermia after more than 35 hours in the water? Even as the thought raced through their minds, Steve and John knew it was unlikely. Both knew that water as warm as the low 80's can soon sap a body of heat and bring on the fatal results. Gustavo had been lost in typically cold spring water now for almost a day and a half! The only fact that made sense was that the water being warmer meant the corpse might be badly bloated. The recovery team would have to take extra weights with them.

After making their final plans and gearing up, the two flipped a coin to see who would lead the way. Orlowski won. Typically, the pair loaded up with redundant equipment. In this sport, gear failure is fatal. Spares is the name of the game. Each carried two air tanks, spare regulators and hoses, along with five lights apiece. Over-weighted as they were, they sank quickly into the ooze as they entered the muddy pool. Gerrard told Fernando earlier that they might not find the body in all that mud. The thought of Gustavo's parents being deprived the chance to even properly bury their son's remains was almost more than Fernando could take. He just shook his head, his red-rimmed eyes brimming.

Before they submerged, their big reel of line was secured to a rock outside the cave, then Orlowski led the way, paying out the line from the cave diving reel. Behind him, Gerrard followed the line, letting it slide easily through his circled thumb and forefinger. He might not be able to see his partner in the opaque water, but he would follow him wherever he went. That thin nylon line was their only way back.

Orlowski swam with the left wall of the cave always on his left side. Whether he could see it or not, he routinely touched its slimy surface with his hand to make sure it was always there.

At first they half crawled, half swam along the muddy passageway from one domed chamber to another. Then as the passageway deepened, they were aware of the expanding area. But visibility was still just a few inches. Orlowski's fin tips moved just inches in front of Gerrard's face mask, but he was unable to see them. Lights were useless in this soup. These divers were trained to move just as quickly and accurately in the dark by feel alone.

After working their way through this liquid murk for what seemed like an hour, they surfaced in a small air pocket, one of the many domes in the cave's roof. Both flashed their lights around the chamber, half expecting to find Gustavo's bloated body wedged against the ceiling. But the pocket was empty.

"I can't believe anyone would come this far back," said Orlowski. "This is pure crazy!"

The passageway had been deepening. This could be the last domed room. If Gustavo was dead in the muddy passageway ahead, there was a good chance that Orlowski would bump into the body head-on before realizing what it was. He didn't relish having to go on, but go on they both knew they must.

Orlowski continued along the passageway. Periodically his tank scraped the ceiling. Better that he keep himself high and out of the muck, than low and blundering into God knows what before he was ready for it.

Suddenly, John sensed that he was about to enter another domed air chamber ahead. He saw the glimmer of a light.

"How come?" he wondered in surprise. "How in the world did I get so turned around that I'm seeing Steve's light *ahead* of me?"

But as he approached it, he realized the light was too dim to be Gerrard. Poking his head through the surface, Orlowski was astonished to see a bulbous-eyed apparition covered with mud stumbling toward him.

"My God, Gustavo? Alive?"

"*Si, si! Madre de Dios, si!*" the apparition responded weakly.

John thrust his light back underwater and wagged it furiously, signaling Gerrard. Seeing the wildly gyrating light, Steve guessed his buddy had found the body and was maybe about to freak out. "Keep your cool, ol' buddy," he thought, surfacing just in time to hear Orlowski shout, "*Habla Inglis? Habla Inglis?*"

"Yes, yes, I speak English!"

Gerrard could hardly believe what he was seeing. Gustavo, alive! My God, it was impossible!

"We're Americans!" he shouted. "Are you okay?"

"Yes, yes." Gustavo was deliriously overjoyed.

The muddied figure in the bedraggled wet suit overwhelmed Orlowski first, hugging him and pounding him weakly with his hands, then he was on Gerrard and for the next few minutes the trio hugged and slapped each other, sharing the delirium of this totally unexpected outcome.

Once everyone regained their composure, they deliberated more calmly on what should be done next. They decided that since Gustavo was seriously dehydrated, Gerrard would go back the way they came for some drinking water, and possibly bring back another air tank. Orlowski would stay with Gustavo. Now that they had found him, he didn't want to chance losing him again.

As Gerrard carefully followed the lifeline back to the cave's entrance, the words, "We found him alive! We found him alive!" kept pounding through his mind. By now his adrenalin was really pumping. He could hardly wait to tell the incredible, the miraculous good news to those waiting outside.

Exiting the cave, he spit out his regulator and shouted across to the waiting crowd, "He's alive!"

The people stared at him in stunned disbelief.

Gerrard repeated it. "He's alive! We found him alive!"

Suddenly, the crowd erupted in jubilation, swarming forward to overwhelm Gerrard, dragging him ashore as he breathlessly explained what had happened.

Steve decided against taking a spare tank back into the cave for Gustavo. He and Orlowski had plenty of air for the three of them. He took only a large bottle of sugar water. It would give Gustavo the liquid boost of energy he needed in his dehydrated condition.

Back again in the domed chamber, after Gustavo drained the bottle of its fluid, they prepared to exit the system. Orlowski would lead with Gustavo behind him, breathing off his spare regulator. Gerrard would bring up the rear, keeping a firm hand on the diver to make sure nothing happened on their way out. Both rescuers were amazed at the calm composure exhibited by Gustavo considering his long ordeal.

When the trio emerged from the cave the waiting crowd went wild. Spectators plunged into the pool and waded through the mud to help the rescuers and the beaming Gustavo ashore. Maria Helena embraced Gustavo and cried. Vivian and Fernando and all the others swarmed over him with the unbridled joy shared by those who have seen loved ones survive death against all odds. It was 8 o'clock Monday morning, 36 hours after Gustavo and Eduardo had entered the cave.

In time, the big question was asked: "How had he done it? How had he survived?"

Gustavo said that while he was untangling himself from the loose guideline, Eduardo left to retie it. Once Gustavo untangled himself he was unable to find the exit from the air chamber he was in. He started swimming in different directions and found 16 similar air chambers, some large, some small, but none led back the way he had come. Eventually he ended up with only 1,000 pounds of air left in his tank.

"In the last chamber the water moved like a river," he said, "so I went underwater and looked for another chamber. When I found the next chamber it was bigger than all the others. It looked like a lake. This is the one where Steve and John found me. I noticed it had a small mud island in the middle. When I got to the island I became happy because I could leave the water. I took the equipment off my body and sat down in the mud."

In the long hours that followed, Gustavo alternately prayed, called out, or beat on his tank with his dive knife in the hope that someone would hear him and come to his rescue. He tried to conserve what battery life he had in his flashlights, but soon they failed and all he had was the light from a camera strobe. In the process of removing his wet suit to urinate, he accidentally lost his dive watch in the water. Eventually he found it by strobing the flash. Upon recovering it he learned he had been lost now for 30 hours.

With this realization came the cold clammy fear that no one was ever going to find him, that any rescuers had probably already given him up for dead. With the thought that he was now totally alone, sitting in the center of an unknown lake in the middle of a mountain cave that no one knew existed, Gustavo felt that his agonizing death was not far off. Rather than wait for it, he wondered if he should commit suicide. Surely that was preferable to going crazy and suffering through a long miserable death.

Unsheathing his dive knife, Gustavo tried making some tentative cuts on his arms. He thought of Maria and all of his family and friends, the fact that they now were probably quite sure that he was drowned to death. No one would ever again come looking for him. How much better to simply plunge the knife into his heart and end it all.

But as that morbid thought began to weigh heavier on his mind, so too did the realization that he couldn't take his own life. And to avoid any further temptation, in a burst of anguish,

Gustavo hurled his knife out into the darkness of his underwater tomb, hearing it splash loudly as it sank into the depths. After that, there was little left except to continue praying until the end.

Suddenly, the water around him began glowing a strange whiteness. At first he thought he was seeing things, the way people describe near-death situations where they find themselves moving toward a bright light at the end of a dark tunnel. Was this finally death coming to claim him? Then he heard the rush and popping of bubbles. A burst of light blinded his sensitive eyes, then the thunderous sound of someone speaking to him in English.

"I thought I had died and that they were angels coming to get me and that in Heaven they spoke English," Gustavo recalled later. In a tremendous surge of joy he staggered toward his rescuers who were equally overjoyed to find him still alive.

A helicopter air-lifted Gustavo to the hospital and except for some dehydration and a brief period of readjusting his eyes to daylight again, he came out of the ordeal surprisingly well. Steve Gerrard and John Orlowski flew back to Florida, feeling better than they had ever felt about a body recovery, knowing that had they not made the effort, this diver surely would have died. It was a new experience for both of them, rescuing not another dead diver, but instead, a very lively survivor.

A week later, Gustavo returned to the small mountain town to give the people there a few gifts in appreciation for their help in his rescue. He went to the entrance of the cave where the near tragic events reeled through his mind like scenes from a movie. He vividly remembered sitting in the blackness of the cave wondering if he had done any harm to anyone in his life, and that was the reason God was punishing him. Now, as all of the events of his life and the people in it scrolled before his mind's eye, Gustavo made himself a promise to somehow do something significant with the life he had left. He fervently believed that his life had been spared by the prayer given to him by Maria Helena just as he was about to enter the cave, the small plastic prayer that he had lost in the cave, but not forgotten. It was the Virgin del Carmen that had brought Steve and John to save him. After all, she was the Virgin of Miracles.

23

THE CAVE TIGER

As mentioned earlier, the first time I met Sheck Exley was a sobering experience. It was at Florida's Little Salt Spring in 1972 as we were descending single file with other divers on an archaeological dive to view human bones, when I developed a touch of vertigo.

Exley was my stabilizing influence. Had he not been there to help by placing his hands on my shoulders, I suspect I would have just kept on "spinning."

What I didn't learn until years later was that Exley was a different person from the one I had known briefly during those Little Salt Spring dives. Indeed, since I never saw him in his "natural guise," it's difficult for me to imagine Sheck as others knew him, teaching algebra at Suwannee High School in Live Oak, Florida. Certainly, the Sheck I knew could be called "mild mannered." But whether he fit the Clark Kent persona, I cannot say. I do, however, see some similarities between the Sheck Exley I knew, and Clark Kent's alter ego. Nothing about his demeanor suggested the powerfully controlled methodical personality behind his outward facade. But Sheck Exley was one very extraordinary individual.

Sheck's introduction to the underwater world began in 1965 when he became scuba certified at the age of sixteen. As a young, eager student, his first open water dive at Crystal River, Florida led to his investigating the shallow but interesting cave at Kings Bay. The experience so impressed him that from that moment on, cave diving was to be his primary avocation. But not one that he was to take lightly.

With young Exley, the idea of being able to explore this alien world of inner space and to penetrate places in the underwater world—caverns, grottoes, mysterious tunnels—leading deep into the earth where no man had ever gone before, was simply too tantalizing to resist. Cave diving became his greatest compelling ambition.

Just how compelling it was can best be judged by the fact that only seven years after he was certified, at the age of 23, he logged his 1,000th cave dive. No one else had ever accomplished anything like that before.

It takes no degree in algebra to figure out that to establish such a record during those years, Sheck had to average almost three cave dives a week! All this during a period in which he graduated from high school, and later the University of Georgia at Athens, which is 600 miles round-trip from the north Florida spring caves he was diving so frequently. Talk about hustling! Nothing ever diminished Exley's obsession with cave diving.

Periodically over the years I read about his exploits. He was always leading the way somewhere deeper and further into sunken caves than anyone had ever gone before. Most times he had dive buddies who were capable of accompanying him. But sometimes, they were physically incapable of keeping up with him. Some perished trying. Sheck Exley was one of the first who felt there were times when it was justified for a diver to dive alone, without a companion. Where he went was doubly difficult to bring one's self back safely without taking on the added responsibility of another person's life.

In his continued compulsion to penetrate caves deeper and further than anyone had gone, Sheck began setting records, the kind that sometimes lasted briefly before he broke his own record to establish a new one.

Exley's first notable record was established May 11, 1975 at Manatee Springs, Florida. Accompanied by Lewis Holtzendorff and Court Smith, he set a penetration record of 4,110 feet. Four years later, divers Lewis Henk and Dave Manor bested Exley's record and pushed the cave to 5,326 feet. Two years later, Sheck Exley and Bill Main broke this existing record by pushing the cave to 5,914 feet. A month later they went to 6,867 feet in that system, and just 15 days after that, on August 23, 1981, Exley and Bill Main explored Manatee Springs to a distance of 7,665 feet. At the farthest point of penetration, the divers reached an impassable constriction too small to negotiate. That particular dive took four hours to accomplish with an additional six hours of decompression.

Dr. William Stone, who was later to develop the innovative Cis-Lunar rebreather, accompanied Exley when he recovered his spent staged air tanks after the record-making penetration. It was a memorable experience for Stone, himself a highly accomplished cave diver and explorer. His account of that tank recovery provides some idea of what this environment is like.

Right from the beginning, Stone was impressed with the entrance to the cave. It was called Friedman Sink which he said was a nice-sounding name for a manhole-sized entry hidden in the woods by palmettos and live oak trees.

The opening was so tight that the divers had to hang their stage bottles (reserve tanks of air) beneath them as they slid down the 50-foot limestone shaft before it deposited them into a 40-foot-wide underground river flowing like a mill race.

"At first you are mesmerized at the transition," Stone said, "and the fact that you are hovering 40 feet off the floor of a gin-clear tunnel. The second thing to hit you is usually the ceiling as you are swept downstream by the incredibly forceful flow."

Exley had warned Stone in advance to completely deflate his buoyancy compensator upon reaching the tunnel, which he had done. But upon entry into this mill stream, they had 2,000 feet to go up-current, crawling along the bottom, pulling themselves from boulder to boulder as they pushed with their fins. It wasn't long before their fingers were raw.

Stone was relieved when they finally reached the cache of empty tanks left when Exley and the others returned from their record penetration. He was amazed to see the tanks and regulators already covered with a patina of silt.

Stone grabbed four of the tanks; Exley took six. The current blasted them downstream to where they had dropped their own reserve tanks at 1,300 feet on their way in. Once they collected all of those, Stone said:

"Riding that current on the way out, we were really nothing but humans riding uncontrollable bundles of tanks down this wild subterranean river. Most of the time it was dream-like. You just loaded your buoyancy compensator so that you and the mass of tanks were neutral and the current did the rest...until the passage took a sharp turn...and there were many. There, despite the strongest finning and mental willing, you still unceremoniously smashed into the wall and rolled sideways, the current spinning you along, until the river shot you back into the mainstream where you had a little maneuvering room."

Once they reached the Friedman entrance which Stone said looked like a ridiculously small soda straw leading out of the roof, they had another problem: how to get the tanks and themselves back up through that soda straw.

Fortunately, a number of small crevices radiated off that narrow exit and the divers slid their tanks into them as if racking bottles of fine wine.

"As we decompressed," said Stone, "every ten feet would find Exley passing tanks up to me one at a time until we found more shelves and crevices. Despite the constricted quarters—it was so tight that Exley was always one stop deeper than me—our little tube had a benign and friendly ambience about it, giving plenty of pleasant time to reflect on a most unusual journey."

This penetration record of Manatee Springs in one continuous push, stood as a world record for over seven years. It was only bested in October 1987 by Sheck Exley at Cathedral Canyon, a spring he recognized years earlier as having so much potential that he bought the property on which the spring existed, and put his house there. Now, this cave diving explorer, with a penchant for diving deeper and further into underwater caves than anyone else in the world, had taken residence over what would prove to be one of the world's longest subterranean systems. He could explore Cathedral Canyon's outer limits to his heart's content, right in his own backyard.

Before that, however, there had been another very pressing record to break. This involved man's deepest vertical descent into the earth in an underwater cave. In 1981, Europe's best underwater cave explorer, Jochen Hasenmayer of Germany, electrified the divers of the world by descending 476 feet into France's Fountain of Vaucluse, the same system that once had almost claimed the lives of Jacques-Yves Cousteau and Frederic Dumas in 1946.

Hasenmayer had gone over 100 feet deeper than Exley's existing cave depth record, making a new world record for surface to surface diving on scuba. He had accomplished this feat by breathing heliox, a mixture of helium and oxygen that divers were using experimentally in those years to avoid nitrogen problems with air.

Ever since scuba diving began, divers relied on the Navy's decompression tables as the standard procedure for preventing decompression sickness or bends. These tables applied only to air—21 percent oxygen and 79 percent nitrogen. When that breathing mixture was a combination of helium and oxygen, then new tables had to be devised. They were not always successful. Decompressing divers on this mix sometimes suffered severe results.

For that reason, Sheck was not too keen on heliox. Hal Watts, one of the first of the truly deep diving pioneers, used a helium mixture during a body recovery in Florida's Mystery Sink. Not only did he fail to find the body, but on his way back to the surface, complications caused him to miss his 60-foot decompression stop. As a result, he was severely bent. He described the pain as feeling as if his lower spine had been injected with hot lead. He said he agonized and vomited constantly for the two and a half hours it took to get him to a recompression chamber at Cape Canaveral. Recovery from the painful injury took a year.

Exley well remembered that his closest friend, Lewis Holtzendorff, died in 1975 when he and a companion tried to set a world record cave dive using heliox. The tragedy occurred during decompression on oxygen after a 265-foot depth record had been established. At 40 feet, both divers abruptly could not breathe. Holzendorff convulsed and drowned. His companion, Court Smith, miraculously made it to the surface and survived.

Sheck kept up with all these events but had his own personal prejudice about some of the exotic gas mixtures. In 1983, when Hasenmayer set a vertical cave diving depth record of 656 feet on heliox, this plunge got Sheck Exley's attention.

After participating in the successful 1987 Wakulla Spring project using a heliox mix that had caused no decompression problems among the 12 divers using it, Exley decided that heliox was at least part of the equation for success. By combining it with the same decompression computation program developed for that project by Bill Hamilton and Dave Kenyan of Tarrytown, New York, Sheck believed he could better Hasenmayer's record in a deep system he had already investigated in Mexico named Mante.

The spring called Nacimiento Del Rio Mante located in northern Mexico west of Tampico was first visited by Sheck and his experienced cave diving companion, Paul DeLoach in 1979 when the two were exploring Mexico's underwater cave systems.

The divers had penetrated Mante 150 feet, pulling themselves down a narrow, sometimes no wider than three-foot shaft that descended into the depths. Unlike the other caves they had explored, however, this one did not turn into a horizontal passageway at that depth. Instead, it continued to plummet straight down through a limestone fissure.

Pursuing its course by pulling themselves down the slender shaft until they were 330 feet below the surface, the two finally stopped. The sharp-edged tight shaft still descended into the black abyss below them. How far would it go?

With their minds already reeling from the vertigo associated with those depths, the pair turned back for their over-an-hour decompression trip to the surface.

In 1979, Exley returned to this seemingly bottomless shaft and explored it even further, reaching a point where he felt sure that Mante might be one of the deepest vertical caves in the Western Hemisphere. But to reach its uncharted depths required a lot more technology than was available in 1979.

After his 1987 Wakulla dives, however, Exley felt this technology was now within his grasp. Moreover, another pressing truth had to be recognized: Sheck was no longer the young man he had been when making so many of those physically debilitating pushes into the unknown. He was now 39, and fully aware that having passed the mid-30 mark, his chances of being bent increased with age. He logged his 3,000th cave dive in May 1987.

Now, on April 1, 1988, as he and his companion, Ned DeLoach, (no relation to Paul DeLoach) left Live Oak, Florida in Sheck 's van, loaded to its bottomed-out springs with 34 air tanks, it was time to see what deeper mysteries Mante had to offer.

DeLoach and Exley intended making a marathon drive

straight through to their destination, no small feat in itself considering the ordeal ahead. This was not to be a high-profile bring-on-all-your-experts-with-their-support-crews type of expedition. It was to be about as low-profile as you get. Exley had arranged for only two other accomplished Mexican divers to meet them. Other than that, it was largely a one-on-one operation: Sheck Exley against the Mante.

Ned DeLoach, an author and accomplished diver in his own right, was a perfect partner to document this low-key expedition. The account he wrote titled *The Deepest Dive*, subtitled, *A Study in Controlled Paranoia*, is one of the most insightful ever written in detailing the moods, fears, tensions and psychological preparations successful divers must experience to achieve maximum results.

Exley may have statistically passed his physical peak for this type of endeavor, but what he had now that he didn't have before was the magic combination he felt would spell success— oxygen, helium and computerized decompression tables tailored for these mixed gases.

As the two drove across country, DeLoach learned something about Exley's preparation for the final push down Mante.

Sheck told DeLoach that after Hasenmayer's 656-foot record, he knew that helium was the key to achieving great depth. In Florida he tried the mix, descending first to 130 feet, and later to 260 feet. Then the year before, he and Mary Ellen Eckhoff headed for Mexico's Mante River Springs.

Two days before the dive, they placed five reserve air tanks in the system. The dive that followed took him to a depth of 520 feet with over 7 hours in the water and 27 decompression stops before he surfaced.

Two months later, he and Eckhoff, returned to the springs with slightly modified tables to try and eliminate some oxygen toxicity problems—facial muscular spasms, tunnel vision, etc.— Sheck had experienced during his previous dive.

This plunge took 24 minutes for him to reach 660 feet, with a price tag of 11½ hours of decompression time. After 12 hours underwater, feeling extremely cold and weak, with hands and face both raw and wrinkled from the exposure, Exley knew the meaning of being water-logged. But he didn't know until it was all over how deep he had dived!

His depth gauge had only recorded to 515 feet. He tied it off at that point and attached a pre-measured line to his previous line. When he reached the deepest point he felt he cared to go, he cut the attached line. Later, on the surface, when he measured the addition, he found that he had exceeded Hasenmayer's record depth but it was so close to it, he didn't bother claiming the record.

Now, he and DeLoach were headed back so that Sheck could break Hasenmayer's record once and for all with a wide margin.

When DeLoach asked Exley how far he thought he could go, Sheck said without hesitation, "At least 700 feet, maybe more."

He then explained that he was using the new computerized tables from the Wakulla project. The new tables would allow him to customize his gas blend. Since he felt he had a high oxygen tolerance, he planned to use Tri-mix during the deepest part of his dive. He hoped this would let him avoid certain uncomfortable side effects of diving deep on heliox—extreme cold and nervous system disorders.

In discussing his preparation for this record dive, DeLoach was impressed by the complex details Sheck's mathematical mind had worked out for this extremely critical undertaking. Using the computerized tables required Sheck to have 16 reserve gas bottles placed at strategic points along his return route while he carried four additional tanks with him. During the dive, he would be breathing 11 different blends of gas, mixtures he had worked out as being the best for the job he had to do. He would make 52 decompression stops, the first one beginning 520 feet down, and the last one ending at the surface where he would breathe oxygen for a half hour.

How long Exley would remain at each of the decompression stops depended entirely upon how long it took him to descend and what his maximum depth would be. These factors would all have to be entered into his dive plan during the time he was actually experiencing the dive.

Not the kind of calculations your average diver could make. Especially one that is hundreds of feet underwater down a narrow rock crevice where if your calculations are incorrect and you have a problem, no one and nothing is going to come down and get you. Not even a body recovery team.

And whether or not Sheck returned from this trip depended entirely upon how deep he went, how long he was there, and whether he calculated the mathematics of all this accurately. One thing, however, was especially in his favor: from Sheck's years of experience in all kinds of difficult cave diving conditions, he knew how to handle stress. Once during a deep dive, he lost his dive watch. Not seemingly too significant a loss until one realizes it meant he had lost the means to determine how long he remained at his decompression stops on the way back. With some ten hours of decompression to do, Sheck did the only logical thing left—he mentally counted off the time. He continued counting until he was finally able to recover a second watch he had thoughtfully left at one of his intended decompression stops. Otherwise, his only alternative to survival would have been to count and remember each minute of those ten long decompression hours while hanging suspended in the cold water blackness of a narrow stone shaft deep within the bowels of the earth. Remembering such details as a spare watch had saved Sheck's life more than once.

It was during this discussion on a long ride to Mexico that DeLoach asked Sheck how he would decide when he had gone deep enough?

Sheck quickly replied that his fear would tell him that. He said it was all a mind game. He knew some cave somewhere was out to get him, and that it probably would catch up to him some day. In fact, his being alive even then was a miracle considering how many close calls he'd had. But it wasn't chance or just luck.

As Sheck talked, DeLoach learned why his unique friend always came out the winner. Sheck told him that he spent hours thinking of every possible thing that could go wrong, then, during his dive preparations, he did whatever he could to prevent them happening. He mixed his own gases, checked every piece of equipment repeatedly, memorized every aspect of the dive plan, then dived it exactly as he planned. The dive itself was like hunting a tiger, he said. Fear kept him alert. He was constantly attuned to every feeling in his body, every function of his equipment, every happening in his surroundings. He fully believed that the moment he went off guard—just once—the tiger would have him.

Sheck said he had learned to handle his fear with what he called controlled paranoia. To him this was a combination of meditation and experience. Meditation cleared his mind of tension, allowing him to achieve a high level of alertness, one that constantly monitored his reaction to stress during a dive.

Sheck told DeLoach that in his 23 years of cave diving, he had somehow managed to escape every life-threatening situation anyone had ever gotten into including the bends, being lost, light failures, running out of air, buddies who panicked, entanglements, getting trapped in restricted passageways, and more. Sheck said that when something went wrong, the first thing he did was control his fear. After that, he let experience take over. Plenty of problems could occur, and those he could cope with. But an error in judgment was fatal.

His plan of attack for Mante: From the beginning, plunge down the shaft as quickly as possible without losing control. Use gravity and pull on the wall to keep from using legs and wasting energy. Passing through the deepest part of the shaft is his greatest risk. Each breath there makes the pressure gauge needle dip lower in marked increments. His mind is constantly on the lookout for emergencies. Each new projection coming toward him he evaluates as a place to tie off in the event of an emergency. If something occurs, his experience kicks in and takes over. The problem must be solved on his first try, or Sheck immediately aborts the dive. If the dive proceeds as planned, he turns around at a point dictated by how long he stays down and how much gas he uses, plus what he calls, "an indefinable coalition of sensory perceptions that tells me to get the hell out."

When the pair finally arrived at Ciudad Mante, Sheck drove straight through town and followed a narrow road leading toward a distant mountain range and the Rio Mante. He wanted to check on the condition of the spring and how much water was flowing.

When they arrived at the spring, they saw two fully equipped dry-suited scuba divers emerging from the water. They were Sergio Zambrano and Angel Soto, the two Mexican divers who were Sheck's support crew. Everyone greeted each other amiably.

The divers had just returned from a 180-foot dive into the spring cave and reported 50-foot visibility with a moderate flow. Sheck was pleased to hear that conditions were fine for his dive.

In fact conditions were so good Sheck moved the dive date up a day which meant, that afternoon he had to make a difficult 330-foot dive into the system to place the deepest reserve tank.

There was nothing outwardly spectacular about Mante. It flowed out of the bottom half of its cave entrance into a bluish green spring pool 150 feet wide where local bathers gathered to enjoy the cool waters.

It took Sheck two hours to gear up for his staging dive. He entered the spring at 6 P.M., placed the bottle at depth, and spent the remaining time decompressing on his way back to the surface, emerging long after dark.

The following day, everyone worked hard to place the reserve tanks in the upper cave passage where Sheck would need them for decompression. Sergio and Angel diligently placed spare tanks each 20 feet apart from 160- to 80-foot depths, and at 10-foot intervals from 70 feet to 30 feet.

Sheck dived again to depth leaving a pair of tanks at 270 feet, one at 240 feet, and another at 210 feet. DeLoach accompanied him documenting details with photographs, stopping only at 100 feet as Sheck, silhouetted behind his powerful light, disappeared into the watery blackness.

The last thing DeLoach remembered seeing that evening before retiring was Sheck still up tying knots in a line and double-checking charts. When he awoke the next morning, he found Sheck cleaning regulators and checking repeatedly all of his equipment.

The group arrived at the spring shortly before 8 o'clock. There was no conversation at all. Sheck was mentally reviewing the details of the dive, the dozens of important things that had to be remembered to prevent the effort failing. As DeLoach described it later, they acted like a team whose pitcher was going into the ninth inning with a no-hitter. They sat 20 yards away on their truck's tailgate watching Sheck ready his equipment.

As DeLoach saw his friend methodically and mentally preparing both his equipment and his mind-set for the effort ahead, he reflected on the dangers of the dive and what he knew about this man who was now going to try to beat the odds.

The professionals who knew the dangers of mixed gas diving under these conditions gave Sheck a 50/50 chance of surviving the attempt. But in DeLoach's mind, there was no question whether or not he would survive. The only question was how far down he would go this time.

DeLoach saw Exley not as a daredevil but an explorer who had spent 20 years preparing himself both mentally and physically for this kind of underwater challenge. In those years that he had known him, DeLoach said, "I've acquired almost a mythical confidence in his ability to accomplish amazing dives. He is simply the best and most experienced diver in the world. If it were physically possible to pull off a 700-foot plus dive, Sheck was the one who could do it."

Geared up, Sheck entered the water at 10:45 A.M. The last his support crew saw of him was as he pulled himself into the entrance of the dry cave. Eight minutes later he was 100 feet back in the dry chamber, kneeling on a rock ledge mentally calming his mind, forcing his pulse to settle as his body calmed down from its pre-dive stress. Periodically, he bent down and pushed his maskless face into the cool, chilling spring water.

Two minutes later, Sheck turned on his four backup lights and his bright primary light designed especially for this record attempt. Gripping the air tank's regulator firmly between his teeth, he pushed off from the ledge, submerged and swam 50 feet to the drop-off. Reaching this point, he checked the exact time, entered the figures on his slate, purged the last bit of air from his buoyancy compensator, and began descending into the crevice.

The upwelling current was so strong he pulled himself down arm over arm, head-first without finning, following a fixed line on the south wall. Three minutes later at 190 feet, he angled left from a projecting rock and continued down. At this point the crevice widened to 15 feet and the walls were smoother.

Now, Sheck kicked his fins to maintain his forward momentum. His pulse increased with the exertion. He eased off his efforts as he passed his reserve tanks placed at 210 and 240 feet.

Two hundred and seventy feet down, he paused momentarily to switch from his air tank to the waiting cylinder of Tri-mix. Ten minutes into the dive he knew he had reached 400 feet down when he spotted a marker left by Mary Ellen Eckhoff the June before. It was a blue garter. At this point the crevice walls stretched 30 feet apart, the widest area in the shaft. Everything was going as planned.

At a depth of 520 feet, Sheck stopped briefly to clip his backup watch and two spare depth gauges to the down line. Now, he began breathing the tri-mix he carried. His depth gauge and watch were now the only two vital monitoring instruments he carried.

Six hundred and sixty feet below the surface, Sheck arrived at the end of the fixed line. It had taken him 17 minutes to reach this point. He attached his reel line to the fixed line and continued his descent, dropping now into depths where no one had gone before under his own power. As he passed into this unexplored area, Sheck was concerned about his slower than anticipated descent rate. But he forced himself not to pick it up.

At this point, rather than continuing his vertical drop, he found the shaft angling 60 degrees. Sheck now felt the effects of narcosis as the slight attacks of headiness came with more regularity. As he glanced at his depth gauge he realized something was wrong. The needle had not changed since the last time he checked it.

He tapped it against his tank. The indicator jumped several hundred pounds lower. The water pressure had squeezed the gauge's lens against the pointer, jamming it. Had he corrected it, or was it still jammed?

The tunnel now descended at a 45-degree angle. At every good projection, Sheck paused to tie off his descent line. He looked at his pressure gauge. It showed he had consumed one-third of the gas. He had been down now for 22 minutes. It was time to go up.

He spotted a good place to tie off his line about 30 feet beneath him. As he descended to that point he was suddenly shaken by an abrupt concussion that almost knocked him out. Had he ruptured a valve or hose?

As best he could he checked his equipment but failed to find the problem. Something had imploded but whatever it was apparently still worked.

Sheck quickly tied to the rock projection, reeled in the loose line and cut it. He had been down now 24 minutes and 10 seconds.

It was important that he get out of this depth as soon as possible. The current that had slowed him on his descent now lifted him like an elevator. He controlled this rate of ascent as best he could to 120 feet per minute. Then another problem arose.

His regulator began breathing hard. Each breath came with more difficulty. Was he running out of air? Again he rapped his pressure gauge against his tank, but this time the needle remained steady. Sheck had no way of knowing whether it was jammed or whether he had exhausted the gas he was breathing. He knew if he were forced to use the gas in his waist tank he would miss all of his decompression stops to 330 feet where the first air reserve was clipped off.

Sheck switched over to his backup regulator and was relieved when he found he could again draw a full breath.

At 520 feet he started decompressing up. Untying his gas gauges, he remained a minute then began ascending at the rate of 10 feet per minute until reaching 340 feet. Only when he saw his first staged reserve gas tank did he begin to relax a little. With ample gas mixture and plenty of spare time on his hands now, he searched for the cause of the deafening concussion.

It was the large Plexiglas battery housing on his primary light. Intense pressure had squeezed the three-quarter-inch-thick lid into the unit, crushing the battery pack. But surprisingly, the light still worked.

"Next," said Sheck later, "I counted the knots on the line remaining in the reel. I factored in the angle of the cave's lower reaches and estimated that I dived 780 feet—a world's record depth for a surface-to-surface dive."

Three and a half hours after Sheck had disappeared into the cave, Sergio and Angel geared up and dived down to see where he was. They found him at 100 feet with a cluster of 12 empty scuba tanks he was bringing back up with him. The three exchanged greetings and congratulations.

Nine thirty that evening, Sheck finally reached the surface

where the others were waiting with a camp light. He had been underwater for 10 hours and 43 minutes. And he was still decompressing. For the final 30 minutes, he remained in the spring pool breathing pure oxygen.

"When he emerged from the water," wrote Ned DeLoach, "he resembled an old man. His face and hands were severely wrinkled, his walk faulty. Three times on the way to the van, he stopped to calm his racing pulse. Later, while struggling to free himself of the dry suit I saw weariness set deep in Sheck 's face like I'd never seen on another man. What came to mind was Hemingway 's description in *The Old Man and the Sea* of Santiago's utter exhaustion after his battle with the sharks."

No sharks had bothered Sheck Exley, but he had met the tiger in the cave again. And as he had done so often in the past, once again he bested it.

In March 1989, Exley returned to Mante and pushed his depth record to 867 feet. And in December 1991, at Florida's Cathedral Canyon Springs, Sheck Exley, diving alone using 14 staged reserve bottles, and a staged Aqua-Zepp underwater propulsion vehicle, dived into Cathedral Canyon and at an average depth of 160 feet, penetrated that system for a well-deserved world record 10,939 feet.

In his book, *Cave Passages: Roaming the Underground Wilderness*, author Michael Ray Taylor wrote that when he asked Sheck Exley what his motivation was for going to Mante and why do such deep dives, he said, Exley's response was, "'I held both the world depth and distance records in 1970...I thought it would be nice to hold them both again before I retire. It just took me nearly twenty years to do it,' he paused before adding, 'I'm not sure I'll go back to Mante. I'd wanted to reach a thousand feet. It's a nice round number. But that might be pushing it. I'm going to have to hang up my tanks—at least for that sort of thing—pretty soon. I guess the real reason I'm doing it is I just want to know what's down there." '

Sheck did not return to Mante. Instead, in April 1994, he went to Zacaton. The same way the unconquered Mt. Everest once attracted mountain climbers with "high fever," this 1,080-foot-deep flooded pit in northeastern Mexico attracts record-setting cave divers with "deep fever."

On April 6, 1994, Exley was joined by a similarly afflicted deep-diving devotee, 55-year-old Texan Jim Bowden. The two planned to set the 1,000-foot depth record in this system.

Descending rapidly into the blackness of the pit on two separate lines and switching gas mixtures all the way down, the divers headed toward their world record. Due to limited visibility, neither diver was able to see the other.

Bowden's swift descent went well, but the gas mixture for the deepest part of his dive was being consumed faster than he planned. Because of this, he turned his dive at the 925-foot mark on his descent line and began his ascent. Bowden carried three digital depth gauges. One showed his maximum depth as 915, the second as 924 feet. The third gauge failed.

At his first decompression stop, as Bowden monitored his gas consumption he realized he was using it too quickly and that he might not have enough to complete his entire required decompression time.

Near the surface, Bowden's support team saw his bubbles and knew he was on his way up. But there were no bubbles rising from Exley's line.

Exley's companion, Mary Ellen Eckhoff descended on his line to 279 feet, searching for him. This was the limit of light from above. As she stared down into the darkness at Exley's disappearing line, she glimpsed two small white squares rising through the water toward her. Suddenly she realized they were laminated pages of Sheck's dive profile, something he would never turn loose intentionally. With heavy heart, she returned to the surface and made arrangements for notifying Sheck's parents.

Meanwhile, Bowden trimmed time off his decompression stops trying to conserve air. A free-flowing regulator accidentally dumped more of his precious air. When he reached 250 feet below the surface without seeing Exley, he knew something was wrong. Then, 100 feet below the surface one of his support divers gave him the sad news. Bowden had to hang in the cold water for several more hours of decompression with this terrible knowledge.

When he finally emerged that night after breathing pure oxygen at ten feet, he was hit by his second case of the bends. His support team treated him with a controversial French technique and by morning he was able to be on his feet. Having reached at least 915 feet, Jim Bowden established the world open circuit depth record.

Before all this occurred, however, Mary Ellen Eckhoff was driven the two-hour trip to Tampico where she telephoned Sheck 's parents and arranged for someone to fly in and drive Sheck 's van home.

No one believed Sheck 's body would ever be recovered. But three days later when the support team hauled up Exley's unused decompression tanks, they discovered his body entangled in the dive line. The only dive gauge he carried read 904 feet.

No one knows what happened. In 4,000 cave dives Sheck had always managed to extricate himself from many life threatening circumstances. This time he could not. Theories abound, but no one really knows what caused him to drown.

Sheck 's father flew to Mexico to claim his son's body. Within 24 hours it was cremated. Sheck was 45 years old.

The news of Sheck 's death stunned the diving world. In a fitting eulogy to his close friend and fellow diver, Ned DeLoach closed his tribute with these words:

"As I remember Sheck, I don't immediately think of dual manifolds, mixed gases, and long decompression stops. Instead, I fondly recall profound conversations about Arctic explorer Ronald Amundsen, his love of Beethoven's bold symphonies, Mexican food, boisterous laughter, and his extraordinary devotion to friends. Without question Sheck Exley is the most remarkable man I have ever known, and I know I am not alone."

24

DIAMONDS IN THE ROUGH

Glittering through the emerald green jungle foliage, hundreds of half-hidden pools of water dot Mexico's Yucatan Peninsula. From a bird's eye view, they sparkle like diamonds in the rough.

They are Mexico's cenotes, water-filled sink-holes and caves formed ages ago in our geological past. As attractive as they are from above, nothing can compare to the underwater beauty concealed beneath their glittering exteriors.

What makes some of these so different from other underwater systems in the world is that these were once dry caves. Water percolating down through the limestone soon dissolved the harder parts and created cavities that became caves. Continued dripping soon created subterranean formations, their shapes further sculpted on occasion by air currents and winds that eventually molded the dripping stone into the unimaginable shapes.

Once surface runoff waters eventually flooded the caverns, this protective barrier, which might have occurred over 12,000 years ago with the end of the last Ice Age, kept the cave's secrets intact. From that time until modern times, no human intrusion occurred. The cave formations, exactly as they were many thousands of years ago, remained literally frozen in time.

Since the Mayan civilization flourished on the Yucatan Peninsula for centuries, many of their religious ceremonies were associated with these deep, dark, mysterious pools of water. Some cenotes, such as that at Chichen Itza, were closely connected to the Mayan way of life. It takes no stretch of the imagination to suspect that before they were flooded, early man may have used these dry caves for his own purposes. Indeed, one theory persists that at one time, as the caverns were slowly being flooded, they once provided a subterranean canal system through which the Mayas could travel by boat, linking them to important Mayan cities. True or not, some archaeological finds suggest that early Mayan ancestors may have performed rituals in some of these now sunken caves.

For the most, however, time and rising waters kept them sealed from the eyes of man for countless millenniums, until one day, along the jungle trail came a man with a scuba tank over his shoulder. That day marked the end of the long-kept secret of the cenotes.

After some of the sink-holes whose roofs had collapsed and created featureless open water pits were investigated briefly by such early-comers as Luis Marden and Bates Littlehales in 1956, most scuba explorers who came later were self-styled archaeologists/treasure hunters looking for valuable artifacts.

Throughout that period, however, divers from Pablo Bush Romero's CEDAM (Club of Exploration and Water Sports of Mexico) looked into the various diveable sites. Most found that few of the cenotes were ever as interesting as they looked from the surface. Many were silt-filled pools of muddy water about as compelling to divers as a sewage settling pond.

In the 1970's, however, American divers with the experience and equipment to make deeper penetrations into some of these systems, soon became aware of their inner beauties. What they found in some systems was a fairyland of natural formations rivaling man's wildest imaginations. In 1979, writer/photographer Ned DeLoach persuaded Sheck Exley to accompany him on an exploratory dive expedition to the Yucatan. Both returned impressed by the incredible clarity of the water, the shallowness of the cave systems, and the beauty of the formations they found there. Certainly, their reports should have started a stampede of cenote diving enthusiasts anxious to see this many-splendored wonderland. But it was not until the 1980's that American cave divers got serious about sampling what was there. These divers included Dr. John Zumrick, Noel Sloan, Gary Storrick, Parker Turner, Steve Gerrard, Danny Atkinson, Lalo Fiorelli, Ron Winiker, and local resident divers, Jim Coke and

Michael Madden, the latter being the owner of the CEDAM Dive Center at Adventuras Akumal. Madden soon was the one person largely responsible for introducing groups of American cave divers to these Mexican systems.

During one excursion in 1987, Lalo Fiorelli reported that in the 11 months they were there, with Madden serving as their guide, they spent a total of 61 days in the caves exploring them.

"Just getting to the first five caves—Cristol Cenote, Mayan Blue, Naharon, Temple of Doom, and Sac-Actun—was not easy," said Fiorelli. "Including our double tanks, our dive equipment alone averaged 110 pounds per person, not to mention cameras, strobes and provisions. All this equipment had to be carried into the jungle to the dive site."

During that expedition, Fiorelli photographed some of the most exquisite underwater cave photographs of geological formations that have ever been seen. No divers intruded in the beauty of these scenes. But by using carefully placed slave strobes in the hands of his assistants, Fiorelli recorded forever these magnificent scenes of nature in its most pristine elegance in underwater caves. Many of these haunting limestone shapes were caused by corrosion from saltwater. Some caves have a top layer of freshwater with a bottom layer of saltwater. Where the two layers meet is the halocline.

Not all of the spectacular systems are difficult to reach. Carwash is so accessible by gravel road that it was named this because locals washed their vehicles there. And one can see by names as Temple of Doom, Mayan Blue, and Giant Birdhouse that these titles reflect individual characteristics of the systems.

The most popular cenotes are located about three miles in from the coast. All are typical karst formations filled with fresh water whose temperatures in the cave systems generally averages 77°F. The pools outside the caves are several degrees warmer.

So far, no significant archaeological finds have been made in these systems, however, in the one called Carwash, which locals named Cenote Cristol, divers exploring some 650 feet into its limestone corridors found the passageway opened up into a large chamber at a depth of 100 feet. There, they found a pyramid-shaped rock containing what looked like a carved out place filled with material resembling charcoal. The divers believed they had found some kind of altar or ceremonial site that might be thousands of years old. A human skull has been found and divers in the Temple Cenote recently found a complete human skeleton 500 feet back in the system. Proper Mexican Cultural Resource authorities were informed.

As more exploration continued, divers discovered links between some systems. In the late 1980's, local diver Mike Madden accompanied by Johanna DeGroot, while penetrating almost a mile of underwater passageways in a cenote named Mayan Blue, came upon a cave diver's line reel left by caver Parker Turner the day before while he was exploring a cave named Naharon near Tulum. Indeed, because of the honeycombed nature of the Yucatan Peninsula's limestone foundation, one suspects that there may well be considerable connections found between all of these coastal systems.

During 1988, the Naharon/Mayan Blue system was explored for almost three miles. On the nearby island of Cozumel just offshore, divers Parker Turner, Jeff Bozanic and Dennis Williams were among those who pushed through the Quebrada Cave system there to almost three miles as well.

Achieving a first in November 1987, local divers Mike Madden and Jim Coke, loaded their gear onto pack mules and trudged across a jungle trail to penetrate for the first time a spectacular system locally named Na-Hoc-Nay-Chic which in Mayan means "Giant Birdhouse." A year later, Madden was joined by Steve Gerrard and others for a major push into that system. Finding an average depth of only 16 feet, the divers progressed an astonishing distance of 4,500 feet from the cave entrance by using two reserve stage bottles each and carrying seven reels of line intended to connect to that which was already in place. The penetration was scheduled to take at least six hours.

As the explorers finned through some of the most spectacular underwater scenery consisting of passageways and chambers filled with elaborate stalactites and stalagmites in a setting of crystal clear water, they finally reached the 4,500-foot end of their fixed line left from their first penetration. Tying off their additional line, the trio now progressed through passageways that still remained shallow. Said explorer Mike Madden, the route was "awesomely pretty" throughout. "Formations are brilliant white, in every shape, size and dimension, with mountains of ivory white silt that call up thoughts of sparkling snowdrifts."

The three divers called a halt to their exploration halfway through their sixth reel of line. At that point they had laid 3,100 feet of new line and progressed into the system for 8,600 feet. In 1990, explorers pushed this cave to an astonishing 30,000 feet through some of the most spectacular underwater scenery in the world. If not in length, for sheer ethereal beauty, Na-Hoch-Nay-Chic is surely one of the world's most beautiful cave systems either above or below water. But to be able to swim through this beauty is such a surrealistic experience that divers have no difficulty finding names for various chambers such as Heaven's Gate, where in a large chamber divers are surrounded by dazzling white spires rising from the floor or descending from the ceiling providing an overall dream-like suggestion of the entry to heaven.

But then so too do similarly breathtaking scenes in some of the other cenotes. For instance, in a page from Lalo Fiorelli's log dated March 3, 1987 in which he did a 60-foot dive for 68 minutes into Cenote Cristol (Carwash) to a chamber called Room of Tears, Lalo wrote: "An absolutely magnificent dive. The single most beautiful place I have been on the planet. Like being in the most beautiful cathedral ever! I could hear the organ playing!! A penetration of about 1,100 feet, past the Chamber of Blocks and the Chamber of Horrors into a very technical tunnel known as 'Madden's Tunnel Passage'. This passageway is approximately 150 feet long and is after the 'Curtain' and 'Luke's Hope'. The room is all white, very crystalline, with many magnificent columns. The ceiling has thousands of soda straw stalactites...."

In 1988, Lalo Fiorelli returned to the Yucatan not long after the new system, Na-Hoch-Nay-Chic (Giant Birdhouse), had been discovered. The entrance to this system was probably overlooked by earlier cenote searchers because it was on a private ranch two miles into the jungle. Once permission was granted to dive the cave, the group of divers that included Fiorelli was unable to use vehicles in this primitive area. As Fiorelli described it:

"Each day for 10 days, we would trek in, suit up, dive an average of 100 minutes, then hike out using horses to carry the heaviest equipment."

Another totally spectacular wonderland is Sistema Sac Actun. When first explored by local resident diver, Jim Coke, the sheer splendor of this grotto must have almost overloaded his capacity to appreciate beauty. Some of the most magnificent photographs of its chambers were made by veteran writer/photographer, cave diver, Ned DeLoach. The roof of these chambers are hung so thickly with long, slender icicles of the most fragile kind that as a dry cave it must have literally rained saturated lime water constantly to have formed such a complex mass of cream-colored drip stones. Here and there, great monarch columns buttress the heavy ornate ceiling. These massive formations are the results of eons of drip-stone growths, gradually reaching from the ceiling to their counterpart stalagmites rising up from the cave floor. At some time in the past, the two joined as one and continued thickening from the continued flow of concentrated lime-saturated water from above.

Had this process not been interrupted by the system being flooded by fresh water, all the ceiling spires would have eventually joined with the floor formations and welded themselves into one solid mass. Today, unlike our slowly but surely changing dry cave formations, these remain forever frozen in time.

Ever since the discovery of this unique system, exploration of it has continued with astounding results, thanks to those who are spearheading the effort, and to the fact that the system is relatively shallow. For example, in the early summer of 1996, with the help of their back-up team and under the direction of Mike Madden, Paul Heinerth and Jill Rabjohn got on their scooters in the Na-Hoch-Nay-Chic, and basically ran off with 6 bottles on their back and were underwater for 7 hours at 30 feet with no decompression. As a result, they surveyed 40,000 feet of underwater tunnel in the space of two weeks bringing the total surveyed to approximately 135,000 feet, making it at the time the longest known underwater cave system in the world. And the push goes on....

Hopefully, the splendors of these marvelous jewel-like cenotes on Mexico's Yucatan Peninsula will be as respected and cared for by man as they have been by time. For they are truly Mother Nature's diamonds in the rough.

APPENDIX 1

BIBLIOGRAPHY

Andrews, E. Wyllys. "Dzibilchaltun: Lost City of the Mayas." *National Geographic*, Vol. 125, No. 1, January, 1959.

Benjamin, George J. "Diving Into the Blue Holes of the Bahamas." *National Geographic*, Vol. 138, No. 3, September, 1970.

Casteret, Norbert. *Ten Years Under the Earth.* New York: Graystone Press, 1938.

Ceram, C. W. *Gods, Graves and Scholars.* New York: Alfred A. Knopf, 1969.

Clark, Eugenie. *The Lady and the Sharks.* New York: Harper and Row, 1969.

Cousteau, J. Y. Captain, with Dumas, Frederic. *The Silent World.* New York: Harper and Brothers, Publishers, 1953.

DeLoach, Ned. "The Deepest Dive." *Ocean Realm Magazine*, Summer 1988.

Dixon, Peter L. *The Silent Adventure.* New York: Ballantine Books, 1968.

Dugan, James. *Men Under the Sea.* New York: Collier Books, 1966.

Farr, Martyn. *The Darkness Beckons.* London: Diadem Books, 1991.

Fiorell, E. J., *Hidden Splendors of the Yucatan,* calendar, New York: Aqua Quest Publications, 1990.

Howell, Clark F., and the editors of Life. *Early Man.* New York: Time, Inc., 1968.

Marden, Luis. "Up From the Well of Time." *National Geographic*, Vol. 125, No. 1, January 1959.

Martin, William R., and Reese II, Michael. "Sink-hole Safari: Diving Florida's Underwater Caverns." *Oceans*, March-April, 1973.

Marx, Robert F. *Sea Fever.* New York: Doubleday & Co., 1972.

Olsen, Stanley J. "The Wakulla Cave." *National History,* August-September, 1958.

Royal, William R.. "Trapped in an Underwater Cave." *Underwater,* January, 1962.

Royal, William R., and Shirley E., unpublished manuscript, "Ten Seconds to Death."

Schenck, Jr., Hilbert, and McAniff, John. "An Analysis of Fatal Skin and Scuba Diving Accidents." *Marine Technology Society Journal,* Vol. 6, No. 3, May-June, 1972.

Stone, Dr. William C. "Exploring Underwater with a Failsafe Diving Rebreather." *Sea Technology,* Vol. 31, No. 12, December, 1990.

Ibid., "Huautla Cave Quest," *National Geographic,* Vol. 188, No. 3, September 1995.

Stopinski, Bettie. "Underwater Death Traps." *Orlando Sentinel,* August 18, 1968.

Taylor, Michael Ray. *Cave Passages - Roaming the Underground Wilderness.* New York: Scribner, 1996.

Thompson, Edward Herbert. *People of the Serpent.* Boston: Houghton Mifflin, Co., 1932.

Tooker, D. K. "Trapped." *Skin Diver,* October, 1974.

Vetter, Craig. "Deep, Dark Dreams: Bill Stone." *Outside,* November, 1992.

Wallace, Jim. "Little Salt Springs." *New Vistas,* Vol. 8, No. 3, March, 1972.

Willard, T. A. *The City of the Sacred Well.* New York: Grosset and Dunlap, Publisher, 1926.

← APPENDIX 2 →

CAVE DIVING TRAINING AGENCIES

National Association for Cave Diving
P.O. Box 14492
Gainesville, FL 32604
http://www.afn.org/~nacd

Cave Diving Section
The National Speleological Society
P.O. Box 950
Branford, FL 32008
http://www.caves.org

INDEX

A **boldface** page number denotes a picture or illustration caption.

KI

Other Books by Robert F. Burgess

The Mystery of Mound Key

A Time for Tigers

Where Condors Fly

Sinkings, Salvages and Shipwrecks

Exploring a Coral Reef

The Sharks

Ships Beneath the Sea: A History of Subs and Submersibles

Man: 12,000 Years Under the Sea:
A Story of Underwater Archaeology

The Man Who Rode Sharks

Secret Languages of the Sea

Florida's Golden Galleons

Handbook of Trailer Sailing

Sunken Treasure: Six Who Found Fortunes

Diver's Guide to Old Shipwrecks of Florida's Southeast Coast

Gold, Galleons, and Archaeology

They Found Treasure

Diving Off The Beaten Track

Other Aqua Quest Titles Available

Ask your dive center or book store for other titles by Aqua Quest Publications, publisher of books on dive travel destinations, underwater photography and videography, wreck diving, dive-related fiction, marine life, technical diving and safety. If these books are not available at your local stores, call or write us directly for a catalog of our publications.

Aqua Quest Publications, Inc.
Post Office Box 700
Locust Valley, NY 11560-0700

(800) 933-8989 ■ (516) 759-0476 ■ Fax: (516) 759-4519
E-mail: aquaquest@aol.com   www.aquaquest.com